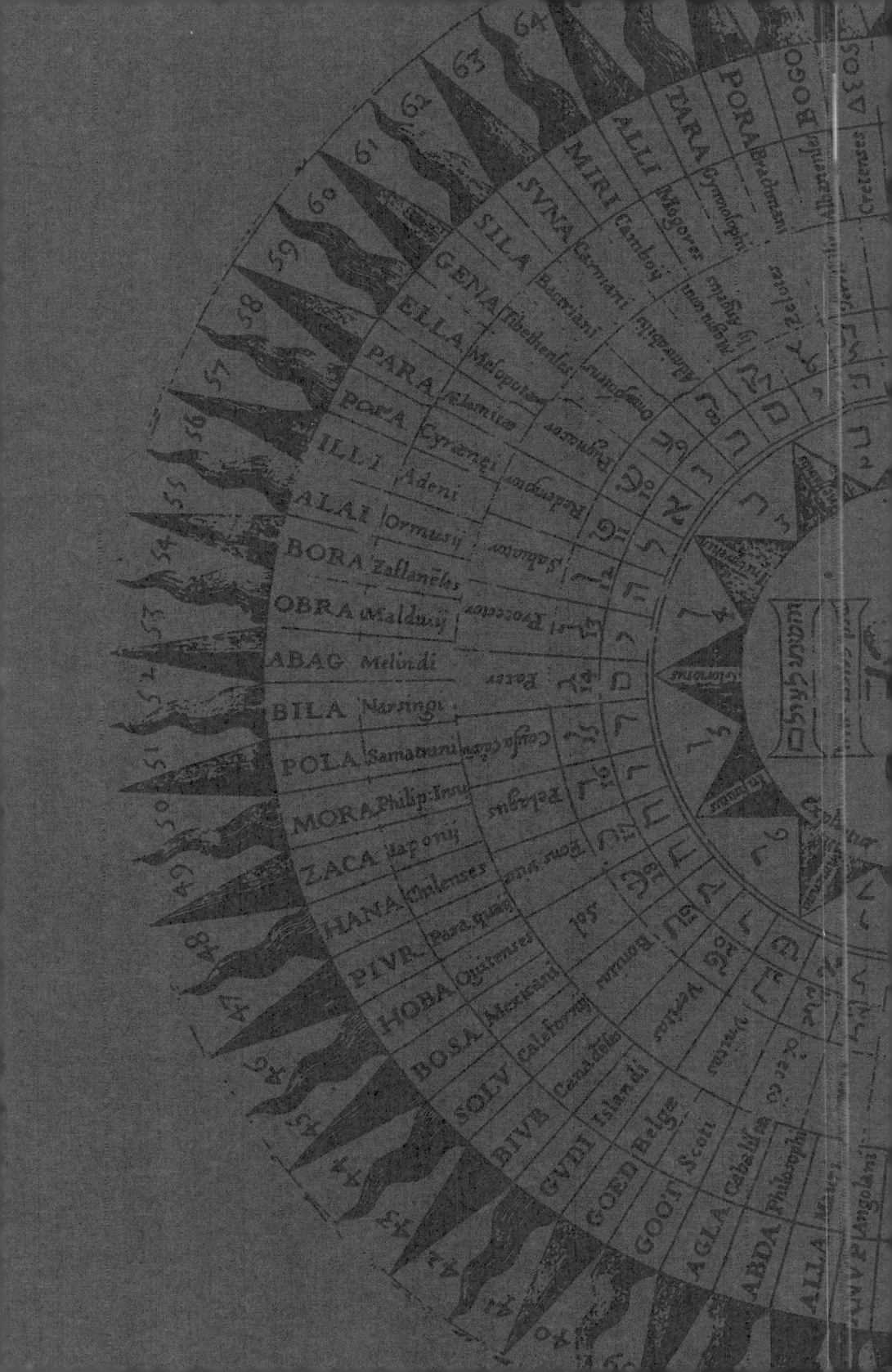

The
Astrological Goetia

"In a decade that has already seen an almost unprecedented resurgence of classical occult knowledge, Jaime Paul Lamb's *The Astrological Goetia* marks a significant new contribution. Lamb has taken one of the neglected corners of magical lore—the symbolism and spirits of the 72 quinaries of the zodiac—and unfolded it into a fascinating and practical system that bridges the space between astrology and ceremonial magic."

JOHN MICHAEL GREER, AUTHOR OF *THE TWILIGHT OF PLUTO*

"By exploring the history of astrology from ancient Babylon, Egypt, and Greece to the medieval grimoire tradition, Jaime Paul Lamb makes the complex subject of astrology easier to understand and, for the skeptic, more plausible. *The Astrological Goetia* bridges the gap between astrology and magic, with Lamb illuminating the meaning of such material as angels and demons. Detailed historical descriptions of planetary angels and demons (and their influences) bring a new dimension to the subject and remind us of the depth of thought of our historical predecessors."

ANGEL MILLAR, AUTHOR OF *TRANSCEND THE CHAOS* AND *THE PATH OF THE WARRIOR-MYSTIC*

"This book breaks new ground with an illumined peek into ancient metaphysics to reveal the highly secretive mappings of the primordial lights of existence as scribed by the ancient Jewish sages in the form of the Shem HaMephorash. *The Astrological Goetia* is poised to be a valuable addition to the library of every seeker, offering insights into both the esoteric knowledge and practical aspects of occult astrology and angelic mysticism."

DAVID PANTANO, AUTHOR OF *ALCHEMICAL HERMETICISM*

"It is well known among occultists that since the appearance of the Testament of Solomon, the hordes of demons found in many grimoires are directly related to the thirty-six astrological decans and the twenty-eight mansions of the moon. But there is scant literature on the spirits behind the seventy-two quinaries of the zodiac. Following Rudd's *Liber Malorum Spirituum Seu Goetia Lemegeton Clavicula Salomonis*, Lamb has done grimoirists and astrologers alike a great service by rendering the demons of the Lemegeton and the angels of the Shem HaMephorash in a practical, workable system that does not fail to emphasize their astrological underpinnings."

P. D. NEWMAN, AUTHOR OF *THEURGY*

"*The Astrological Goetia* is a seminal work—the capstone of a complete astrological and magical corpus and some of Lamb's sharpest writing to date. With this offering, the author provides not only the present but future generations of researchers and practitioners with a tremendous and invaluable resource. This is essential reading and a new classic of astrological magic."

IKE BAKER, AUTHOR OF
ÆTHERIC MAGIC AND HOST OF *ARCANVM* PODCAST

"A valuable addition to the library of an astrologer or student of the Hermetic sciences, bringing to life the connection between an astrological chart and the angels and demons of the Shem HaMephorash."

CHRIS ZALEWSKI, AUTHOR OF
ENOCHIAN CHESS OF THE GOLDEN DAWN

"Lamb's work demands critical examination and holds the potential to unlock fascinating new avenues for astrologers and magicians alike."

DARCY KÜNTZ, EDITOR OF
THE HERMETIC PAPERS OF THE GOLDEN DAWN

THE
ASTROLOGICAL
GOETIA

The 72 Keys to Angelic and
Demonic Astrology

Jaime Paul Lamb

Inner Traditions
Rochester, Vermont

Inner Traditions
One Park Street
Rochester, Vermont 05767
www.InnerTraditions.com

Cataloging-in-Publication Data for this title is available from the Library of Congress

ISBN 979-8-88850-133-7 (print)
ISBN 979-8-88850-134-4 (ebook)

Printed and bound in China by Reliance Printing Co., Ltd.

10 9 8 7 6 5 4 3 2 1

Text design by Virginia Scott Bowman and layout by Kenleigh Manseau
This book was typeset in Garamond Premier Pro with IvyOra Display and ITC Legacy Serif Std used as display typeface
Artwork by Sky Mathis unless otherwise noted

To send correspondence to the author of this book, mail a first-class letter to the author c/o Inner Traditions • Bear & Company, One Park Street, Rochester, VT 05767, and we will forward the communication, or contact the author directly at **jaimepaullamb.com/astrology**.

Scan the QR code and save 25% at InnerTraditions.com. Browse over 2,000 titles on spirituality, the occult, ancient mysteries, new science, holistic health, and natural medicine.

Contents

✻

Foreword

Mark Stavish

AT A 2014 SEMINAR hosted by the Institute for Hermetic Studies (IHS), held one Sunday afternoon at the Free Library in Wyoming, Pennsylvania, instructions were given for an exercise using the angels of the Shem HaMephorash. The approach was simple and designed to help those working with the angels, something very rarely done in contemporary magical groups. In summary, the participants were to write the name of a particular angel and draw its attendant sigil and briefly meditate on it at the start of their day. They were not to read anything about the angel or its areas of influence. These exercises were to be performed daily, with a new angel being used every five days (a *quinarian week*, to use Jaime Paul Lamb's terminology) as the influences changed. At the end of each period, participants were to reflect upon their experiences, write them down, and then—*and only then*—read about the angel governing those five days and its range of action.

What happened next was impressive. The participants reported having the most peculiar synchronicities and encounters. They observed, or rather *encountered*, strange events, some seemingly insignificant, corresponding to the domain of the angel of the period. Despite the ease and simplicity of the exercise given, several participants ceased the angelic rotation as there were, in their words, "too many coincidences." As for myself, I found it *very* exciting. To my knowledge, for the first time, we were able to collect data from a group—not just a single practitioner—on the influences of these elusive spiritual intelligences. Some of our findings were described in *Child of the Sun: Psychic and Physical Rejuvenation in Alchemy and Qabala* (IHS Study Guide Series, 2015) with a narrow look at select angels and their functions.

Among the most memorable personal experiences I had during the experiment with the angels of the Shem was a phone call I received from a former student from whom I had not heard in about ten years. I remember it very clearly—down to where I was standing when the phone rang. After a few minutes of brief pleasantries, my "wayward child" asked me to accompany her and her fiancé on a journey of "independent investigative journalism," which consisted of trespassing on the rural property of a man who had a criminal record and was believed to be involved in some form of dark magic with political overtones. Since that sounded like a fine recipe for ending up dead and being dumped down an abandoned mine shaft, or maybe eaten for whatever passed as a holiday dinner in the fellow's dark magic of choice, I politely declined and wished them luck. I have not heard from her since.

When I looked up the angel of the day it was Hahuiah, angel of the twenty-fourth quinary. As this book points out, this angel protects those who have committed crimes, insofar as they do not fall back on their wicked ways. Thus, if we follow the influence of the angel, the fellow in question may have been a recluse, on his own land, remorseful for what he had done, or a potential serial killer—neither of which were within my wheelhouse or legal authority to address.

While your experiences may not be as movie-of-the-week as mine, I am certain that a patient application of the knowledge contained in the present volume—when wedded to generosity and goodwill—will give the reader a deeper, more applicable, and joyful insight into the roles of the Shem angels not only in theoretical astrology but also practically *in your daily life.*

It is in this spirit, and with great joy, that I introduce *The Astrological Goetia: The 72 Keys to Angelic and Demonic Astrology* by Jaime Paul Lamb. Not only have I been fortunate enough to experience Lamb's expertise in traditional astrology personally, when he taught two courses for the IHS, but I also had the pleasure of coteaching a class with him (along with Ike Baker of *Arcanvm* podcast) on the elusive and at times confounding *Three Books of Occult Philosophy* by Cornelius Agrippa. Lamb took on the formidable task of elucidating the contents of Book II, which deals with the celestial world.

It was in the preparation and execution of these classes that Lamb demonstrated not only the depth of his knowledge of astrology but also his contagious enthusiasm for its practical application. His students eagerly awaited his presentations, many utilized his services as a consulting astrologer, and several others engaged him in personal tutoring on the subject. Why do I tell you this? Because astrology can be difficult and boring at times (ancient astrologers were called *mathematici* for a reason), but Lamb, in his presentations as well as his personality, is neither difficult nor boring. He has a knack for taking notoriously abstruse subjects and making them not only manageable but inspirational. This talent is showcased in the present volume.

It was also during the preparatory sessions for the IHS courses that Lamb and I talked at length about some of the strengths and weaknesses of modern astrology and by extension modern astrologers, the primary deficit being a clear and almost unquestioned separation of astrology from the other Hermetic arts—alchemy and theurgy (magic). Of course, astrologers are very good at pointing out obstacles and opportunities—that is what they get paid to do. But few seem to know how to integrate those other occult sciences into an active, holistic practice, a practice by which one might ameliorate celestial influences. This is where astrological magic comes into play. Lamb emphasizes the synergetic relationship between astrology and magic in the introduction when he asks, "What is magic but the enchanted technology by which we accentuate the positive and mitigate the negative terrestrial effects of the stars and planets?"

From antiquity through the Renaissance, astrology was seen less as a standalone practice than as one part of a suite of enchanted methods. Within the astrological domain, we encounter various branches of the art—natal, mundane, horary, and so on—each with a specific application. Electional astrology figures most prominently in the grimoire tradition. Talismanic magic, particularly, is predicated on elections, and it is by means of these enchanted objects that stellar and planetary influences can be more precisely directed and utilized by the astrological magician. Lamb devotes an entire chapter to the talismanic art in the context of the quinaries.

It is in this capacity that Lamb provides his greatest service to the twenty-first-century astrologer. He contributes to the reintegration of astrology and magic; he points to an active astrology—one made *negotiable* through magic. The 72 quinaries are repurposed as a medium of this negotiation. Here, for the first time, the quinaries are being presented in clear detail, despite being a topic of discussion among advanced ceremonial practitioners for years. In this book, Lamb has outlined the historical development, theory, and practice of a new synthesis in the world of astrological magic, a synthesis he has dubbed *quinarian astrology*. In this system, he has applied the documented significations and attributes of the Shem angels and the goetic demons to astrological interpretation. This is something that should have happened centuries ago.

This book is an effective and meticulously organized guide to freeing astrology from the theoretical confines of the chart and bringing the art into the living domain of the magus. Instead of being the unwitting subject of the Fates—for good or for ill—the reader is exposed to methods by which the very rules of causality may be negotiated, to a greater or lesser degree. *This project is critical and should not be underestimated.*

MARK STAVISH, M.A.
DIRECTOR OF STUDIES
INSTITUTE FOR HERMETIC STUDIES
WEST WYOMING, PENNSYLVANIA
WINTER SOLSTICE

Acknowledgments

Many thanks to Jon Graham and the Inner Traditions team for believing in this project and helping to make it a reality.

A thousand thanks, lots of love, and limitless light to the following individuals and societies without whose friendship, guidance, and support this work would have been impossible: Stephanie Lamb, P. D. Newman, Mark Stavish and the Institute for Hermetic Studies (Wilkes-Barre, Pennsylvania), Piers Vaughan, Adam Goldman, Ben Williams, Justin Ross, Kevin Fuller, Danny Hawkins, Angel Millar, Darcy Küntz, Yoseff Samchuk, Chris Zalewski, Chris Brennan, Christopher Warnock, John Michael Greer, Jake Trayer, Pat Shannahan and *Tria Prima* podcast, Ike Baker and *Arcanvm* podcast, Sky Mathis and *Philosophical Minds* podcast, Greg Kaminsky and *Occult of Personality* podcast, Rudolf Berger and *Thoth-Hermes* podcast, Jenn Zahrt and the *Mountain Astrologer* magazine, the Brethren of Old Well-St John's Lodge no. 6, F. & A. M. (Norwalk, Connecticut) and Ascension Lodge no. 89, F. & A. M. (Phoenix, Arizona), the *Fratres* of the Arizona College of the *Societas Rosicruciana in Civitatibus Foederatis*, and the *Sorores et Fratres* of M∴ Temple of the Hermetic Society of the G∴D∴ (Phoenix, Arizona).

Illuminating the Quinaries

THE NAMES OF THE ANGELS of the Shem HaMephorash, which means "the Explicit Name" of God, are formed from three consecutive verses in the book of Exodus (14:19–21). There are 72 such angels, collectively having mystical significance in the Jewish esoteric tradition known as Qabalah. Similarly, 72 demons are described in an infamous grimoire on nigromancy (demonic magic) known as the *Ars Goetia*, which is the first of the five books comprising the *Lesser Key of Solomon*. Sometime during the early modern period, these angels and demons were organized into pairs, and each pair was assigned to a 5-degree arc segment of the zodiac called a *quinary*—one angel and one demon per quinary.[1] The zodiac is divided into 72 such quinaries. The angels and demons rule and govern their respective quinaries, through which they emanate their astrological influence on the seven visible planets and from the planets to terrestrial life on Earth, or the *sublunar world*.[2]

According to the qabalistic and Solomonic grimoire traditions, each of the 72 angels of the Shem HaMephorash[3] and the 72 demons of the *Ars Goetia*[4] have a set of significations and attributes, as well as a scope of influence and activity unique to them. An array of topics such as memory, fertility, and divination, as well as activities such as finding hidden things, avoiding shipwrecks, and aiding in the study of the liberal arts, fall under the purview of the various angels and demons. And through the medium of the planets, their influence spans all aspects of terrestrial life.

In a traditional astrological figure (or chart), the seven visible planets are arrayed against the twelve 30-degree signs of the zodiac. The natural expression of each planet is modified by the quality of the zodiacal sign in which it is found. Consider a placement such as Mars in Pisces on the tenth house, for instance. The hot, dry, active energy of Mars is tempered by the cold, moist, passive mutability of Pisces, rendering the planet's expression significantly altered in the context of the native's career, symbolized by the tenth house. Similarly, each planet in an astrological figure resides in one of the quinaries and is therefore under the dominion of the angel and demon of that quinary. The angelic and demonic rulers of the quinaries bestow their influence upon any planet found within the *cusps* (borders) of their 5-degree segment of the zodiac.

For example, suppose a given chart shows Venus at 6 degrees Capricorn on the seventh house. This planet is in a quinary ruled by the angel Poiel and the demon Gremory because this pair has dominion over 5° 00'–9° 59' Capricorn. The astrologer will note that Venus's natural significations—love, beauty, the arts, and so on—will be modified by the influence of Poiel and Gremory. Angelic Poiel "serves to obtain what one wants,"[5] and demonic Gremory "procure[s] the Love of Women."[6] Clearly, there are positive, romantic auspices for our hypothetical *native* (the subject of a natal chart) in the context of the seventh house of romantic relationships. *This is the essence of quinarian astrology.*

This method may be applied to natal astrology, as in the example above, as well as to other astrological domains such as *electional* and *horary*. Electional astrology is used to decide the most auspicious time to set a cycle in motion. For instance, suppose you were planning a boating trip; you might choose to set sail at a time when the quinary ruled by the angel Ieiaiel was rising because Ieiaiel protects against storms and shipwrecks.[7] That would be a favorable election, an auspicious moment to commence your voyage.

Horary astrology is used to answer specific questions. A chart is cast for the moment the question is understood by the astrologer. Suppose the querent asks, "Will I get the job at NASA?" A figure is erected, and the astrologer finds that the midheaven (symbolizing the querent's profession, reputation, and status) is in the quinary of Morax, the goetic demon who rules over astronomy.[8] Clearly, this would be a favorable factor in the overall horary delineation.

Despite having a body of clear and defined significations and a ready applicability to astrological analysis and chart delineation, the quinarian angels and demons have heretofore languished in the shadowy environs of the qabalistic and Solomonic grimoire traditions—underground and out of the reach of your typical astrologer. Having been cloistered away in the arcane world of Western occultism, they have never been incorporated into the mainstream astrological current. This book is an attempt to finally present quinarian astrology as a practicable system.

This book contains the names, attributes, sigils, and seals corresponding to each quinary, as well as the zodiacal degrees governed by each of the 72 angels and demons in an easy-to-reference, sequential arrangement. The quinarian pair governing each 5-degree segment of the zodiac is listed in order, beginning at 0 degrees 00 minutes Aries, all the way around the zodiac to 29 degrees 59 minutes Pisces—from the alpha to the omega of the ecliptic. The astrologer need only observe the zodiacal degree of the planet, part,* or angle under consideration, consult that quinary in the reference section of this book, then use the significations and attributes of the angel and demon to enhance their delineation of the placement.

Quinarian astrology is not some trendy new technique—its component parts have been embedded in the tradition for centuries. This book marks the first time the quinaries are being presented as a practicable delineation technique.[9] The astrologer now has unprecedented

---

*The part, also called Arabic part or lot, is a theoretical point, usually the distance between two planets, projected from the ascendant.

access to the body of significations attributed to each of the angels and demons, enabling them to add further nuance to chart interpretation. The scheme of zodiacal rulership is also made clear—one need only know the degree and sign of a planet to determine its quinary, and then assign and assess angelic and demonic influence. In the two-thousand-plus-year history of horoscopic astrology, there have been very few innovations and only a handful of lost techniques that have been reconstructed.[10] The component parts of this quinarian delineation technique are historically and philosophically grounded in the most esoteric corners of the Western astrological tradition, which is why they have managed to elude systemization—until now.

It should be remembered that all serious astrological analysis is multifactorial. The quinaries are not a *substitute* for the common methods of interpretation; they are supplemental to them. The delineation of planets configured in signs and houses is central to the art, but delineation is enhanced when extended techniques such as the quinarian approach are applied. The angelic and demonic dimension afforded by the quinaries simply sheds further light on the existing placements in a figure. When several techniques are wed in this manner, a fuller picture emerges from the puzzle of astrological symbolism; the astrologer's hypotheses are accepted or rejected; and the true nature and character of the chart reveals itself. The depth and complexity of astrology is made clear in such a methodological synthesis.

This book is an attempt to bridge two worlds—the astrological and the magical—as these domains are mutually beneficial and, to some extent, *activate* each other. The qabalist, ceremonial magician, or Solomonic exorcist, approaching the subject with experience in their specialized corner of occultism, will see the underlying cosmic unity that only a developed sense of astrology can make possible. While most magicians working within the grimoire tradition will be familiar with elections, this book may inspire them to apply the angelic and demonic significations to natal and horary astrology. The modern astrologer, not typically conversant with the other Western esoteric traditions, will gain access to a new angelic and demonic dimension to their work, which they may then utilize in chart delineation, adding further detail and nuance to their art. This sort of exposure may even lead the intrepid astrologer into operative magical experimentation, such as the construction and consecration of talismans. *For what is magic but the enchanted technology by which we accentuate the positive and mitigate the negative terrestrial effects of the stars and planets?*

This book was written with the practitioner in mind. It is intended to aid in the practical synthesis of astrology and Western occultism by situating the 72 quinaries at the intersection of the two, in their rightful astrological context, and establishing them as a practicable technique. This is not to say that the quinarian lens should be the only one applied but, as most astrologers can affirm, when an astrologer gains similar results from applying several techniques, they are likely close to the truth. Using the quinaries as one of several metrics employed in judging charts has enriched my personal astrological practice.[11] And, reciprocally, astrological proficiency has greatly enhanced my magical practice, particularly in terms of navigating astrological weather and engaging cosmic momentum in an operation. I feel confident that both the magician and the astrologer stand to gain by this peculiar quinarian synthesis of astrology and magic.

THE STRUCTURE AND USE OF THIS BOOK

Chapter 1 contains a short overview of traditional* astrological doctrine, providing a theoretical foundation for those who are unfamiliar with the art as it was practiced and understood before its New Age recuperation and popular psychologization in the twentieth century. Chapter 2 deals with the angels of the Shem HaMephorash, their emergence and the qabalistic lore built around them, as well as a helpful overview of basic qabalistic

---

*Traditional astrology generally refers to Hellenistic, Perso-Arabic, medieval, and Renaissance astrology, or otherwise as the art existed before the collapse of the enchanted worldview and its subsequent psychologization in the twentieth century.

principles. In the third chapter, I introduce the demons of the *Ars Goetia*, outlining their origins in antiquity and the Solomonic grimoire tradition as well as discussing their pairing with the Shem HaMephorash angels. Chapter 3 also contains a survey of the Solomon Magus tradition, which examines the often-overlooked roles of the king as an exorcist and controller of demons. In chapter 4, the zodiacal degrees ruled by each angel and demon are given, along with their significations, attributes, sigils, and seals. This is the most important chapter for those wishing to immediately employ the quinaries in chart analysis. The reader will likely be in and out of this reference section a lot. It is not necessarily meant to be read page by page as much as it is to be consulted on a case-by-case basis in the context of chart delineation. In chapters 5, 6, and 7, I demonstrate the application of this quinarian technique in the context of natal, electional, and horary astrology, respectively. Chapter 8 examines some of the magical applications of this technique, including the composition and consecration of quinarian talismans. And, finally, chapter 9 is a general summary of the subject along with some parting thoughts on the philosophical implications of quinarian astrology. These implications are quite vast, especially when you consider that, for the first time in the history of the art, we are now able to astrologize on the purely *noetic* plane, beyond the fixed stars and the zodiac. The door is now open to an intellectual, angelic astrology.

I have included a helpful glossary in the back of the book, as the use of some specialized terms was unavoidable. It is hoped that readers will familiarize themselves with the historical context of the angels and demons under consideration, develop a sound theoretical basis, reference their significations and attributes in chapter 4, and, finally, utilize this occult technique in natal, electional, and horary astrology. The intrepid astrologer-magician may also consider using the quinaries in magical operations and talisman making. This book is, after all, oriented toward both the magical and astrological practitioner and is arranged to give them the historical, theoretical, and practical tools necessary to apply these 72 quinarian keys of occult astrology to their own practice.

1
The 72 Quinaries

THE 72 QUINARIES, or 5-degree zodiacal subdivisions, are the technical foundation of our study. They are the astrological system into which the angels of the Shem HaMephorash and the demons of the *Ars Goetia* are fitted. Each quinary is governed by a qabalistic angel and a Solomonic demon. These pairs emanate their *influence** through the quinaries, which modify the expression of any planet, part, or angle placed within their *cusps* or boundaries.

Though a certain degree of technical proficiency in astrology will have to be presumed, we will begin with a short orientation on the elements and scope of the art. This general introduction will include some of the theory and philosophy supporting traditional Western tropical astrology, which in some ways differs from the modern, post-theosophical, psychologized astrology of today. This will help us to contextualize the quinaries—historically and philosophically—and illustrate how they are situated within this system. From there, we will address the celestial mechanics of the quinaries. Finally, we will examine some of the existing material on the quinaries as well as the history of their presence in *astromythology* and stellar lore.

---

*From the medieval Latin *influere* or *influentia*; originally, an astrological term for the stellar emissions of an ætheric fluid, which, in certain configurations, acts upon the character of humankind, altering its fate.

ASTROLOGICAL ORIENTATION

It is impossible to understand traditional astrology without having a grasp of the worldview upon which it is based. The Ptolemaic system[1] was the standing cosmological paradigm for over fifteen hundred years, until the Copernican Revolution in the sixteenth century. It was built upon the foundation of Aristotle's physics. Though this model was geocentric, we need not picture it that way. All we need to digest is that Earth is at the symbolic center because it is the locus of human consciousness; it is our point of observation. We know Earth is not the center of our solar system—as did many of the ancients—but we *experience* the cosmos from this perspective. All that is necessary to astrologize is that we take the imaginary pin out of the sun and stick it in Earth, making it stationary—all the other movements are the same as the modern heliocentric model. This is what we might call the *georeferential* model: Earth is the reference point from which we observe the cosmos. *Astrology is georeferential, not geocentric.*[2]

According to the Ptolemaic cosmology, the sublunary sphere (Earth) is nested inside the sphere of the moon, which is why we call it sublunar: it is the region beneath the moon. The four classical elements—earth, water, air, and fire—comprise the states of all matter in the sublunary sphere, and they are listed here in their pregravitational order, from the density of earth to the rarity of fire. Aristotle referred to this stratification as the doctrine of *natural place*.[3] He observed that the mixed elements, if left undisturbed, will naturally separate in this order, but they are in a constant state of generation and corruption. Being sublunar, the elements are subject to change via the permutations of the four qualities: moisture, coldness, dryness, and heat. This bit of Aristotelian natural philosophy surfaces again in astrology as the doctrine of elemental *triplicities*, which attributes an elemental correspondence to each of the signs.

The spheres of the seven visible planets—the moon, Mercury, Venus, the sun, Mars, Jupiter, and Saturn—are concentrically nested in their

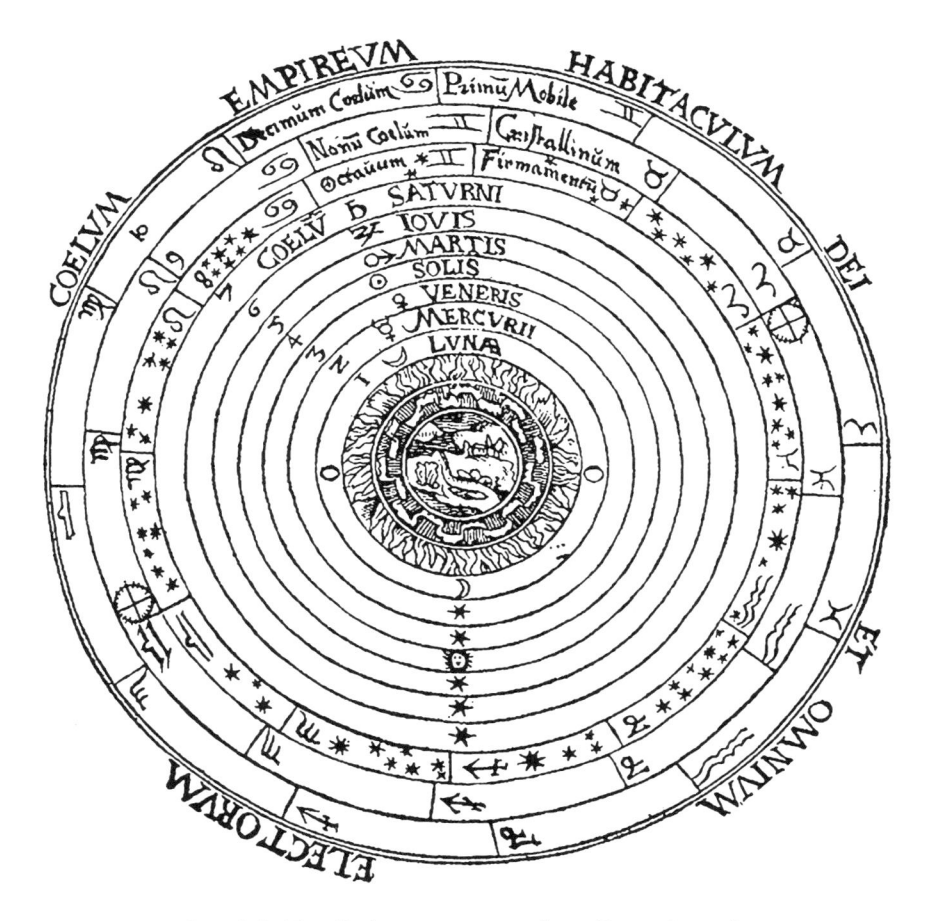

Fig. 1.1. The Ptolemaic system from Peter Apian's
Cosmographia (Antwerp, 1539).

Chaldean order, arranged by their orbital speeds: the slower the planet, the farther away it is. According to Aristotle, the crystalline planetary spheres are composed of incorruptible *æther* (the quintessence or fifth element).[4] There is no æther below the sphere of the moon, and there are no classical elements above it; the lunar sphere separates the terrestrial from the celestial. The moon collects the ætheric influence of the planets and translates it to the elemental world below. Above the furthermost planetary sphere of Saturn—the "seventh heaven"—is the sphere of the fixed stars and the zodiac. This is the starry firmament against which the seven visible planets wander, which is synonymous with the Ogdoad (the Eighth, referring to the eighth sphere of fixed stars above the seven planetary spheres) of the Hermetists and Gnostics and the Chochmah of the qabalists. The *primum mobile* (the first moved, corresponding to the Hermetic Ennead or ninth heavenly sphere) envelops all the inferior spheres. According to this worldview, the stars and seven visible planets communicate supercelestial emanations from the *primum movens* (Aristotle's unmoved or prime mover) to the sublunary sphere and this causes elemental generation and corruption.[5]

Astrology is the study of qualitative, meaningful time. It is predicated on the notion that the terrestrial and celestial spheres are in a sympathetic relationship. The microcosm is mirrored in the macrocosm, as we find echoed in the oft-cited Hermetic axiom: "That which is above is like that which is below."[6] According to astrological doctrine, celestial events and phenomena indicate and/or symbolize terrestrial events and phenomena. The causally mechanistic model, such as that employed by Claudius Ptolemy in his *Tetrabiblos* (second century CE), applies to personal and social affairs (judicial astrology), as well as to medical and meteorological phenomena (natural astrology).[7] Clearly, solar light and heat influence Earth, as do lunar-tidal patterns; ergo, it was only a short leap for the ancients to presume that all planets and stars figure into this system of cosmic influence. But it is not necessary to subscribe to a materialistic perspective of astrological causality; in fact, most ancient astrologers viewed the planets in signs, houses, and aspect as being symbolic and indicative of terrestrial affairs—not their cause, per se. Hellenistic astrologers such as Dorotheus of Sidon (first century CE) and Vettius Valens (second century CE), for example, were more representative of your typical Alexandrian astrologer at the time. They believed that the positions of the planets in signs and houses *symbolized* events and phenomena on Earth rather than *caused* them, as we encounter in the mechanistic causality of Ptolemy's astrology.[8]

Proper horoscopic astrology—as opposed to the omenic protoastrology of the Mesopotamians and the enchanted horoscopic timekeeping of the Egyptians that preceded it—arose sometime around the second century BCE in Alexandria, Egypt, during the Hellenistic period. This is when the concepts introduced by the Mesopotamians and the Egyptians were integrated with Greek natural philosophy. The Greeks also contributed the four elements (Empedocles's *rhizomata* or roots), humoral and temperamental theory (Hippocrates and Galen), and the study of optics (Euclid and others), the latter of which would inform the doctrine of aspects. We call this astrology "proper" because it is the first time we see the codification of the art's four indispensable components—planets, signs, houses, and aspects—fitted together in a complex and comprehensive philosophical system. This was the inception of Hellenistic astrology.[9]

The planets are the seven, visible "wandering stars" (Greek: *astēr planētēs*) that move against the firmament, or the canopy of the fixed stars. They are most commonly viewed as archetypal concentrations who bring their significations to bear in the context of signs and houses. The planets signify the nature of the influence—mercurial, venereal, martial, jovial, and saturnine. The signs of the zodiac are twelve equal divisions of the ecliptic, totaling 30 degrees of celestial longitude (right ascension) each. They qualitatively modify their resident planets. The signs dictate *how* that planetary influence is being expressed, much like the relationship between an adjective (sign) and a noun (planet). The houses are twelve terrestrial areas of life—such as finances, relationships, career, and so on—in which the zodiacally conditioned planets exert their influence and actualize their agendas. Houses illustrate *where* the planetary influence is being expressed. Aspects are the geometrical relationships (conjunction,* sextile, square, trine, and opposition) made by the planets on the ecliptic. Some aspects denote a harmonious

---

*Technically, a conjunction is not an aspect since two conjunct bodies do not form a geometrical relationship when inscribed on the ecliptic.

communication, others dissonant. Aspects express the communication among the planets. These four essential components—planets, signs, houses, and aspects—still form the basis of astrology today, as the art has changed remarkably little over the past two thousand years.

One efficient way to conceptualize the basic structure of astrology is called the *theater analogy.* Unfortunately, the primary source of this analogy is obscure, but it usually goes something like this: *planets in signs and houses in aspect relationships are to astrology as actors in costumes on sets having dialogue are to the theater.* Put differently: the planets are analogous to the actors; the signs are the costumes they wear; the houses are the sets they are on; and the aspects are the dialogue among them. For example, the astrological placement of Mars in Pisces on the second house conjunct the moon is analogous to a scene featuring a Navy SEAL (Piscean Mars) talking to a pregnant woman (conjunct the moon) at the bank (second house). This analogy helps us conceptualize the functionality of and relationships among astrology's four primary elements.

Another important thing to remember is that *signs are not constellations.* In the Western tropical system, the signs are thought of as sectors of space-time, and their boundaries (cusps) do not correspond to the constellations after which they were named. At the inception of horoscopic astrology in the Hellenistic period, the zodiacal signs roughly aligned with their constellational namesakes, but due to a phenomenon known as axial precession—which we will discuss shortly—they gradually slipped out of alignment by about 24 degrees over the last two thousand years or so.[10] The truth is that the signs and constellations never exactly corresponded because, unlike the signs, the zodiacal constellations are not an equal 30 degrees each. In Western tropical astrology, the signs align to the equinoxes and solstices thus making them seasonal, which is why we call this system tropical. Spring always begins at 0 degree Aries, summer at 0 degree Cancer, fall at 0 degree Libra, and winter at 0 degree Capricorn—these are the cardinal signs. The seasonal symbolism of the signs only remains intact in the tropical system; it is absent from the sidereal system. To reiterate: the signs of the zodiac are not the same as the constellations on the ecliptic. The signs are merely regions of the ecliptic that we agreed—long, long ago—to collectively call the zodiac.[11]

This ancient science of the stars may be used in a variety of applications. In natal astrology, for example, the positions of the planets in signs and houses, as well as their relationships by aspect, can tell the astrologer something about the native's past, present, or future. Imagine the following configuration for instance: Saturn in Aquarius on the second house receiving a dexter trine aspect from Jupiter in Gemini on the sixth house. This could indicate that the native has a natural tendency (this is a nativity) to be very disciplined (dignified Saturn) financially (second house), but in their forty-first year of life (a sixth house profection* year), much of their savings (second house) will be spent (dexter trine aspect) on their children's (debilitated Jupiter) medical bills (sixth house) from a respiratory infection (lungs are ruled by Gemini) after contracting an airborne virus (both planets are in air signs). Clearly, the symbolism is multivalent, and there are many ways this particular configuration could play out in the life of the native, but this shows the basic methodology in practice. We will be employing the quinarian technique, as discussed in this book, in the context of natal, electional, and horary astrology in chapters 5, 6, and 7, respectively.

While it is outside the scope of this book to detail the technical minutiae of practical astrology, suffice it to say that planets *always* find themselves in some degree of the zodiac or other and, further, that the ecliptic is itself divided into various groups—arc segments of the great cosmic circle—that affect a planet's ability to actualize its agenda. Planetary influences are modified by the planet's placement in the zodiac, for better or worse. The most common segments are the zodiacal signs, the terms (bounds), and the faces (decans), which bestow *essential dignity* (i.e., the necessary strength to express their

---

*Astrological timing technique that assigns a house to each year, month, day, or hour.

significations) to the planets. The quinaries are one such set of arc segments. Although not being counted among the medieval dignity scheme,[12] they still exert a potent symbolic influence and offer their own unique angelic and demonic significations to those planets, parts, and angles found within their quinarian cusps.

THE QUINARIES

The *quinaries* (sometimes called *pentads* or *quinances*) are somewhat of an astrological mystery. Information on their origin and use is scarce. Oddly, more can be discovered about them in the domains of Hermetic Qabalah and the Solomonic grimoires than in the literature of astrology, despite being an astrological device. They have been variously described as "any of 72 rays associated with the Sun, six for each of the 12 houses of the zodiac"[13] and a "phase of five degrees. In astrology, there are six quinances for each of the twelve zodiacal signs, totaling 72 quinances in all."[14] Aleister Crowley, British occultist and ghostwriter for renowned American astrologer Evangeline Adams, positioned the quinaries between the faces and the *monomoiria*—the 360 individual degrees of the sky in Hellenistic astrology—when describing the astrological segments of the ecliptic.

> First, there is the division into twelve signs of thirty degrees each, these signs corresponding roughly with the principal constellations. Each sign is divided into three parts called decanates, each containing ten degrees. Each sign is divided into six parts called quinaries, each containing five degrees. The degrees themselves are divided into sixty equal parts called minutes, and each minute is divided into sixty parts called seconds.[15]

As we have said above, each of the seven visible planets in an astrological chart find themselves in a particular degree of the zodiac. This arrangement of planets in signs and houses, along with their aspect relationships, is the essence of astrological analysis. The ecliptic is divided into various sets of longitudinal arc segments that specify the nature and strength of each planetary placement. A planet in its own sign, term, and face, for example, is said to be *essentially dignified*: it has access to resources enabling it to realize its agenda or to bring about its significations. A planet in signs opposing its rulership or exaltation is said to be *essentially debilitated*: it is devoid of resources and its ability to express its significations is muted. A planet's natural expression is modified—for better or worse—by its placement in the zodiac.

Beyond signs, terms, and faces, there are several other ecliptical subdivisions, but they are almost never used, except perhaps in the context of a particular technique or in the most technical and anachronistic astrological practice. For clarity's sake, we will list some of the common and the not-so-common zodiacal divisions here:

> The *signs* divide the ecliptic into twelve 30-degree arc segments.
> The *terms* (bounds) divide it into sixty, uneven 2- to 10-degree arc segments.
> The *faces* (decans) divide it into thirty-six 10-degree arc segments.
> The *leitourgoi* (ministers) divide it into one hundred eight 3-degree 30-minute arc segments.
> The *dodecatemoria* (twelve parts) divide it into one hundred forty-four 2-degree 30-minute arc segments.
> The *monomoiria* (individual degrees) divide it into three hundred sixty 1-degree arc segments.

To this list, we add the *quinaries*, which divide each sign into six equal subdivisions and each face in half. In the most direct terms: the quinaries are a set of 5-degree arc segments dividing the 360 degrees of the ecliptic into 72 equal parts ($360 \div 5 = 72$). In chapter 4, we will show how each of the individual quinaries are ruled by an angel of the Shem HaMephorash and a demon of the *Ars Goetia*. But, first, we will discuss how the quinaries came to be.

THE HISTORY OF THE QUINARIES

The quinaries appear to have evolved from a Babylonian calendrical unit consisting of five days. Since the 360 degrees of a circle are based on a solar year,[16] each degree of the zodiac corresponds to approximately one day. Thereby, a five-day period occupies a segment of approximately 5 degrees on the ecliptic, or the apparent path of the sun from the perspective of Earth. There are 72 of these *quinarian weeks* in a year, and as we will illustrate, each is ruled by an angel and demon.

The quinarian weeks are alluded to in a third-century BCE document known as the *Salmeschiniaka*. The name is believed to be etymologically related to the Babylonian word *salmi*, meaning "pictures," which is fitting, considering the images associated with the faces and quinaries with which the book deals.[17] This very work, which survives only in fragments, had been mentioned in late antiquity by the Neoplatonists Porphyry and Iamblichus, as well as by Hephaestio of Thebes, and is also the source of some of the earliest extant material on the faces, as well as the doctrine of astrological houses (anciently, *topoi* or "places").

According to Hephaestio, the calculations in the *Salmeschiniaka* were used by the legendary Greco-Egyptian astrologers Nechepso and Petosiris.[18] Often referred to simply as "the Egyptians" or "the Ancients," Nechepso and Petosiris were (ostensibly) a pharaoh and his priest living in the second to first centuries BCE, whom nearly all Hellenistic astrologers reference but whose work does not survive.[19] In addition to being responsible for such storied techniques as the *length of life*, the pair were also said to have used the *Salmeschiniaka* to work out the face—and perhaps the quinary—governing the moment of birth. These would correspond to either a ten-day period for the face or a five-day period for the quinary. According to the *Salmeschiniaka*, each of these 72 quinarian weeks is associated with "one or more astral rulers." It is speculative but conceivable that these very astral rulers may have evolved into either the 72 angels of the Shem HaMephorash or the demons of the *Ars Goetia*—or both, since one or more entities are mentioned.

A fragmentary manuscript nearly matching Porphyry and Iamblichus' description of the Salmeschiniaka on several points was discovered among the Oxyrhynchus papyri in 1897. In P. Oxy. 465, the twelve months of the Egyptian calendar are coordinated with the signs of the zodiac. Each month/sign is divided into six portions of five days/degrees (i.e., $12 \times 6 = 72$, $72 \times 5 = 360$), and each of these seventy-two pentads is assigned to one or more astral rulers who establish terrestrial conditions during that pentad.[20]

It is also worth noting that another document (P.Lond. 1 98)* from the same period references 36 *horoskopoi* (hour watchers) and 36 decans in a system of 72 segments of the zodiac.[21] The passage is in reference to Egyptian nocturnal timekeeping, so it is likely that the horoskopoi were made visible by 36 decanal *asterisms*, or star groups, in the evening and the decans were 36 divisions of the daylight hours. Regardless of how they were used, this is yet another unmistakable example of 72 quinaries, by any other name. In fact, another ancient document (P.Oxy. LXI 4180, 465 CE, which is cited in the above quote)† corroborates this notion by structurally implying that the 36 decans and 36 hour watchers were indeed synonymous with the 72 astral rulers of the *pentads* (i.e., the quinaries).[22]

In the strictly horoscopic sense—that is, pertaining to the practice of "hour watching" by the observance of rising asterisms—the quinaries would appear to be the Babylonian cousins of the Egyptian decans, which were used as such and were also *associated with distinct images*.[23] The notion that, like the faces and the lunar mansions of the *Picatrix*, the quinaries were associated with certain scenes or images is very interesting from a talismanic perspective. We will expand upon this idea later.

---

*The P.Lond. papyri are a collection of magical, astrological, and Hermetic texts from antiquity housed at the British Library in London.

†P.Oxy. (the Oxyrhynchus Papyri) denotes a collection of antique religious and administrative texts discovered at the site of an ancient trash heap near Oxyrhynchus, Egypt, in the late nineteenth and early twentieth centuries.

QUINARIAN MECHANICS

The quinaries, like the faces, are cast from the ascendant in zodiacal order (counterclockwise) both diurnally and annually. That is to say that they are considered in their order according to both the *primary* and *secondary* motions.[24] Primary motion is a diurnal cycle caused by Earth's rotation on its axis, which is why the planets and stars appear to rise in the east at the *ascendant*, culminate in the south at the local meridian or *medium coeli*, and set in the west at the *descendant*, from the perspective of the Northern Hemisphere. Secondary motion is an annual cycle caused by the revolution of Earth around the sun, which is why the sun and planets appear to travel through the signs of the zodiac. If one were to view our solar system from above (celestial north), perpendicular to the planets' orbital plane, Earth would be rotating counterclockwise on its axis and all the planets would be revolving counterclockwise in their orbits around the sun.

Diurnally, a new quinary rises on the eastern horizon every 20 minutes (1,440 minutes per day divided by 72 is 20 minutes). This is caused by Earth's primary motion, which is to say its rotation. Over the course of a day—one complete axial rotation—the ascendant (the point at the intersection of the ecliptic and the eastern horizon) passes through each of the 72 quinaries, just as it simultaneously passes through all 36 faces and all twelve signs. So, depending on the time of day, the ascendant will be in a certain quinary, as will each of the seven planets. Ergo, each planet will be under the influence of a particular quinary at any given time. We will call this 20-minute period a *quinarian hour*, of which there are 72 per day. This is the diurnal quinarian scheme.

At the annual scale, a new quinary rises at dawn approximately every five days. This is caused by Earth's secondary motion, that is, its revolution. Over the course of a year—one complete orbital revolution of Earth around the sun—sunrise will take place in all 72 quinaries, just as it simultaneously takes place in all 36 faces and all twelve signs. So, depending on the time of year, sunrise will occur in a different quinary every five days.

We will call this five-day period a *quinarian week*, of which there are 72 per year. This is the annual quinarian scheme. Since the planets are orbiting the sun at different rates of speed, their time spent in each quinary varies. Saturn, for example, spends approximately 150 days in each quinary; whereas the moon transits three quinaries in a single day. Planets may even appear to retrogress into a quinary they had recently exited, as they do with the signs. But it is important to remember that *every planet will be under the influence of a particular quinary at any given time.*

THE NUMBER 72

The number 72 is frequently encountered in the context of both astromythology and astrotheology. Tales of 72 angels, demons, and djinn abound, as well as accounts of 72 murderous accomplices and a 72-runged ladder. In this section we will highlight the quinarian archetypes' presence in stellar lore, myth, and religion. But first, we need to consider a certain 25,920-year cycle known as the Great Year.

We discussed the phenomena of primary and secondary motion in the preceding section, but there is an often-overlooked *tertiary* motion.* Due to the imperceptibly slow gyration of Earth's axis, the vernal equinoctial point *precedes* by 1 degree approximately every 72 years. This cycle is known as axial precession, or the precession of the equinoxes. Over the course of 2,160 years, the equinoctial point precedes through the 30 degrees of a zodiacal sign, and in approximately 25,920 years, the equinoctial point returns to its starting point on the ecliptic, thereby completing a Great Year, a phenomenon first hypothesized by Hipparchus of Rhodes (second century BCE). This is the same phenomenon that causes the Pole Star (currently Polaris, also known as Alpha Ursae Minoris) to periodically shift. The zodiacal symbolism of the sign hosting the vernal equinox over this period contributes to the

---

*There is also a *quaternary* motion, which describes the 230-million-year revolution of the sun around the galactic center, currently located at approximately 27 degrees Sagittarius.

stellar lore and mythotheological symbolism of nearly all civilizations since those of ancient Mesopotamia.[25]

This being the case, when one encounters 72 of *anything* in folklore, myth, sacred texts, and elsewhere, one should suspect the presence of either a quinarian or precessional allegory. Take, for example, the 72 accomplices who aided the Egyptian god Set in sealing his brother, Osiris, in a chest or coffin, precipitating the death of the god of the underworld. Although it is unclear as to whether this set of 72 accomplices constitutes some form of cryptic astromythological allusion or a direct commentary on the quinaries themselves, this interpretation is not outside the realm of possibility. When we consider not only the centrality of the Egyptian's conception of the 36 faces, but also an Egyptian creation myth involving Tahuti (or Thoth), the measurer, who gathers 1/72 of each day of the year in consequence of a wager with the moon.[26] The ibis-headed god then uses these parts to assemble the five intercalary days, during which the remaining gods and goddesses are born, which is almost certainly in reference to both axial precession and the quinaries. One seventy-second of the day is a diurnal quinary of twenty minutes; and 1/72 of the year is a quinarian week, consisting of approximately five days. Also worthy of consideration are later quinarian allusions such as the 72 rungs of Jacob's ladder, regarding which, cofounder of the Hermetic Order of the Golden Dawn, Samuel Liddell MacGregor Mathers (1854–1918) said:

> These are also the 72 names of the ladder of Jacob on which the Angels of God ascended and descended. It will presently be shown how the 72 Angelic names are formed from the 72 Names of the Deity, and also how their signification is to be found. The 72 Names of the Deity are thus obtained. The 19th, 20th, and 21st verses of the XIV Chapter of the Book of Exodus each consist of 72 letters.[27]

From the modern astrological perspective, we encounter the number 72 in reference to a minor aspect known as a *quintile*, which is formed by two planets separated by 72 degrees on the ecliptic. This aspect, which inscribes a pentagon in the ecliptic, is evocative of the five-petalled rosette traced by Venus over the course of her synodic period (583.92 days) and, thereby, alludes to the Venusian archetype in its myriad forms, such as the Sumerian Inanna, the Akkadian Ishtar, and the Greek Aphrodite. The five 72-degree sides of the pentagon—and its unicursal cousin, the pentagram—carry a wealth of Pythagorean and occult significance.

The breastplate worn by the high priest of King Solomon's Temple was called the Choshen Mishpat. This "Breastplate of Judgment" was an oracular device consisting of twelve gemstones, which may have been used as (or in conjunction with) a *pinax*, which was an astrologer's board, used by some Hellenistic astrologers to visually illustrate planetary placements in the zodiac and houses. This garment is believed to be the origin of assigning a specific gemstone to each sign of the zodiac.[28] Qabalistic writers, such as Hezekiah ben Manoah (thirteenth century) and Bahya ben Asher (fourteenth century), have drawn parallels between the tribal names on the breastplate and the 72-fold name.[29] Each of the twelve stones on the breastplate were said to be engraved with a six-letter rendering of the twelve Hebrew tribes, thus assigning six letters to each of the twelve stones—*72 letters in all*. This is a clear allusion to the Shem HaMephorash. As each stone represents a zodiacal sign, their division into six equal parts necessarily represents the 72 quinaries.

In Book II of his three-volume *De Occulta Philosophia* (1533), translated into English as *Three Books of Occult Philosophy*, the German Renaissance polymath Heinrich Cornelius Agrippa (1486–1534) masterfully explicates the qualitative or metanumerical powers of numbers, particularly highlighting their occult virtues. He seems to support the theological ubiquity of the number 72 by attributing it to the number's astrological significance. Unmistakably, his "seventy two fives" are none other than the quinaries: six parts of each sign, each ruled by an angel, together constituting the 72-fold name of God—the Shem HaMephorash.

[T]he number seventy two was famous for so many languages, for so many Elders of the Synagogue, for so many interpreters of the old Testament, for so many Disciples of Christ: It hath also a great Communion with the number twelve; hence in the heavens, every sign being divided into six parts, there result seventy two fives, over which so many angels bear rule; and so many are the names of God; and every five is set over one Idiom with such efficacy, that the Astrologers, and Physiognomists can know from thence from what Idiom everyone ariseth.[30]

Intriguingly, Agrippa associates each 5-degree segment with what J. F. translated as an "idiom." In this usage, we might understand the word as denoting a *type* or a *temperament*. He then seems to imply that astrologers and physiognomists (face readers) can know someone's rising idiom by observing their personality (or, perhaps, vice versa?). This is, of course, similar to the standard astrological doctrine of the rising sign signifying the native's character, physique, and temperament. We will pick up this thread again in chapter 5 when we discuss the significance of the rising quinary, as well as the Angel of the Nativity.

As an astromythological and/or astrotheological allusion to the quinaries, the number 72 figures prominently in qabalistic literature and the Solomonic grimoire tradition. Throughout history, various mythologies and religions have made reference to 72 angels, demons, djinn, and other potentially quinarian embodiments.

2
The Angels of the Shem HaMephorash

EACH QUINARY OF THE ZODIAC is ruled by one of the 72 angels of the Shem HaMephorash. When a planet, part, or angle is placed in a certain quinary, it is modified by the influence of the angel who presides over that 5-degree subdivision. This is similar to the archangelic influence on a planet found in any particular term or face. For instance, suppose a given natal planetary placement is found in 15 degrees Libra; that planet is in Saturn's face and is thereby under the influence of Zaphkiel, the archangel of Saturn.[1] Similarly, the ruling Shem angel bestows its influence—for better or worse—upon the planet found within its quinarian cusps. Throughout the ensuing qabalistic and Solomonic grimoire traditions, various powers and attributes have been associated with these entities.

In this chapter, we will discuss how the angelic names were qabalistically derived from the Shem HaMephorash or 72-fold name of God, along with some commentary on that topic. We will also examine the textual history and the development of the angelic significations. But before we begin, it will be necessary to develop a cursory sense of qabalistic thought, as this body of interpretive techniques informs how we approach Judaic scripture and apocrypha and their commentary. A working knowledge of basic qabalistic doctrine will make the angelological and cosmological significance of the Shem HaMephorash more accessible.

QABALISTIC ORIENTATION

Qabalah (meaning "reception, tradition") is a Jewish mystical tradition that arose during the medieval period, further developing many of the concepts found in the preceding *Hekhalot* (Palaces) and *Merkabah* (Chariot) mystical literature of late antiquity. The word is alternately spelled Kabbalah, Cabala, or Qabalah, depending on the context. Kabbalah is usually used in the Jewish tradition; the Latinization Cabala is used in the Christian tradition; and Qabalah in the syncretized hermetic context. Because we are employing the term in the context of astrology and magic—two of the three hermetic arts, excluding alchemy—we will be using the spelling with a *q*.[2]

Qabalistic cosmogony is of the emanationist variety, common to other esoteric traditions emerging in Alexandria, Egypt, during the Hellenistic era, such as Hermetism, Gnosticism, and Neoplatonism. Angels figure heavily into qabalistic lore, particularly regarding the transmission of the system. While there is a developed mystical and contemplative component to Qabalah, we will limit our focus to the tradition's cosmogony and its set of exegetical interpretive methods whose purpose is to reveal the esoteric import of sacred and magical texts.

Qabalists use *gematria, temurah, notariqon,* and other cryptographical techniques to uncover the occult significance of scripture and other texts. *Gematria* is an alphanumerical cipher system that assigns a number value to each letter of the Hebrew alphabet (*aleph* = 1, *beth* = 2, etc.). *Temurah* consists of a set of substitution ciphers that replace the first letter of the Hebrew alphabet with the last, the second with the second to last, and so on (*atbash*), or with the preceding letter (*avgad*), or with the twelfth letter ahead (*albam*). *Notariqon* is an interpretive method and system of encryption using acronyms and abbreviations. The most common type of notariqon uses the individual letters of a word to form full sentences. The notariqonic sentence is thought to expound upon the underlying hidden nature of the root word. For example, the word *cat* may be interpreted to conceal the message: "canines are terrible." Thus, any word may be viewed as an acronym concealing its occult virtue. These three methods are employed to access the esoteric substratum of words and phrases.[3]

There is a sort of *sacred algebra* to qabalistic cosmogony, in that the very letters of the Hebrew alphabet are central to the creation and form of the cosmos. In the protoqabalistic *Sefer Yetzirah* (Book of Creation, circa second to fifth century), for example, the Hebrew alphabet plays an important part in the mystical emanation of the four worlds. Jah, the Lord of Hosts, is described as creating the cosmos, *ex nihilo*, by means of the three seraphim: number, writing, and speech. Issuing from this alphanumerical fiat are the Sephirot (emanations) and *netivot* (paths) of the Etz Chaim (Tree of Life). Like the planets in astrology to which they correspond, the Sephirot are archetypal concentrations and the netivot are the paths by which they progress and communicate.[4]

The Etz Chaim is a visual representation of the qabalistic cosmological model and is directly patterned on the Ptolemaic system, which was the standing cosmological paradigm at the time of the tradition's inception. Whereas the Ptolemaic system is composed of a series of concentrically enveloped ætheric spheres, the Tree of Life diagram depicts the Sephirot in a more linear configuration. At the top is the Sephirah Keter (crown), which is associated with Aristotle's primum mobile. Keter "overflows" into Chochmah (wisdom), which corresponds to the firmament, or the sphere of the fixed stars and the zodiac. This particular juncture represents the engagement of causality and the bounds of fate (an important point to remember when we begin to examine the philosophical implications of the quinaries in the conclusion). The primum movens is the uncaused cause, and its influence on—or emanation into—the stellar-zodiacal sphere gives rise to the notions of space and time and, thereby, to mechanical causality and resultant fate. The rest of the Sephirot descend in the Chaldean planetary order: Binah (understanding) represents Saturn;

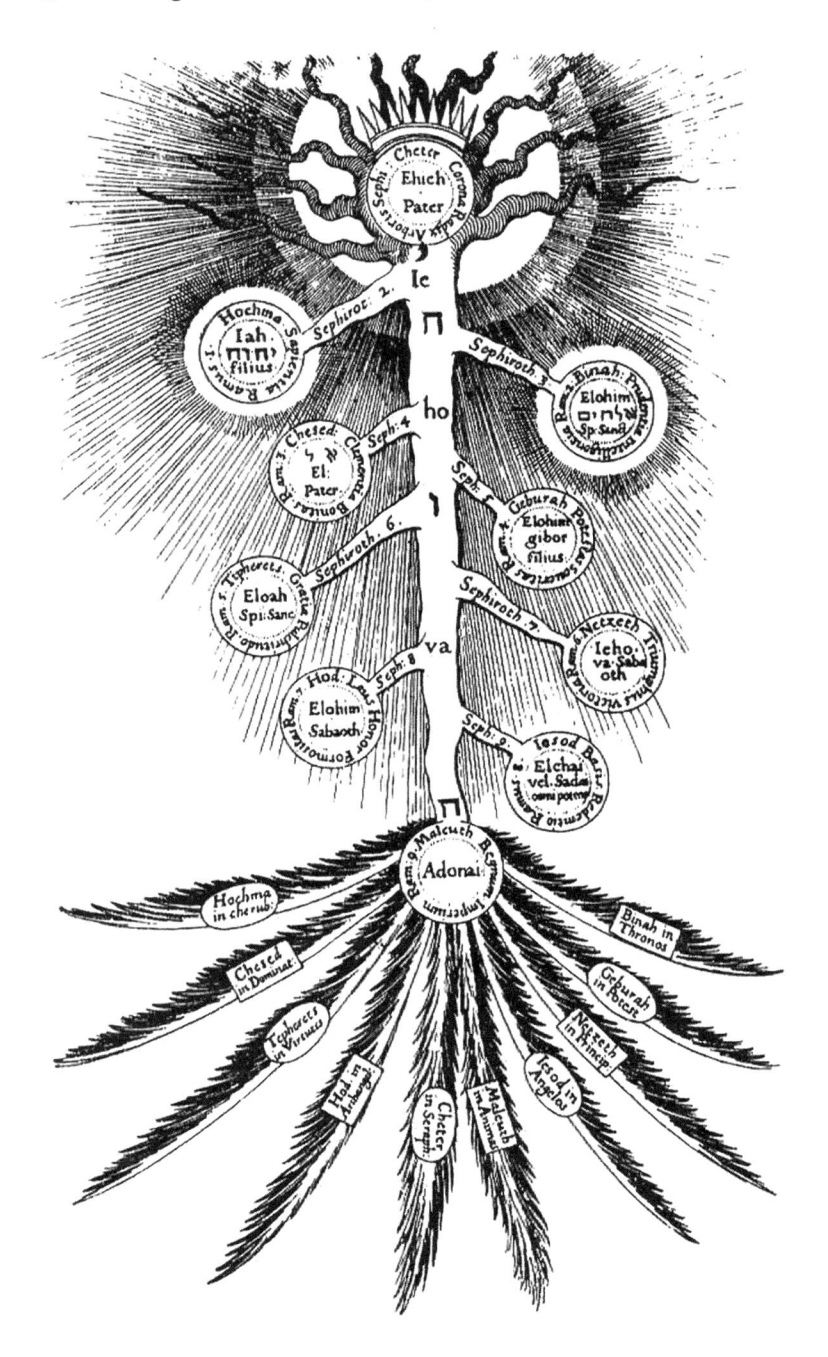

Fig. 2.1. The Tree of Life from Robert Fludd's *De præternaturali utriusque mundi historia* (1621).

Chesed (mercy) Jupiter; Gevurah (strength) Mars; Tiferet (beauty or glory) the sun; Netzach (victory) Venus; Hod (splendor) Mercury; Yesod (foundation) the moon; and Malchut (kingdom) represents Earth—the sublunary, elemental sphere of generation and corruption.[5]

The emanation of the primum movens—an expression of divine will—is first communicated to the stars and zodiac, which then distribute the supernal effluvia downward through the seven planetary spheres. Each planet further modifies the expression until it penetrates the sublunary sphere, which is the ætheric membrane separating the celestial realm from the terrestrial. Finally, the *empyrean* emanation, having been conditioned by the stars and planets and distributed by the moon, reaches the sublunary sphere, where it acts upon the four terrestrial elements causing change, growth, and decay. The classical elements are stratified in their pregravitational order known as *natural place*: fire, air, water, and earth (descending from rarity to density).[6] These are the essential features the Aristotelian-Ptolemaic causal cosmology. This is the system upon which the qabalistic Tree of Life was superimposed, with the Sephirot representing the Ptolemaic spheres.

Qabalistic exegetical methods, cosmogony, and cosmology offer us a potent hermeneutic with which we may unlock the secrets surrounding the Shem HaMephorash. In qabalistic theurgy, the angels and divine emanations represented by the Sephirot may be petitioned by working with the 72 inferior angels of the Shem HaMephorash. Much of this supernal contact is made possible by the qabalistic manipulation of the letters of the Hebrew alphabet.[7]

THE NAME

Jewish cultural convention forbids the pronunciation of God's name (Yahweh, Jehovah). This is made clear in the third commandment, which states that "you shall not take the name of the Lord your God in vain" (Exodus 20:7). The twelfth-century, Sephardic Jewish philosopher Moses Maimonides said that in the event that the name were to be pronounced, it should immediately be followed by praise, such as "blessed be He for all eternity" or "He is great and exceedingly praiseworthy."[8] We see this sort of reverential practice extended into Islam wherein, after the mention of the prophet Mohammed's name, it is customary to say, "peace be upon him." Alternate names such as Adonai (my Lord) and Elohim (God or gods) were used in lieu of pronouncing the tetragrammaton or YHVH, the four-letter Hebrew name for God. The name of God was considered ineffable and could only legally be uttered once per year by the high priest of the temple.

The term *Shem HaMephorash* (Explicit Name) was coined by a group of rabbinical sages known as the Tannaim. It is first encountered in the written collection of the oral Torah known as the *Mishnah*. Though it was originally used in reference to the tetragrammaton,[9] it most commonly refers to the 72-fold name of God. However, in the interim between these two applications, the Shem HaMephorash was also used in reference to names of God consisting of twelve, twenty-two, and forty-two letters. A tractate of the Mishnah called Qiddushin 72a recommends a twelve-letter name (YHVH-EHIH-ADNI)[10] as well as a forty-two-letter name that is now apparently lost.

> Those two names [the twelve- and forty-two-letter names] must have included some metaphysical ideas. It can be proved that one of them conveyed profound knowledge, from the following rule laid down by our Sages: "The name of forty-two letters is exceedingly holy; it can only be entrusted to him who is modest, in the midway of life, not easily provoked to anger, temperate, gentle, and who speaks kindly to his fellow men. He who understands it, is cautious with it, and keeps it in purity, is loved above and is liked here below; he is respected by his fellow men; his learning remaineth with him, and he enjoys both this world and the world to come."[11]

The thirteenth-century *Sefer Raziel HaMalakh* (Book of Raziel the Angel) mentions a twenty-two-letter name of mysterious origins and etymology. The name Anaktam Pastam Paspasim Dionsim appears to have no relation to Hebrew, Aramaic, or Arabic, nor is there any known connection to Greek of Zoroastrian origins. It is possible that this name is a form of magical glossolalia such as one encounters in the Gnostic and Hermetic incantations of the *Greek Magical Papyri*. The twenty-two-letter name was employed in amulets and talismans and, in the seventeenth century, was incorporated into a prayer preceding the reading of the priestly benediction in the ritual of the synagogue.[12]

The notion of a 72-fold name seems to emerge from the account of Moses parting the Red Sea from the book of Exodus. Medieval qabalists affirm that he used the angelic powers of the Shem HaMephorash to accomplish this miraculous feat of *thaumaturgy*. The Explicit Name was qabalistically derived from the nineteenth, twentieth, and twenty-first verses of Exodus 14. These three verses contain exactly 72 letters each—a feature that did not escape the notice of the authors of the *Sefer Raziel HaMalakh* and the *Zohar* and later the German theologian Johann Reuchlin (1455–1522) and the Renaissance polymath Athanasius Kircher (1602–1680). They recognized this as being an unusual and significant phenomenon. The qabalistic method known as *temurah* was applied, which has to do with the rearranging of letters and, in this case, sentences to reveal the occult substratum of the verses in question. In their qabalistic exegesis, attempting to find the esoteric meaning of the passages, they arranged the sentences *boustrophedonically*, which is to say, "as the ox plows the field." The nineteenth verse was read from right to left, which is typical in Hebrew. They then reversed the order of the letters of the twentieth verse, from left to right, as the ox would turn when plowing a field. The twenty-first verse was ordered from right to left again, per usual Hebrew. When the three rows of letters are stacked in this manner, they yield 72 columns consisting of three letters each. After the set of 72 three-letter angelic roots is produced, Reuchlin adds the suffixes *el* or *iah*, both Hebrew words for God, in order to *angelicize* the names. Angel names ending in *el* are masculine and those ending in *iah* are feminine. Reuchlin's conventions further influence Agrippa's and Kircher's (and everyone else's) approach to working with the angels of the Shem HaMephorash.[13]

The explanation of this name may be found in the works of several medieval commentators, such as the French rabbi Rashi (Shlomo Yitzchaki, eleventh century),[14] as well as in the qabalistic *Sefer HaBahir* (Book of Brightness, twelfth century).[15] The formula for its derivation is best elucidated in Reuchlin's *De art cabalistica* (1517).[16]

It is also worth noting that the *Zohar* attributes each of these three verses to a specific Sephirah: verse 19 corresponds to Chesed, verse 20 to Gevurah, and verse 21 to Tiferet. The total gematriac value of the word *chesed* (חסד) is 72. The gematriac value of the word *gevurah* (גברה) is 216, which is the total number of letters in the three verses from Exodus ($72 \times 3 = 216$). And Tiferet (beauty or glory) is the balance between the mercy of Chesed and the severity of Gevurah. There are further qabalistic proofs attesting to the occult veridicality of the 72-fold name. Reuchlin goes on to offer another proof from the Pythagorean perspective.

> It is enough that you read the three words that I have just resolved into the seventy-two names of the angels with reverence and veneration, in the order the holy spirit laid down, and that you press on directly through love of them in the names of God most high, in burning ardor and fearful adoration, taking great care to bear in mind that just as the number seventy-two is derived arithmetically from the numerical value of the Tetragrammaton, so the seventy-two angels are produced from the sign of the creator, as if by divine issue. Any Hebrew letter you take stands for a particular number. Thus, in this way, YHVH equals seventy-two; Y means ten, H five, V six, H five again. Put together arithmetically, Y is ten, YH fifteen, YHV is twenty-one, YHVH twenty-six. Now add ten, fifteen, twenty-one and twenty-six, and the answer is seventy-two.[17]

The qabalistic formula described above is a method by which the tetragrammaton is adapted to the *tetraktys*, revealing the number 72. In essence, the formula uses the tetraktys as a Pythagorean key, linking the tetragrammaton to the Shem HaMephorash through speculative mathematics.

The tetraktys is a mystical figure first utilized in the teachings of Pythagoras of Samos (circa 570–495 BCE). The philosopher and his followers held the symbol in such high regard that they deemed it holy and were said to have taken their oaths upon it.[18] The tetraktys consists of ten regularly spaced points arranged in an upward-pointing equilateral triangle, having one point on the top tier, two on the second, three on the third, and four at the bottom. It is a cosmogonical model illustrating the organization of space through the emanations of the Grand Geometer: from a point to a line, to a superficies, and, finally, to a solid. In this sense, the tetraktys prefigures the emanationist cosmogony of the theosophical qabalah, revealing a clear Pythagorean influence. In Reuchlin's arrangement, the letter *yod* occupies the uppermost point, *yod heh* on the second tier, *yod heh vav* the third, and the tetragrammaton is spelled out in full—*yod heh vav heh*—on the bottom tier consisting of four points. When the total gematriac value of the four tiers is calculated, the sum is 72. Reuchlin posits this as a sort of *metageometrical* proof for the angels of the Shem HaMephorash, whom he gives power over the 72 divisions of Earth.

> These are the angels strong over the whole earth. Through them, it is thought, did Moses the miracle-worker divide the sea with his hand down to the sea-bed, for these are the angels of division, and God divided the earth in accordance with the number of angels.[19]

In his *Oedipus Aegyptiacus* (1652), Kircher assigned a verse from Psalms to each one of the 72 angels. These are presented as the means by which the angels of the Shem HaMephorash may be invoked. The occult logic behind his selections and attributions was that each verse must contain

Fig. 2.2. The 72 names of God from Athanasius Kircher's
Œdipus Ægyptiacus (1652–1654).

not only the four letters of the tetragrammaton but also the three letters of the angelic name to which it corresponds. For example, in Hebrew, Psalm 3:3 ("But thou, O Lord, art a shield for me; my glory, and the lifter up of mine head") contains a yod, heh, vav, and heh, the letters of the tetragrammaton, as well as a separate vav, heh, and vav, which are the three root letters of the angel name Vehuiah (והויה). The invocatory verses from Psalms (except the seventieth, which is from Genesis) are given with their corresponding angel in chapter 4.

As we have illustrated, the Shem HaMephorash was qabalistically derived from three verses in the book of Exodus. The angels of the 72-fold name were the source of Moses's *thaumaturgical* or wonder-working power, such as his miraculous parting of the Red Sea. Qabalistic legend maintains that this name grants the bearer thaumaturgical power, such as the ability to exorcise demons, heal the sick, prevent natural disasters—and kill enemies.[20] But Moses is not the only magician in the Old Testament. In the next chapter, we will draw parallels between Moses's control of the 72 angels of the Shem HaMephorash and King Solomon's control of the 72 demons of the *Ars Goetia*.

3

The Demons of
the *Ars Goetia*

LIKE THE 72 ANGELS of the Shem HaMephorash, each of the 72 demons of the *Ars Goetia* presides over a quinary. This means that each placement in a given astrological figure is governed by a quinarian pair consisting of an angel and a demon. This is astrologically valuable because each of these entities has a unique set of significations, attributes, and powers that modify the expression of any planet placed within their cusps. Each angel and demon also has a particular scope of activity and influence, such as being able to assist the astrologer-operator in projects like memorization, achieving invisibility, or finding lost objects.

In this chapter, we will first discuss the notion of the demon in general before turning our attention to the Solomon-magus tradition. Rooted in antiquity, this tradition situates the son of David not only as the wise monarch of ancient Israel with which most are familiar but also as an exorcist and nigromancer or controller of demons. For, just as Moses thaumaturgically harnessed power of the 72 angels of the Shem HaMephorash to work wonders, such as parting the Red Sea, King Solomon is said to have employed their 72 demonic counterparts, commanding them to build the First Temple at Jerusalem. We will then outline the development of the standard demon catalog as found in the *Ars*

Goetia, one of the five books comprising the mid-seventeenth-century grimoire known as the *Lesser Ley of Solomon*.

DAIMŌN, DÆMON, DEMON

Though demons tend to be perceived as malevolent entities from the modern perspective, in the ancient conception they tended to be morally ambivalent. A distinction was also sometimes drawn between a good demon (*agathodaimōn*) and a bad demon (*kakodaimōn*), but over time, the difference between the two seems to have blurred and eventually most of the positive significations were allotted to angels, while the negative qualities were relegated to demons.

Demons figure into the cosmological, mythological, and theological systems of both the ancient Mesopotamians and Egyptians.[1] Much like angels, they were thought of as intercessors and messengers between the terrestrial and celestial worlds as well as the guardian spirits of sacred locations, as we encounter them later in the Roman concept of a *genius loci*.

From the very beginning, demons in the various systems appear to have a specific scope of activity. They presided over the realization of certain projects and could be petitioned, also like the angels, to aid in the achievement of mortal aims. Demons were often thought to represent various abstract concepts such as justice or love, as we see in Plato's *Symposium* (202d-e) wherein Diotima, in teaching Socrates the art of love, argues that love is a demon because it binds together the mortal and immortal as an intermediary. In fact, the concept of the *daimōn* figures prominently in Plato's and Socrates's philosophy, where it represented both the general notion of divine inspiration as well as a personal tutelary spirit—an incorporeal *mystagogue*, guiding and counseling its mortal host. This understanding was echoed by the third century BCE dramatist Menander, who thought it preposterous that one might be guided by an evil demon.

> A daimon stands by every man, straightway from his birth, to guide him into the mysteries of life, a good daimon, for one must not imagine that there is an evil daimon injuring good life.[2]

It is the latter definition that carries perhaps the most astrological significance, since the demon has long been associated with an individual's fate and fortune, as well as one's higher genius. For example, in Plato's "Myth of Er," the final sequence of Book X (616c–17e) of his *Republic*, the preincarnate human soul stands outside the cosmos where it chooses its daimōn. This psychopompic entity then guides the soul down through the seven planetary spheres, at each of which vices and virtues corresponding to the planets are allotted. At the sphere of Mars, for instance, qualities such as aggression, stamina, or bravery are meted out, depending on the condition of the planet at the time of the descent. This descent and distribution of qualities and characteristics endowed the soul with personality. *This mechanism may be seen as the very essence of natal astrology's predictivity*, at least from the Hermetic and Neoplatonic perspectives, because people tend to act within the confines of their character and, if their character were calculable through astrological delineation, then one could make inferences based on their planetary placements and condition.[3]

There are ancient methods of calculating the planetary affiliation of one's personal demon, there being seven orders of planetary daimōnes. In the Hellenistic astrology practiced by the Alexandrian Hermetists, Neoplatonists, and Stoics, this entity was known as the Kyrios Geneseos or Lord of the Geniture or Nativity.[4] Accounts of the various techniques differ, but the demon was generally represented by the planet possessing the most essential and accidental dignity in the five *hylegical places*.* In the later medieval Perso-Arabic and Renaissance astrological traditions, the personal demon became associated with the Almuten Figuris (Winner of the Figure), which was the most dignified planet

---

*That is "the places of life," namely the degrees of the sun, moon, ascendant, part of fortune, and prenatal syzygy.

in the nativity. This entity was later conflated with the holy guardian angel—a tutelary guide and protector encountered in ceremonial magic traditions.[5]

Prefiguring the goetic demons of the 72 quinaries, there is a system of demons associated with the 36 faces of the zodiac. In the *Testament of Solomon*, the king encounters and interviews a widely syncretized cast of Egyptian, Greek, Jewish, Christian, and Arabic demons.[6] This, in fact, may be seen as the origin of all subsequent astrological demon catalogs. The 36 decanal demons each preside over their 10-degree segment of the zodiac, just as the 72 goetic demons each rule a segment of 5 degrees.

The demons of the *Ars Goetia* are a specific group of nonhuman, supernatural entities—sometimes referred to as spirits or spiritual creatures—that evolved into their present form over the course of approximately fifteen hundred years. In the next section, we will first examine the Solomon-magus tradition, which situates King Solomon as an exorcist and nigromancer. We will then move on to the development of the goetic demon catalog as it evolved in the Solomonic cycle of grimoires.

THE SOLOMON-MAGUS TRADITION

When most people think of King Solomon (regnal years: 970–931 BCE), they think of the son of David, the great and wise monarch of ancient Israel and builder of the First Temple at Jerusalem. This perspective is not wrong—*but it is incomplete*. Another, fuller picture begins to emerge when we read in 1 Kings 11:4 that under the influence of his foreign wives, Solomon's heart was turned toward gods other than Yahweh. That is to say that pagan idolatry was not entirely outside the king's purview. In fact, Solomon went so far as to build temples to pagan gods, such as Ashtoreth of the Sidonians and the Ammonitish Milcom. For these infractions, the King incurred the wrath of the Lord, who removed most of the Judaic tribes from his rule (1 Kings 11:30–34).

There is a long and developed literary history of Solomon the magus beginning as far back as Josephus's historiographical *Antiquities of the Jews* from the first century CE. This depiction is continued in a likely second century CE apocalyptic work known as the *Apocalypse of Adam*. This apocryphal text of Sethian Gnostic provenance depicts the king as being in control of an army of demons who are nigromantically compelled to do his bidding. Solomon's control over demons is also noted in the pseudepigraphal *Testament of Solomon*, which, as mentioned above, is where we begin to see the development of the elaborate Solomonic demonology.[7] In the *Testament*, the king is given a magical seal ring by the Archangel Michael. He uses the ring to control a veritable parade of demons of Egyptian, Greek, Jewish, and Christian pedigree, who he compels to build the First Temple. He interrogates a host of demons, imprisons them, and forces them to perform a variety of labors, from hewing and setting stones to carrying water for the demonic workforce.

There are accounts contributing to the Solomon-magus literary tradition spanning many centuries, in such diverse works as the Talmud (third to sixth centuries), the Qur'an (seventh century), and the *Alf LayLah wa Laylah* (*One Thousand and One Nights* or *Arabian Nights*, eighth to fourteenth centuries). But nowhere is Solomonic magic more explicitly and practicably presented than in the European grimoire tradition, to which we will presently turn our attention.

ANGELS AND DEMONS IN THE GRIMOIRE TRADITION

Grimoires are textbooks of magic covering subjects such as the construction of magical equipment such as altars, pentacles, and talismans; the casting of spells; the performance of divination; and the invocation and conjuration of supernatural entities such as angels and demons. As the name implies, grimoires are essentially *grammars* of magic.[8] Cuneiform tablets and papyri of magical incantations date back to ancient

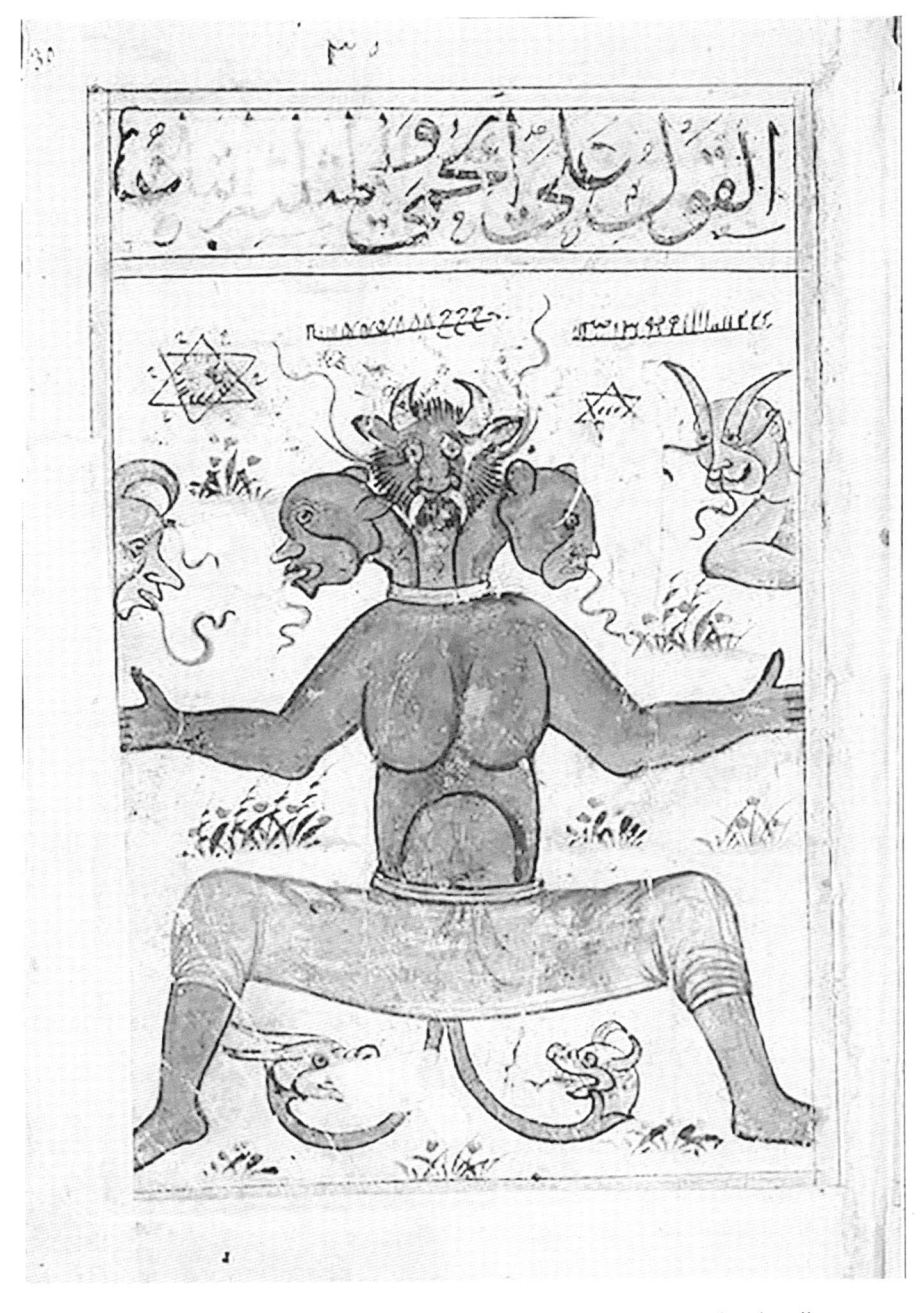

Fig. 3.1. A demon from the late fourteenth-century *Kitab al-Bulhan* (Book of Wonders). Note the Seals of Solomon on either side of the demon's heads.

Mesopotamia and Egypt. These documents evolved throughout the Hellenistic period and often took the form of *pseudepigrapha* or works falsely attributed to notable personages. It was very common for magical texts to have been attributed to figures such as Zoroaster, Hermes Trismegistus, Moses, and King Solomon. This would, of course, add a level of authority to the work, as opposed to attributing the work to an anonymous scribe.

Most grimoires have an astrological component in that they utilize *electional astrology*. This branch of astrology is used to maximize auspicious planetary and stellar configurations by *electing* to perform activities at astrologically meaningful times. An election could be as simple as using the planetary rulers of the days of the week in a corresponding operation. For instance, a love spell may be executed on a Friday, which is governed by the planet Venus, whose purview includes love, sex, and relationships. Thereby, a more romantically efficacious causal cycle is engaged. The next level of electional granularity would be the planetary hours: the magician may choose to consecrate a talisman at the hour governed by the appropriate planet. Elections can also become quite complicated, such as making sure the planet in question is not only in its day and hour but in its own domicile, face, and term, as well as either *rising* (conjunct the ascendant) or *culminating* (conjunct the midheaven) and being free from malefic aspects. Great elections can be very difficult to find, and it may be years before a planet is suitably dignified. The overall rationale supporting electional astrology is that the strength of a planet's energetic emanation is proportionate to its degree of essential and accidental dignity. A dignified planet is more likely to manifest its significations and actualize its agenda. The concentrated planetary influence may then be captured and retained in a seal, pentacle, or talisman. Another less materialistic way to view this phenomenon is that an occult link is forged between the terrestrial object and the spirit of the planet. In Book II of his *Three Books of Occult Philosophy*, Agrippa explains the importance of considering the essential and accidental dignities in an election.

Whosoever will work according to the Celestiall opportunity, ought to observe both or one of them, namely the motion of the Stars, or their times; I say their motions, when they are in their dignities or dejections, either essential or accidentall; but I call their times, dayes and hours distributed to their Dominions.[9]

The 72 angels of the Shem HaMephorash have their origin in medieval commentaries on the book of Exodus such as the *Sefer HaBahir*[10] and the *Sefer Raziel HaMalakh*. In the various works of Jewish magic, qabalistic angelology is communicated to the likes of Adam, Noah, Moses, and Solomon by the angel Raziel, whose name means "Angel of Secrets" or "Angel of the Mysteries." The *Sefer HaRazim* (Book of Secrets), for example, is a Jewish magical text communicated from Raziel to Noah. The book instructs the reader how to call upon angels, rather than God, to perform thaumaturgical operations.[11] Scholars have dated at least portions of the text to the late third or early fourth century.[12] The book contains an angel catalog as well as the operations meant to invoke them in theurgical rites. The book is divided into seven sections, each corresponding to one of the planetary spheres. It contains rituals for gaining fortune, defeating enemies, and attaining divinatory powers.

The Shem HaMephorash figures prominently in the *Sefer Raziel HaMalakh*, which was given to Adam by Raziel. It is a qabalistic grimoire of practical magic, probably dating back to late antiquity but surviving in a thirteenth-century Latin translation called *Liber Razielis Archangeli*, a translation produced by Alfonso X of Castille. It draws heavily on the *Sefer Yetzirah* and on the *Sefer HaRazim*. The book is a mystical *midrash* (rabbinical exegesis) on the creation account as well as containing an elaborate angelology. It contains protective spells and utilizes astrological and gematriac methodology to prepare talismans and also uses the various names of God, such as the Shem HaMephorash. The *Sefer Raziel HaMalakh* in turn influenced Peter d'Abano's (1257–1316) fifteenth-century grimoire the *Heptameron* (Magical Elements). The work deals with the summoning of angels corresponding to the days of the week, as the title implies, and contains sigils, ruling planets, and other astrological magic.

As we discussed in the last section, the Solomon-magus tradition begins with the account in Josephus's *Antiquities* and runs all the way through the Islamic golden age—a period of over one thousand years. But this sort of Solomonic magic does not enter the grimoire tradition until the *Hygromanteia*, or *Magical Treatise of Solomon*. This first of the Solomonic grimoires was composed between the sixth and fourteenth centuries CE in various iterations and recensions.[13] It is a pseudepigraphal account of Solomon's instructions to his son Rehoboam on subjects such as astrology, divination, magical uses of herbs, and, of course, controlling demons. The *Hygromanteia* contains electional instructions on how to create planetary talismans by both day and hour, as well as invocations of the seven planetary archangels. The work is considered the bridge between the ancient *Testament of Solomon* and the Renaissance *Lesser Key of Solomon*.[14]

The *Lesser Key of Solomon* (*Lemegeton Clavicula Salomonis*) was compiled during the late fourteenth century, though most surviving manuscripts date from the late sixteenth and seventeenth centuries. It, along with the *Hygromanteia*, is among the first of many pseudepigraphal grimoires attributed to Solomon. Also, like the *Hygromanteia*, it is presented as instructions to Rehoboam. While it contains no demon catalog, the *Lesser Key of Solomon* is replete with conjurations and invocations to summon demons and command them to do the exorcist-operator's bidding. The demon catalog had long been under development by this time, however. We, of course, encounter a number of demons under Solomon's control in the *Testament*—Ornias, Beelzebul, Ephippas, Asmodeus, the seven star sisters (the Pleiades), the 36 decanal demons, and approximately twelve others—but it is incomplete. A demon catalog begins to take shape, but it would be about a millennium before we encounter the 72 demons of the *Ars Goetia*.

In the interim, we encounter three important documents in the evolution of the goetic demon catalog: *Livre des Esperitz* (Book of Spirits, fifteenth century), *Liber Officiorum Spirituum* (Book of the Office of Spirits, 1583), and *De praestigiis dæmonum* (On the Tricks of Demons, 1577). *Livre des Esperitz*, which is attributed to Solomon, contains a catalog consisting of forty-six demons. The hierarchy of hell is given as well as the appearance and functions of the demons. The *Livre* contains no prayers, invocations, or conjurations.[15] The *Liber Officiorum Spirituum* contains a catalog of eighty-two demons and incorporates material from the *Livre*, Agrippa's *Three Books of Occult Philosophy*, the famous but non-Solomonic *Arbatel* (1575), and the qabalistic *Sefer Raziel HaMalakh*, thereby creating perhaps the first concrete link between the angels of the Shem HaMephorash and the then-burgeoning goetic demons. It contains practical nigromancy involving the use of magic circles, as well as a variety of spells, geomantical figures, talismans, and notes on the lunar mansions.[16] Johann Weyer's *De praestigiis dæmonum*, while directly influenced by the *Livre* and the *Liber Officiorum Spirituum*, was somewhat different in tone. It argues *against* the existence of witchcraft and maintains those who have been deemed witches are actually individuals suffering from potentially treatable mental illnesses. In some ways, *De praestigiis* may be seen as an early example of the psychologization of the magical worldview, supporting the notion that occult phenomena are psychological rather than supernatural (a subject we will revisit later). Whatever the case, it contains an appendix known as the *Pseudomonarchia Dæmonum* (False Monarchy of Demons), which contains the demon catalog that would most influence that of the *Ars Goetia*. In fact, the only differences between the two are that Pruflas appears among the sixty-nine total demons of the *Pseudomonarchia*, which lacks the *Goetia*'s Vassago, Seere, Dantalion, and Andromalius.[17]

The *Lesser Key of Solomon* is a seventeenth-century grimoire usually consisting of five books: *Ars Goetia*, *Ars Goetia Theurgia*, *Ars Paulina*, *Ars Almadel*, and *Ars Notoria*. Though the five books were compiled in the seventeenth century, as noted earlier, most of the material can be traced back to the fourteenth century.[18] While the *Lesser Key* is perhaps the most famous of the Solomonic grimoires, its authorship is not attributed to the king. The *Ars Theurgia Goetia* deals primarily with the spirits of the four cardinal directions and leans heavily on *Steganographia* (1499), written by German Renaissance polymath Johannes Trithemius (1462–1516), Agrippa's teacher. The *Ars Paulina* is also derived from the *Steganographia* as well as d'Abano's *Heptameron*. It details the angels of the twenty-four hours of the day as well as the 360 spirits who govern the individual zodiacal degrees (the Hellenistic monomoiria). The *Ars Almadel* instructs the magician in angelic scrying as well as the construction of a special tablet designed for that purpose. The *Ars Notoria* (sometimes *Ars Nova*) is a collection of prayers designed to foster the development of *eidetic* or photographic memory in the mind of the magician. This book, which borrows from *The Sworn Book of Honorius* (fourteenth century), is omitted from some iterations of the *Lesser Key*.

The *Ars Goetia* deals principally with the astrologically elected conjuration of the 72 goetic demons. In addition to the *Pseudomonarchia*, it bears the influence of Reginald Scot's *The Discovery of Witchcraft* (1584), Agrippa's *Three Books of Occult Philosophy*, d'Abano's *Heptameron*, and the *Magical Calendar* (1620).[19] The *Ars Goetia* is particularly important to our study because it contains the first complete catalog of 72 demons. Each demon is ranked and their significations, scope of activity, and influence are neatly attributed, allowing for a ready application to astrological delineation via the quinaries, as we shall see shortly.

The angel catalog of the Shem HaMephorash was ultimately collated with the complementary demon catalog by English mathematician Thomas Rudd (1583–1656) in his recension of the *Ars Goetia*.[20] Rudd had previously referenced the goetic demon's association with their corresponding Shem angels in his *Nine Keys* and *Tabula Sancta cum Tabulis Enochi* (Harley MS 6482). In Rudd's usage (and presumably that of his peers), this method was meant to insulate the goetic operator-exorcist from the unpredictable and potentially hazardous adverse effects of working with the demons alone. The angels would bind (*ligatio*) the demons and protect the exorcist when performing the

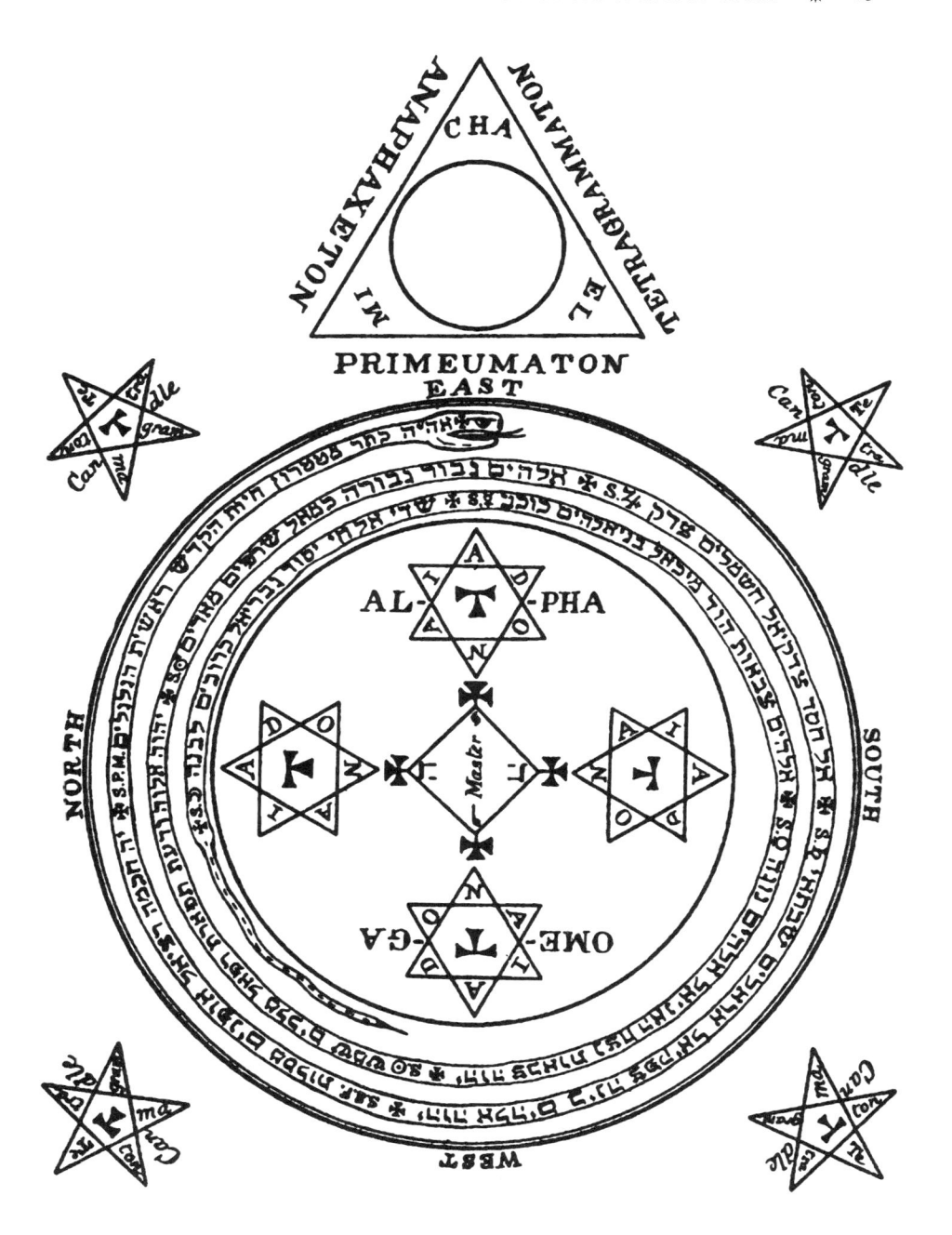

Fig. 3.2. The circle and triangle of Solomon from Samuel Liddell MacGregor Mathers's *The Goetia: Lesser Key of Solomon the King; Clavicula Salomonis Regis* (1904).

operations detailed in the *Lesser Key*. Rudd gives the 72 seals for the demons combined with those of the angels, rendering his goetic invocations safer and more energetically balanced. The operator-exorcist is instructed to wear the pentacle as a *lamen* or magical pendant on their breast during the conjuration. The demon's seal is facing outward and the seal of the corresponding angel is worn toward the operator's heart, protecting them from possible mischief set in motion by the demon. This appears to have been Rudd's major contribution to spirit conjuration in the angelic and demonic magic of the early modern period, though there may be a precedent in the idea of "thwarting angels" in antiquity.[21]

We know that Rudd was not alone in his pairing of the angels and demons, however, as we see evidence of this practice in the work of French cryptographer and alchemist Blaise de Vigenère (1523–1596), as well as Henry Dawson Lea, copyist of Wellcome MS 3203, which is based on manuscript copies of the *Goetia* belonging to Ebenezer Sibley (1751–1799) and Frederick Hockley (1809–1885). Indeed, it begins to appear that the practice of using the Shem angels in conjunction with the goetic demons may have been customary among the operative angel magicians of the early modern period.

4
The Significations
of the Quinaries

THE 72 ANGEL-DEMON PAIRS emanate their influence through the 72 quinaries of the zodiac. Every planet, part, point, and angle in an astrological chart is inhabiting one of the quinaries and is thereby under the shared rulership and influence of an angel and a demon at any given time. From a traditional perspective, the central project of each planet is to express its significations and actualize its agenda. A planet's ability to accomplish its promise is contingent on its level of essential and accidental dignity. A dignified and well-placed moon, for example, is more likely to bring about her expressions in the context of the figure. These planetary expressions are further modified by the angel and demon under whose dominion they are placed. These are the *quinarian keys* to astrological delineation. The balance of this book will be devoted to the practice of quinarian astrology, as well as to integrating this technique into a traditional practice of chart delineation.

This chapter is an easy-to-use reference, containing the significations and correspondences relative to each of the 72 angels and demons. These are culled from traditional qabalistic and grimoiric sources. The sequence and alignment of the Shem HaMephorash angels and the goetic demons as they were presented and juxtaposed in Thomas Rudd's recension of the *Ars Goetia* have been adopted here.[1] Since we are somewhat reimagining the system in an astrological context, we need not think of these entities in such polarizing terms. Rather, we may view the angel and demon pair as actualizing their agendas in the context of a shared quinary, for better or worse. We are simply assessing how the angelic and demonic influences—singularly and in tandem—affect planetary placements in an astrological figure and how delineation is impacted.

In keeping with convention, we have the quinaries begin at 0 degree Aries (the vernal equinox) in the annual scheme and at 6:00 a.m. (equinoctial sunrise, at the local meridian) in the diurnal. According to the primary motion, the degree of the ascendant cycles through each quinary once daily, spending twenty minutes in each—this is a *quinarian hour*, and there are 72 per day. The equinoctial or *equal hours* of the day are given here. These are given as they would fall on the days of the equinoxes, as opposed to the *temporal hours*, which expand and contract by tropical season (long daytime hours in summer, long nighttime hours in winter).* In the secondary motion, which is annual, sunrise occurs in each quinary for a period of approximately five days—a *quinarian week*. The zodiacal degrees and sign corresponding to each quinary are given, followed by the equinoctial hour. These temporal parameters are under the rulership of the quinarian pair listed.

Vehuiah, the first Shem angel, and Bael, the first goetic demon, are both assigned to the first quinary, beginning at 0 degree Aries. This is, by far, the most common configuration, though others may be encountered. For instance, in the Golden Dawn tradition, Samuel Lidell MacGregor Mathers had both beginning at 0 degree Leo. Another configuration has the angels and demons beginning at 12 degrees Leo, due to the heliacal rising of Sirius, a significant agricultural event in ancient

---

*The temporal, expanding, and contracting quinarian hours may be used as well, with a modicum of mathematical calculation.

Egypt. These are all fine attributions, depending upon your goal, but we are most concerned with astrological efficacy in this case. We have also disregarded the Golden Dawn's diurnal and nocturnal distinction between quinaries, which appears to have been adopted to make them fit into the order's existing decanal scheme. In any case, that distinction is irrelevant to the present study.

ABOUT EACH ENTRY

Each of the following 72 entries represents a 5-degree segment of the zodiac. They are laid out in order beginning at 0 degree Aries (annually) and 6:00 a.m. (diurnally). The name of the angel is given, in English and Hebrew, along with its total gematriac value, its ruling archangel, and the choir to which it belongs. The invocatory Psalm is given in English (KJV) and Latin—except for the seventieth quinary, whose invocation is from Genesis and is given in English and Hebrew. The pertinent passages from Savedow's translation of the *Sefer Raziel HaMalakh*,[2] Robert Ambelain's *Practical Kabbalah*,[3] and Lazare Lenain's *Science of the Kabbalah*[4] are given. The passages from the *Sefer Raziel HaMalakh* can be frustratingly cryptic but may be of value to the qabalist and the mystically inclined. A selection of attributes follows. The attributes are my distillations from the extant source material. Finally, the angelic sigil is reproduced.

The corresponding demon is listed under the same quinary number. The name is given in English and Hebrew, along with its gematriac value. The demonic classification is listed along with the planetary and metallic correspondence. Suffumigations are also given for each demon; these are especially useful should the astrologer-magician wish to compose appropriate ritual and consecrate talismans (see chapter 8). The pertinent passage from Mathers's translation of the *Ars Goetia*[5] is given, as are attributes I have distilled from the source materials. Finally, the demonic seal is reproduced. The sigils and seals will be useful to those who wish to create talismans, which we will further address in chapter 8.

The transliterations of the names of each angel follow Lenain's *Science of the Kabbalah* and the transliterations of the names of each demon follow the *Ars Goetia*. Note that ׳ (*yod*) as the initial letter of a name may be better represented with a *Y* for the purposes of pronunciation, but I have chosen to stick with the source spellings.

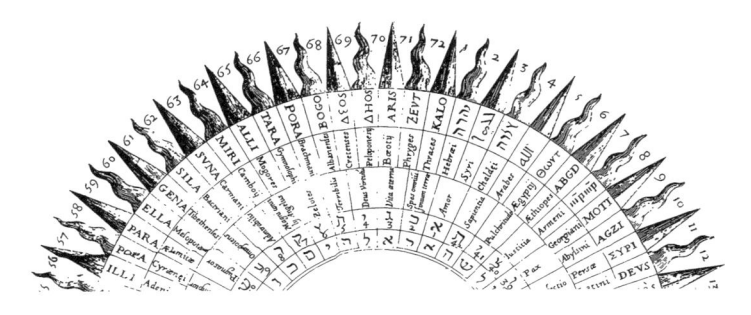

The 72 Quinaries

A Reference Guide to the 72 Angels and Demons

⊰ THE FIRST QUINARY ⊱

Degrees and Sign: 0° 00'–4° 59' Aries
Equinoctial Hour: 6:00–6:19 a.m.

Shem HaMephorash Angel: VEHUIAH

Hebrew: והויה

Gematria: 32

Ruling Archangel: Metatron

Angelic Choir: Seraphim

Invocation: "But thou, O Lord, art a shield for me; my glory, and the lifter up of mine head." [Psalm 3:3 (KJV)] *Et tu Domine susceptor meus et gloria mea et exaltans caput meum.*

Passage from *Sefer Raziel HaMalakh*: Guide the great name. The glory binds the image of four powers. Be guided in perfection. By things, be adorned of beauty. Proclaim the Lord and speak, blessed is he. The abundance descends to the temple of יהוה. From the name, descend to all the universe.

Ambelain: The person who is born under the influence of this angel has a skillful nature; being blessed with great wisdom, a lover of the Arts and Sciences, capable of undertaking and executing the most difficult things; having a love for military service, due to the influence of Mars; having abundant energy, due to the dominance of fire.

Lenain: Subtle spirit. Endowed with great wisdom, enthusiastic for science and the arts, capable of undertaking and accomplishing the most difficult things.

Attributes: Enlightenment, expanded consciousness, arts and sciences, skillful, wise.

Goetic Demon: BAEL

Hebrew: באל

Gematria: 33

Demonic Classification: King

Planet: Sol

Metal: Gold

Suffumigation: Frankincense

Description from *Ars Goetia*: The First Principal Spirit is a King ruling in the East, called Bael. He maketh thee to go Invisible. He ruleth over 66 Legions of Infernal Spirits. He appeareth in divers shapes, sometimes like a Cat, sometimes like a Toad, and sometimes like a Man, and sometimes all these forms at once. He speaketh hoarsely.

Attributes: Invisibility, protean, hoarse voice.

⊰ THE SECOND QUINARY ⊱

Degrees and Sign: 5° 00'–9° 59' Aries
Equinoctial Hour: 6:20–6:39 a.m.

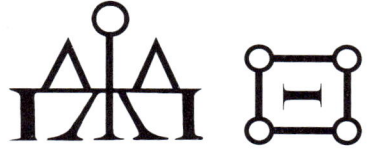

Shem HaMephorash Angel: IELIEL or JELIEL

Hebrew: יליאל

Gematria: 81

Ruling Archangel: Metatron

Angelic Choir: Seraphim

Invocation: "But be not thou far from me, O Lord: O my strength, haste thee to help me." [Psalm 22:19 (KJV)] *Tu autem Domine ne elongaveris auxilium tuum a me ad defensionem meam conspice.*

Passage from *Sefer Raziel HaMalakh*: The Lord indicates the highest blessing. Rise up to the highest compassion. The Perfection is complete. Therefore, from it, the strength of the highest strength. Cover the blessing and images of four powers. Guide the word עזאבה. It is the ancient of all ancients. Bind the image, guided by the word.

Ambelain: This angel rules over kings and princes, and keeps their subjects obedient; he has influence over the generation [of] all beings which exist in the animal realms; he reestablishes peace between spouses and maintains conjugal fidelity. Those born under this influence have a cheerful spirit, agreeable and genteel manners; they are passionate in sex.

Lenain: To quell popular uprisings. To obtain victory over those who attack unjustly. Sprightly spirit, agreeable and courteous manners, passionate for sex.

Attributes: Repress revolutions, fidelity, marital harmony, generation, passionate, courteous, cheerful.

Goetic Demon: AGARES

Hebrew: אגאראש

Gematria: 506

Demonic Classification: Duke

Planet: Venus

Metal: Copper

Suffumigation: Sandalwood

Description from *Ars Goetia*: The Second Spirit is a Duke called Agreas, or Agares. He is under the Power of the East, and cometh up in the form of an old fair Man, riding upon a Crocodile, carrying a Goshawk upon his fist, and yet mild in appearance. He maketh them to run that stand still, and bringeth back runaways. He teaches all Languages or Tongues presently. He hath power also to destroy Dignities both Spiritual and Temporal, and causeth Earthquakes. He was of the Order of Virtues.

Attributes: Running, returns runaways, foreign languages, earthquakes.

⊰ THE THIRD QUINARY ⊱

Degrees and Sign: 10° 00'–14° 59' Aries
Equinoctial Hour: 6:40–6:59 a.m.

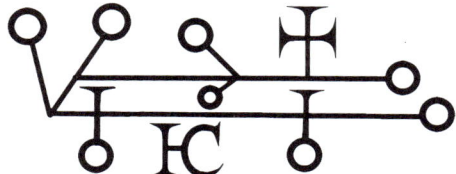

Shem HaMephorash Angel: SITAEL

Hebrew: סיטאל

Gematria: 110

Ruling Archangel: Metatron

Angelic Choir: Seraphim

Invocation: "I will say of the Lord, He is my refuge and my fortress: my God; in him will I trust." [Psalm 91:2 (KJV)] *Dicet Domino: susceptor meus es tu et refugium meum: Deus meus, sperabo in eum.*

Passage from *Sefer Raziel HaMalakh*: Guide the greatest compassion. Be complete by it. Justice and righteousness is in the living Earth. Bind three powers guided by the word and image. The powers of the Lord support Beth and Beth is in the middle. The Shekinah is in the center dwelling. There are five of them. Seven guide in the place of living in victory. Of עזאבה, live and exist in victory.

Ambelain: He rules over nobility, magnanimity and great works; he protects again arms and ferocious beasts. A person born under this influence loves truth; keeps his word and takes pleasure in helping those who need assistance.

Lenain: Against adversities. Protects against weapons and wild beasts. Loves truth, will keep his word, will oblige those in need of his services.

Attributes: Magnanimity, nobility, against adversity, truth, helpful.

Goetic Demon: VASSAGO

Hebrew: ושאגו

Gematria: 316

Demonic Classification: Prince

Planet: Jupiter

Metal: Tin

Suffumigation: Cedar

Description from *Ars Goetia*: The Third Spirit is a Mighty Prince, being of the same nature as Agares. He is called Vassago. This Spirit is of a Good Nature, and his office is to declare things Past and to Come, and to discover all things Hid or Lost.

Attributes: Divination, fortunes, recovers lost items.

⊰ THE FOURTH QUINARY ⊱

Degrees and Sign: 15° 00'–19° 59' Aries
Equinoctial Hour: 7:00–7:19 a.m.

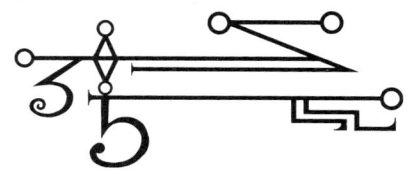

Shem HaMephorash Angel: ELEMIAH

Hebrew: עלמיה

Gematria: 155

Ruling Archangel: Metatron

Angelic Choir: Seraphim

Invocation: "Return, O Lord, deliver my soul: oh save me for thy mercies' sake." [Psalm 6:4 (KJV)] *Convertere Domine, et eripe animam meam: salvum me fac propter misericordiam tuam.*

Passage from *Sefer Raziel HaMalakh*: Guide by the second existing. Being in the place, complete Yod Heh Yod. Sublime in the highest judgement, understand all judgement. The image of seven powers join to guide all understanding. עזאבה sees authority by making judgement in Egypt, with three scriptures from them all. The foundation binds Yesod. Adorn in splendor by the highest beauty in the center. They guide over the word

Ambelain: This angel rules over travel, maritime expeditions, and he rules over useful discoveries. The person born under its influence will be industrious, happy in his enterprises, and will have a passion for travel.

Lenain: Against mental troubles and for the identification of traitors. Governs voyages, sea travels. Industrious, successful, keen for travel.

Attributes: Spiritual peace, sea voyages, discovery, industrious, travel.

Goetic Demon: GAMIGIN or SAMIGINA

Hebrew: גאמיגין

Gematria: 667

Demonic Classification: Marquis

Planet: Luna

Metal: Silver

Suffumigation: Jasmine

Description from *Ars Goetia*: The Fourth Spirit is Samigina, a Great Marquis. He appeareth in the form of a little Horse or Ass, and then into Human shape doth he change himself at the request of the Master. He speaketh with a hoarse voice. He ruleth over 30 Legions of Inferiors. He teaches all Liberal Sciences, and giveth account of Dead Souls that died in sin.

Attributes: Liberal arts, necromancy, hoarse voice.

⊰ THE FIFTH QUINARY ⊱

Degrees and Sign: 20° 00'–24° 59' Aries
Equinoctial Hour: 7:20–7:39 a.m.

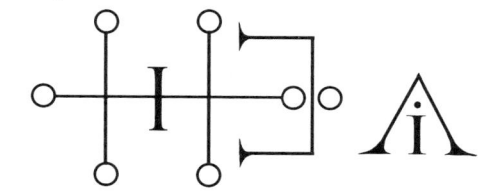

Shem HaMephorash Angel: MAHASIAH

Hebrew: מהשיה

Gematria: 360

Ruling Archangel: Metatron

Angelic Choir: Seraphim

Invocation: "I sought the Lord, and he heard me, and delivered me from all my fears." [Psalm 34:4 (KJV)] *Exquisivi Dominum, et exaudivit me: et ex omnibus tribulationibus meis eripuit me.*

Passage from *Sefer Raziel HaMalakh*: Guide the four secret houses in prayer. Reach to the Lord in the highest light, concealed and bound. Be guided to adorn. תת תתא. In the center is the Heh. Complete the prayers. Of Shin, the image guide between the vestment of the priest. Guide by the word עזאבה. By the power of victory, the Heh is the image of the Lord. Reach in righteousness to the fathers by them.

Ambelain: He rules over the high sciences, occult philosophy, theology and the liberal arts. The person born under this influence learns all that they desire with ease; has an agreeable physiognomy and character, and will be keen on honest pleasures.

Lenain: To live in peace with everyone. Governs high science, occult philosophy, theology, and the liberal arts. Learns easily, keen for honest pleasures.

Attributes: Peace, magic, occultism, theology, agreeable, honest, science.

Goetic Demon: MARBAS

Hebrew: מארבש

Gematria: 543

Demonic Classification: President

Planet: Mercury

Metal: Quicksilver

Suffumigation: Storax

Description from *Ars Goetia*: The fifth Spirit is Marbas. He is a Great President, and appeareth at first in the form of a Great Lion, but afterwards, at the request of the Master, he putteth on Human Shape. He answereth truly of things Hidden or Secret. He causeth Diseases and cureth them. Again, he giveth great Wisdom and Knowledge in Mechanical Arts; and can change men into other shapes.

Attributes: Secrets, causes and cures diseases, wisdom, hidden things, mechanical arts.

⊰ THE SIXTH QUINARY ⊱

Degrees and Sign: 25° 00'–29° 59' Aries
Equinoctial Hour: 7:40–7:59 a.m.

Shem HaMephorash Angel: LEHAHEL

Hebrew: ללהאל

Gematria: 96

Ruling Archangel: Metatron

Angelic Choir: Seraphim

Invocation: "Sing praises to the Lord, which dwelleth in Zion: declare among the people his doings." [Psalm 9:11 (KJV)] *Psallite Domino, qui habitat in Sion: annuntiate intergentes studia ejus.*

Passage from *Sefer Raziel HaMalakh*: Guide the Merkabah. Of the Merkabah of unity in two secrets, rise up and bind beauty, beauty of the greatest compassion. Reach to the unity of one. The image of six powers is guided by the word עזאבה. Create the universe in compassion by the ten commandments. From the commandment, reveal the one brother. Support to understand the word.

Ambelain: This angel rules over love, renown, sciences, arts and fortune. The person born under this influence will love to converse, and will acquire fame through his talents and actions.

Lenain: To acquire knowledge and cure disease. Governs love, renown, science, arts and fortune. Features (include) ambition, fame.

Attributes: Cures disease, love, ambition, fame, arts and sciences, fortune.

Goetic Demon: VALEFOR or VALEFAR

Hebrew: ואלפהר

Gematria: 322

Demonic Classification: Duke

Planet: Venus

Metal: Copper

Suffumigation: Sandalwood

Description from *Ars Goetia*: The Sixth Spirit is Valefor. He is a mighty Duke, and appeareth in the shape of a Lion with an Ass's Head, bellowing. He is a good Familiar, but tempteth them he is a familiar of to steal.

Attributes: Theft, temptation, punishment, loud voice.

⊰ THE SEVENTH QUINARY ⊱

Degrees and Sign: 0° 00'–4° 59' Taurus
Equinoctial Hour: 8:00–8:19 a.m.

Shem HaMephorash Angel: ACHAIAH

Hebrew: אכאיה

Gematria: 37

Ruling Archangel: Metatron

Angelic Choir: Seraphim

Invocation: "The Lord is merciful and gracious, slow to anger, and plenteous in mercy." [Psalm 103:8 (KJV)] *Miserator et misericors Dominus: longanimis et multum misericors.*

Passage from *Sefer Raziel HaMalakh*: Guide in the foundation, all the souls and the Sabbaths. By the sign of living in victory, reach the Neshemeh. Of the name, bind to guide three sephiroth. Guide by the three vowels, Cholem, Shoreq, and Chireq. The image of seven powers guides to reach in the middle. עזאבה guides to atonement in a quiet moment. Of life and death, understand the power of the actions by measures and thus complete.

Ambelain: This angel rules over patience; he reveals the secrets of nature; he influences the propagation of knowledge and industry. The person born under this influence will love to learn about useful subjects; he will glory in executing the most difficult works, and will discover many useful practices of the arts.

Lenain: Governs patience, secrets of nature. Loves learning, proud to accomplish the most difficult tasks.

Attributes: Useful knowledge, secrets, patience, temperance, skillful.

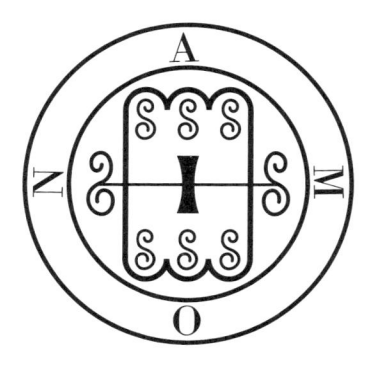

Goetic Demon: AMON or AAMON

Hebrew: אמון

Gematria: 747

Demonic Classification: Marquis

Planet: Luna

Metal: Silver

Suffumigation: Jasmine

Description from *Ars Goetia*: The Seventh Spirit is Amon. He is a Marquis great in power, and most stern. He appeareth like a Wolf with a Serpent's tail, vomiting out of his mouth flames of fire; but at the command of the Magician he putteth on the shape of a Man with Dog's teeth beset in a head like a Raven; or else like a Man with a Raven's head (simply). He telleth all things Past and to Come. He procureth feuds and reconcileth controversies between friends.

Attributes: Divination, love, diplomacy, friendship, mediation.

⊰ THE EIGHTH QUINARY ⊱

Degrees and Sign: 5° 00'–9° 59' Taurus
Equinoctial Hour: 8:20-8:39 a.m.

Shem HaMephorash Angel: CAHETEL or CAHETHEL

Hebrew: כהתאל

Gematria: 456

Ruling Archangel: Metatron

Angelic Choir: Seraphim

Invocation: "O come, let us worship and bow down: let us kneel before the Lord our maker." [Psalm 95:6 (KJV)] *Venite adoremus, et procidamus: et ploremus ante Dominum, qui fecit nos.*

Passage from *Sefer Raziel HaMalakh*: Guide as the Lord of the action speaks. The image of five powers guides. Complete by Yod. Of the understanding of vestments, and also the images coming forth from the Torah, support to understand and rise over the rewards of the righteous. Of the righteous, speaks. Blessed is he. Of the covenant of Elohinu in heaven, is purity by the highest wisdom.

Ambelain: This angel rules over all agricultural production, and principally those which are necessary to the existence of men and animals. He inspires man to raise himself towards God, to thank Him for all the goods He sends to the earth. The person born under this influence will love work, agriculture, the countryside and hunting, and will be very active in business.

Lenain: To obtain the benediction of God and to drive away evil spirits. Governs agricultural production. Inspires man to rise towards God.

Attributes: Blessings, theology, protection, rural, agriculture, business acumen, hunting.

Goetic Demon: BARBATOS

Hebrew: ברבטוש

Gematria: 519

Demonic Classification: Duke

Planet: Venus

Metal: Copper

Suffumigation: Sandalwood

Description from *Ars Goetia*: The Eighth Spirit is Barbatos. He is a Great Duke, and appeareth when the Sun is in Sagittary, with four noble Kings and their companies of great troops. He giveth understanding of the singing of Birds, and of the Voices of other creatures, such as the barking of Dogs. He breaketh the Hidden Treasures open that have been laid by the Enchantments of Magicians. He is of the Order of Virtues, of which some part he retaineth still; and he knoweth all things Past, and to come, and conciliateth Friends and those that be in Power.

Attributes: Animals, birdsong, divination, treasures, friendship, reconciliation.

⊹ THE NINTH QUINARY ⊱

Degrees and Sign: 10° 00'–14° 59' Taurus
Equinoctial Hour: 8:40–8:59 a.m.

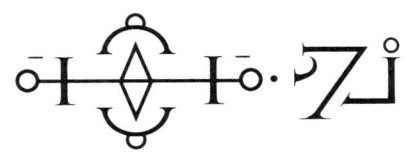

Shem HaMephorash Angel: HAZIEL or AZIEL

Hebrew: הזיאל

Gematria: 53

Ruling Archangel: Jophiel

Angelic Choir: Cherubim

Invocation: "Remember, O Lord, thy tender mercies and thy loving kindnesses; for they have been ever of old." [Psalm 25:6 (KJV)] *Reminiscere miserationum tuarum, Domine, et misericordiarum tuarum quae a saeculo sunt.*

Passage from *Sefer Raziel HaMalakh*: Guide to unity. Reach by mercy. עזאבה The Lord over all the heights and over the measures. The image of four powers guides by the word in unity. Bind the Heh by Yod. Guide and lead by the word of enlightenment. The Yod rises up to the Lord. Both are in victory of the unity of one.

Ambelain: He serves to obtain God's mercy, the friendship and favours of the great, and the execution of promises made by a person. He rules over good faith and reconciliation. Those born under this influence will be sincere in their promises, and will easily pardon those who commit an offence against them.

Lenain: Mercy of God, friendship and favor of the great, execution of a promise made. Governs good faith and reconciliation. Sincere in promises, will easily extend pardon.

Attributes: Promises, friendship, faith, sincerity, forgiving.

Goetic Demon: PAIMON

Hebrew: פאימון

Gematria: 837

Demonic Classification: King

Planet: Sol

Metal: Gold

Suffumigation: Frankincense

Description from *Ars Goetia*: The Ninth Spirit in this Order is Paimon, a Great King, and very obedient unto LUCIFER. He appeareth in the form of a Man sitting upon a Dromedary with a Crown most glorious upon his head. There goeth before him also an Host of Spirits, like Men with Trumpets and well sounding Cymbals, and all other sorts of Musical Instruments. He hath a great Voice, and roareth at his first coming, and his speech is such that the Magician cannot well understand unless he can compel him. This Spirit can teach all Arts and Sciences, and other secret things. He can discover unto thee what the Earth is, and what holdeth it up in the Waters; and what Mind is, and where it is; or any other thing thou mayest desire to know. He giveth Dignity, and confirmeth the same. He bindeth or maketh any man subject unto the Magician if he so desire it. He giveth good Familiars, and such as can teach all Arts.

He is to be observed towards the West. He is of the Order of Dominations. He hath under him 200 Legions of Spirits, and part of them are of the Order of Angels, and the other part of Potentates. Now if thou callest this Spirit Paimon alone, thou must make him some offering; and there will attend him two Kings called LABAL and ABALI, and also other Spirits who be of the Order of Potentates in his Host, and 25 Legions. And those Spirits which be subject unto them are not always with them unless the Magician do compel them.

Attributes: Arts, secrets, natural philosophy, honor, obscurity, loud voice.

⊰ THE TENTH QUINARY ⊱

Degrees and Sign: 15° 00'–19° 59' Taurus
Equinoctial Hour: 9:00–9:19 a.m.

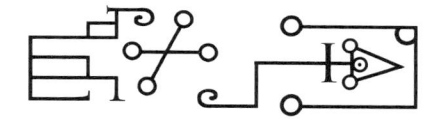

Shem HaMephorash Angel: ALADIAH

Hebrew: אלדיה

Gematria: 50

Ruling Archangel: Jophiel

Angelic Choir: Cherubim

Invocation: "Let thy mercy, O Lord, be upon us, according as we hope in thee." [Psalm 33:22 (KJV)] *Fiat misericordia tua Domine super nos: quemadmodum speravimus in te.*

Passage from *Sefer Raziel HaMalakh*: Guide the Merkabah. Of Merkabah, Aleph adorns עזאבה. Rise up and bind three powers, mercy and beauty of the highest beauty, by understanding six images of crowns, the beauty of one.

Ambelain: This angel rules against rabies and plague, and influences recovery from illnesses. The person who is born under this influence enjoys good health, and will be happy in his enterprises, esteemed by those who know him; he will frequent the most sophisticated societies.

Lenain: Good for those guilty of hidden crimes and fearing discovery. Governs rage and pestilence, cure of disease. Good health, successful in his undertakings.

Attributes: Secrets, diseases, health, healing, sophisticated, success.

Goetic Demon: BUER

Hebrew: בואר

Gematria: 209

Demonic Classification: President

Planet: Mercury

Metal: Quicksilver

Suffumigation: Storax

Description from *Ars Goetia*: The Tenth Spirit is Buer, a Great President. He appeareth in Sagittary, and that is his shape when the Sun is there. He teaches Philosophy, both Moral and Natural, and the Logic Art, and also the Virtues of all Herbs and Plants. He healeth all distempers in man, and giveth good Familiars.

Attributes: Philosophy, morality, logic, herbs, plants.

⊰ THE ELEVENTH QUINARY ⊱

Degrees and Sign: 20° 00'–24° 59' Taurus
Equinoctial Hour: 9:20–9:39 a.m.

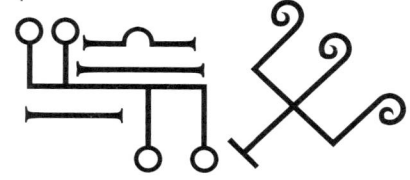

Shem HaMephorash Angel: LAUVIA or LAVIAH

Hebrew: לאויה

Gematria: 52

Ruling Archangel: Jophiel

Angelic Choir: Seraphim

Invocation: "The Lord liveth; and blessed be my rock; and let the God of my salvation be exalted." [Psalm 18:46 (KJV)] *Vivit Dominus et benedictus Deus meus, et exultatur Deus salutis meae.*

Passage from *Sefer Raziel HaMalakh*: Guide by the second actions received from the understanding עזאבה. The Yod rises up. Judge in Egypt from the place of governing dominion. The image of six powers supports the Aleph. Guide by the word. Bind in Unity.

Ambelain: He serves against lightning and to obtain victory. This angel rules renown; he influences great persons, the wise, and all those who become famous through their talents.

Lenain: Against lightning and for the obtainment of victory. Governs renown. Great personage, learned, celebrated for personal talents.

Attributes: Protection from lightning, victory, fame, talented.

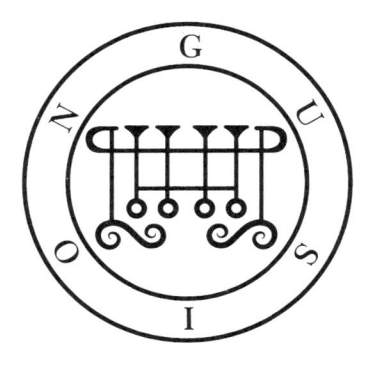

Goetic Demon: GUSION

Hebrew: גוסוין

Gematria: 785

Demonic Classification: Duke

Planet: Venus

Metal: Copper

Suffumigation: Sandalwood

Description from *Ars Goetia*: The Eleventh Spirit in order is a great and strong Duke, called Gusion. He appeareth like a Xenopilus. He telleth all things, Past, Present, and to Come, and showeth the meaning and resolution of all questions thou mayest ask. He conciliateth and reconcileth friendships, and giveth Honour and Dignity unto any.

Attributes: Divination, reconciliation, friendship, honor, dignity.

⊰ THE TWELFTH QUINARY ⊱

Degrees and Sign: 25° 00'–29° 59' Taurus
Equinoctial Hour: 9:40–9:59 a.m.

Shem HaMephorash Angel: HAHAIAH

Hebrew: ההעיה

Gematria: 95

Ruling Archangel: Jophiel

Angelic Choir: Seraphim

Invocation: "Why standest thou afar off, O Lord? why hidest thou thyself in times of trouble?" [Psalm 10:1 (KJV)] *Ut qui Domine recessisti longe, despicis in opportunitatibus, in tribulatione.*

Passage from *Sefer Raziel HaMalakh*: Guide the Lord of the action. Bind to guide as twenty actions.

Ambelain: He rules over depths, and reveals hidden mysteries to mortals. He influences wise, spiritual and discreet persons. A person born under this influence has affable habits, a pleasant physiognomy and agreeable manners.

Lenain: Against adversity. Governs dreams. Mysteries hidden from mortals. Gentle, witty, discreet manners.

Attributes: Against adversity, charity, dreams, mysteries, gentle, agreeable.

Goetic Demon: SITRI

Hebrew: שיטרי

Gematria: 529

Demonic Classification: Prince

Planet: Jupiter

Metal: Tin

Suffumigation: Cedar

Description from *Ars Goetia*: The Twelfth Spirit is Sitri. He is a Great Prince and appeareth at first with a Leopard's head and the Wings of a Gryphon, but after the command of the Master of the Exorcism he putteth on Human shape, and that very beautiful. He enflameth men with Women's love, and Women with Men's love; and causeth them also to show themselves naked if it be desired.

Attributes: Love, luxury, nudity, lust.

⊰ THE THIRTEENTH QUINARY ⊱

Degrees and Sign: 0° 00'–4° 59' Gemini
Equinoctial Hour: 10:00–10:19 a.m.

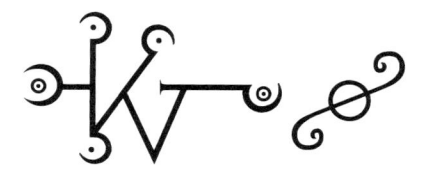

Shem HaMephorash Angel: IAZALEL or IEZALEL

Hebrew: יזלאל

Gematria: 78

Ruling Archangel: Jophiel

Angelic Choir: Cherubim

Invocation: "Make a joyful noise unto the Lord, all the earth: make a loud noise, and rejoice, and sing praise." [Psalm 98:4 (KJV)] *Jubilate Deo omnis terra: cantate, et exultate, et psallite.*

Passage from *Sefer Raziel HaMalakh*: Guide the Yod by the great name in the power of victory. The image of four powers guides the word. עזאבה By Yod, all actions. By desire of all powers of the wheel and angel. By the power of victory, bind to guide by two actions, the dominions in every power by the power victory.

Ambelain: He rules friendship, reconciliation and conjugal fidelity. A person born under this influence will learn everything he desires with ease; he will have happy memories and will distinguish himself through his speech.

Lenain: Governs friendship, reconciliation, conjugal fidelity. Learns easily. Adroit.

Attributes: Reconciliation, marital fidelity, memory, learning, eloquent, rhetoric.

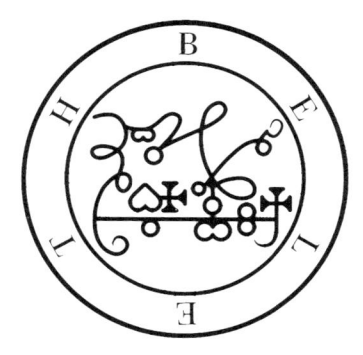

Goetic Demon: BELETH, BILETH, or BILET

Hebrew: בלאת

Gematria: 433

Demonic Classification: King

Planet: Sol

Metal: Gold

Suffumigation: Frankincense

Description from *Ars Goetia*: The Thirteenth Spirit is called Beleth (or Bileth, or Bilet). He is a mighty King and terrible. He rideth on a pale horse with trumpets and other kinds of musical instruments playing before him. He is very furious at his first appearance, that is, while the Exorcist layeth his courage; for to do this he must hold a Hazel Wand in his hand, striking it out towards the South and East Quarters, make a triangle without the Circle, and then command him into it by the Bonds and Charges of Spirits as hereafter followeth. And if he doth not enter into the triangle at your threats, rehearse the Bonds and Charms before him, and then he will yield Obedience and come into it, and do what he is commanded by the Exorcist. Yet he must receive him courteously because he is a Great King, and do homage unto him, as the Kings and Princes do that attend upon him. And thou must have always a Silver Ring on the middle finger of the left hand held against thy face, as they do yet before AMAYMON. This Great King Beleth causeth all the love that may be, both of Men and of Women, until the Master Exorcist hath had his desire fulfilled.

Attributes: Love, desire, furious.

⊰ THE FOURTEENTH QUINARY ⊱

Degrees and Sign: 5° 00'–9° 59' Gemini
Equinoctial Hour: 10:20–10:39 a.m.

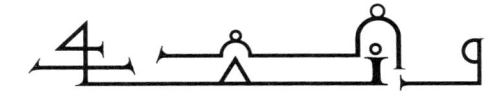

Shem HaMephorash Angel: MEBAHEL

Hebrew: מבהאל

Gematria: 78

Ruling Archangel: Jophiel

Angelic Choir: Cherubim

Invocation: "The Lord also will be a refuge for the oppressed, a refuge in times of trouble." [Psalm 9:9 (KJV)] *Et factus est Dominus refugium pauperis: adjutor in opportunitatibus, in tribulatione.*

Passage from *Sefer Raziel HaMalakh*: Guide the great name, the name of power by 70. Proclaim unity. Of the image of six powers, guide by six ends and by the word עזאבה. The power of God sends forth to Moses by the power and the glory. Bind beauty by wisdom in the crown. In every word is one and the one power. Extend the powers to understand the power of the actions.

Ambelain: He rules over justice, truth and liberty; he delivers the oppressed and makes truth to be known. The person born under this influence will love jurisprudence and will distinguish himself at the Bar.

Lenain: Against those who seek to usurp the fortunes of others. Governs justice, truth, liberty. Delivers the oppressed and protects prisoners. Loves jurisprudence, affinity for law courts.

Attributes: Against greed, justice, truth, liberty, law, protection, prisoners, influence.

Goetic Demon: LERAIKHA, LERAJE, or LERAIE

Hebrew: לראיך

Gematria: 741

Demonic Classification: Marquis

Planet: Luna

Metal: Silver

Suffumigation: Jasmine

Description from *Ars Goetia*: The Fourteenth Spirit is called Leraje (or Leraie). He is a Marquis Great in Power, showing himself in the likeness of an Archer clad in Green, and carrying a Bow and Quiver. He causeth all great Battles and Contests; and maketh wounds to putrefy that are made with Arrows by Archers. This belongeth unto Sagittary.

Attributes: Wars, wounds, contests.

⊰ THE FIFTEENTH QUINARY ⊱

Degrees and Sign: 10° 00'–14° 59' Gemini
Equinoctial Hour: 10:40–10:59 a.m.

Shem HaMephorash Angel: HARIEL

Hebrew: הריאל

Gematria: 246

Ruling Archangel: Jophiel

Angelic Choir: Cherubim

Invocation: "But the Lord is my defense; and my God is the rock of my refuge." [Psalm 94:22 (KJV)] *Et factus est mihi Dominus in refugium: et Deus meus in adjutorium spei meae.*

Passage from *Sefer Raziel HaMalakh*: Guide the name of the unity. Bind all by the Yod. Bind three powers of the one word. Proclaim the living Earth. Reach and the image of four powers guides by the word עזאבה by the highest one.

Ambelain: This angel rules over the arts and sciences; he influences useful discoveries and new methodologies. The person born under this influence will love the company of good people; he will love religious sentiment and will distinguish himself through the purity of his morals.

Lenain: Against the impious. Governs sciences and arts. Religious sentiments, morally pure.

Attributes: Religion, arts and sciences, pure, morality, discoveries.

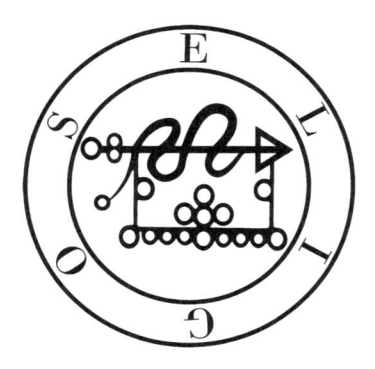

Goetic Demon: ELIGOS or ELIGOR

Hebrew: אליגוש

Gematria: 349

Demonic Classification: Duke

Planet: Venus

Metal: Copper

Suffumigation: Sandalwood

Description from *Ars Goetia*: The Fifteenth Spirit in Order is Eligos, a Great Duke, and appeareth in the form of a goodly Knight, carrying a Lance, an Ensign, and a Serpent. He discovereth hidden things, and knoweth things to come; and of Wars, and how the Soldiers will or shall meet. He causeth the Love of Lords and Great Persons.

Attributes: Hidden things, divination, fame, the future, strategy.

⸭ THE SIXTEENTH QUINARY ⸬

Degrees and Sign: 15° 00'–19° 59' Gemini
Equinoctial Hour: 11:00–11:19 a.m.

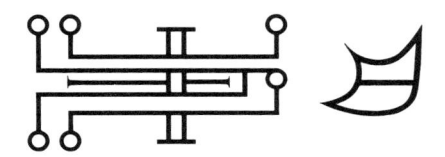

Shem HaMephorash Angel: HAKAMIAH

Hebrew: הקמיה

Gematria: 160

Ruling Archangel: Jophiel

Angelic Choir: Cherubim

Invocation: "O lord God of my salvation, I have cried day and night before thee." [Psalm 88:1 (KJV)] *Domine Deus salutis meae, in die clamavie, et nocte coram te.*

Passage from *Sefer Raziel HaMalakh*: Guide by two actions. By Yod, the diagonal border. Swear an oath by them and bind to the crown. Reach the understanding, and עתת guides over the word. The image of six powers guide by the understanding of the oath. Of two actions עזאבה. Remember the Lord by the name.

Ambelain: This angel rules over crowned heads and great captains; he gives victory and warns of sedition; he influences fire, arsenals and all things connected with the genie of war. The man who is born under this influence has a frank, loyal and brave character, susceptible to honor, faithful to his obligation and passionate in love.

Lenain: Against traitors and for deliverance from those who seek to oppress us. Governs crowned heads, great captains. Gives victory. Frank, loyal, brave character, sensitive to points of honor, an affinity for Venus.

Attributes: Against traitors, dignitaries, war, loyal, brave, passionate, victory, honor.

Goetic Demon: ZEPAR

Hebrew: זאפר

Gematria: 288

Demonic Classification: Duke

Planet: Venus

Metal: Copper

Suffumigation: Sandalwood

Description from *Ars Goetia*: The Sixteenth Spirit is Zepar. He is a Great Duke, and appeareth in Red Apparel and Armour, like a Soldier. His office is to cause Women to love Men, and to bring them together in love. He also maketh them barren.

Attributes: Love, lust, infertility.

⊰ THE SEVENTEENTH QUINARY ⊱

Degrees and Sign: 20° 00'–24° 59' Gemini
Equinoctial Hour: 11:20–11:39 a.m.

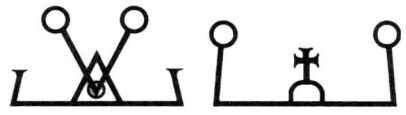

Shem HaMephorash Angel: LAUVIAH or LOVIAH

Hebrew: לאויה

Gematria: 322

Ruling Archangel: Zaphkiel

Angelic Choir: Thrones

Invocation: "O Lord our Lord, how excellent is thy name in all the earth!" [Psalm 8:9 (KJV)] *Dominus Deus noster, quam admirabile est nomen tuum in universa terra.*

Passage from *Sefer Raziel HaMalakh*: Guide three in beauty. Of the image of six powers, the crown. תיית reaches the beauty between two wisdoms. Speak from between two Cherubim. By the word עתת, complete all. All are divided in three holy things. עזאבה guides by the holy words of degrees. Bind the one name to them.

Ambelain: He serves against spiritual torment, sadness and to sleep well at night. He rules over the high sciences, marvelous discoveries, and gives revelations in dreams. The person who is born under this influence will love music, poetry, literature and philosophy.

Lenain: To be invoked while fasting. Against mental anguish, sadness. Governs high sciences, marvelous discoveries. Gives revelations in dreams. Loves music, poetry, literature and philosophy.

Attributes: Rest, sciences, music, poetry, philosophy, discoveries, dreams.

Goetic Demon: BOTIS

Hebrew: בוטיש

Gematria: 327

Demonic Classifications: President and earl

Planets: Mercury and Mars

Metals: Quicksilver, copper, and silver

Suffumigations: Storax and dragon's blood

Description from *Ars Goetia*: The Seventeenth Spirit is Botis, a Great President, and an Earl. He appeareth at the first show in the form of an ugly Viper, then at the command of the Magician he putteth on a Human shape with Great Teeth, and two Horns, carrying a bright and sharp Sword in his hand. He telleth all things Past, and to Come, and reconcileth Friends and Foes.

Attributes: Divination, reconciliation, friends, enemies, herbs, stones.

⊰ THE EIGHTEENTH QUINARY ⊱

Degrees and Sign: 25° 00'–29° 59' Gemini
Equinoctial Hour: 11:40–11:59 a.m.

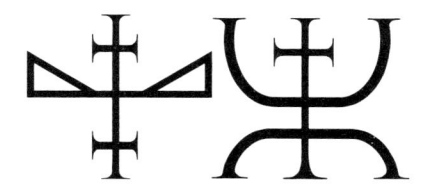

Shem HaMephorash Angel: CALIEL

Hebrew: כליאל

Gematria: 91

Ruling Archangel: Zaphkiel

Angelic Choir: Thrones

Invocation: "Judge me, O Lord my God, according to thy righteousness; and let them not rejoice over me." [Psalm 35:24 (KJV)] *Judica me Domine secundum justitiam meam, et secundum innocentiam meam super me.*

Passage from *Sefer Raziel HaMalakh*: Guide by the name. Complete the four gates of the highest universe. עזאבה completes in compassion. The image of four powers guide by the word. Bind the crown of beauty. Of wisdom, guide by all understanding.

Ambelain: This angel allows knowledge of truth in proceedings, and allows innocence to triumph, he confounds the guilty and false testimony. The person born under this influence will be just and possess integrity, love truth, and will distinguish himself in magistracy.

Lenain: To obtain prompt aid. Makes truth known in law suits, causes innocence to triumph. Just, honest, loves truth, judiciary.

Attributes: Truth, innocence, integrity, just, trials, witnesses.

Goetic Demon: BATHIN

Hebrew: באתין

Gematria: 1113

Demonic Classification: Duke

Planet: Venus

Metal: Copper

Suffumigation: Sandalwood

Description from *Ars Goetia*: The Eighteenth Spirit is Bathin. He is a Mighty and Strong Duke, and appeareth like a Strong Man with the tail of a Serpent, sitting upon a Pale-Coloured Horse. He knoweth the Virtues of Herbs and Precious Stones, and can transport men suddenly from one country to another.

Attributes: Herbs, stones, international travel.

⊰ THE NINETEENTH QUINARY ⊱

Degrees and Sign: 0° 00'–4° 59' Cancer
Equinoctial Hour: 12:00–12:19 p.m.

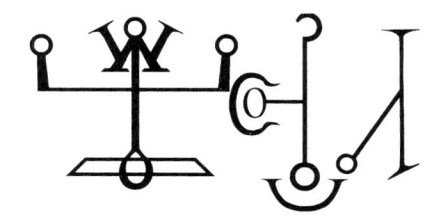

Shem HaMephorash Angel: LEUVIAH or LEVUIAH

Hebrew: לוויה

Gematria: 57

Ruling Archangel: Zaphkiel

Angelic Choir: Thrones

Invocation: "I waited patiently for the Lord; and he inclined unto me, and heard my cry." [Psalm 40:1 (KJV)] *Expectans expectavi Dominum, et intendit mihi.*

Passage from *Sefer Raziel HaMalakh*: Guide by the commandment. The power of the oath by the Yod. The image guides. thus engraving in twelve signs of the zodiac of Israel.

Ambelain: His attribute is "God Who Forgives Sinners." He corresponds to the name "Bogy" of the Hungarian language.

Lenain: To be invoked while facing South. To obtain the grace of God. Governs memory, human intelligence. Amiable, lively, modest, bearing of adversity with resignation.

Attributes: Obtaining grace, memory, joviality, intelligence, amiable, stoic.

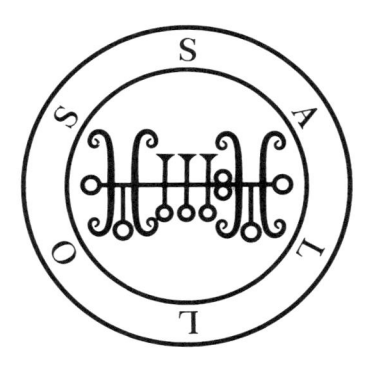

Goetic Demon: SALLOS or SALEOS

Hebrew: שאלוש

Gematria: 637

Demonic Classification: Duke

Planet: Venus

Metal: Copper

Suffumigation: Sandalwood

Description from *Ars Goetia*: The Nineteenth Spirit is Sallos (or Saleos). He is a Great and Mighty Duke, and appeareth in the form of a gallant Soldier riding on a Crocodile, with a Ducal Crown on his head, but peaceably. He causeth the Love of Women to Men, and of Men to Women.

Attributes: Love, lust, desire.

⊰ THE TWENTIETH QUINARY ⊱

Degrees and Sign: 5° 00'–9° 59' Cancer
Equinoctial Hour: 12:20–12:39 p.m.

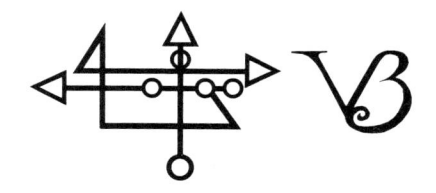

Shem HaMephorash Angel: PAHALIAH

Hebrew: פהליה

Gematria: 130

Ruling Archangel: Zaphkiel

Angelic Choir: Thrones

Invocation: "In my distress I cried unto the Lord, and he heard me. Deliver my soul, O Lord, from lying lips, and from a deceitful tongue." [Psalm 120:1–2 (KJV)] *Domine libera anima mean a labiis iniquis, et a lingua dolosa.*

Passage from *Sefer Raziel HaMalakh:* Guide by two actions. In the midst is עזאבה. The compassion of the Lord is eternal. Follow them in the midst and bind to guide. The image of six powers guides the crown. Reach and bind in mercy and compassion. Bring near the highest.

Ambelain: He serves against the enemies of religion, and to convert people to Christianity. This angel rules religion, theology and morality; he influences chastity and piety in those whose vocation is towards the ecclesiastical state.

Lenain: Against enemies of religion, for the conversion of nations to Christianity. Governs religion, theology, morality, chastity, purity. Ecclesiastical vocation.

Attributes: Conversions, theology, chastity, morals, purity.

Goetic Demon: PURSON

Hebrew: פורשון

Gematria: 1292

Demonic Classification: King

Planet: Sol

Metal: Gold

Suffumigation: Frankincense

Description from *Ars Goetia*: The Twentieth Spirit is Purson, a Great King. His appearance is comely, like a Man with a Lion's face, carrying a cruel Viper in his hand, and riding upon a Bear. Going before him are many Trumpets sounding. He knoweth all things hidden, and can discover Treasure, and tell all things Past, Present, and to Come. He can take a Body either Human or Aërial, and answereth truly of all Earthly things both Secret and Divine, and of the Creation of the World. He bringeth forth good Familiars.

Attributes: Hidden things, treasures, secrets, divination, honesty.

⊰ THE TWENTY-FIRST QUINARY ⊱

Degrees and Sign: 10° 00'–14° 59' Cancer
Equinoctial Hour: 12:40–12:59 p.m.

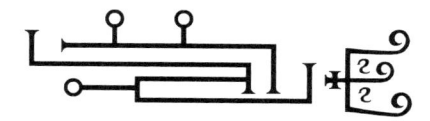

Shem HaMephorash Angel: NELCHAEL

Hebrew: נלכאל

Gematria: 131

Ruling Archangel: Zaphkiel

Angelic Choir: Thrones

Invocation: "But I trusted in thee, O Lord: I said, Thou art my God." [Psalm 31:14 (KJV)] *Ego autem in te speravi Domine: dixi Deus meus es tu: in manibus tuis sortes meae.*

Passage from *Sefer Raziel HaMalakh*: Guide by the great name. The oath is in the power of the staff of Moses, of the power of actions of marvelous deeds. Bind to guide from the understanding of two. The image of powers guide by the word. This is received from that. From the midst, the actions go forth remembered.

Ambelain: He serves against caliomnators, charms, and works to destroy the power of evil spirits. This angel rules over astronomy, mathematics, geography and all abstract sciences; he influences the wise and philosophers. The person born under this influence loves poetry and literature, and [has] a passion for study; he will distinguish himself in mathematics and geometry.

Lenain: Against calumniators and spells and for the destruction of evil spirits. Governs astronomy, mathematics, geography and all abstract sciences. Loves poetry, literature, avid for study.

Attributes: Against slander, astronomy, mathematics, geography, poetry, studious.

Goetic Demon: MARAX or MORAX

Hebrew: מאראס

Gematria: 302

Demonic Classifications: Earl and president

Planets: Mercury and Mars

Metals: Copper, silver, and quicksilver

Suffumigations: Storax and dragon's blood

Description from *Ars Goetia*: The Twenty-first Spirit is Marax. He is a Great Earl and President. He appeareth like a great Bull with a Man's face. His office is to make Men very knowing in Astronomy, and all other Liberal Sciences; also he can give good Familiars, and wise, knowing the virtues of Herbs and Stones which be precious.

Attributes: Astronomy, herbs, stones, arts and sciences.

⊰ THE TWENTY-SECOND QUINARY ⊱

Degrees and Sign: 15° 00'–19° 59' Cancer
Equinoctial Hour: 1:00–1:19 p.m.

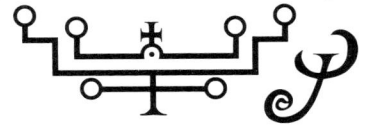

Shem HaMephorash Angel: IEIAIEL

Hebrew: ייאל

Gematria: 61

Ruling Archangel: Zaphkiel

Angelic Choir: Thrones

Invocation: "The Lord is thy keeper: the Lord is thy shade upon thy right hand." [Psalm 121:5 (KJV)] *Dominus custodit te; Dominus protection tua, supermanum dexteram tuam.*

Passage from *Sefer Raziel HaMalakh*: Guide by three secrets of three vowels. Of the unity of אהיה. The highest path is a line on the center until the Yod. Reach in three places. עזאבה follows the highest. Reach the resting place in the universe. Make the oath to all the nation by the ram's horn. Of one power, indicate the power of the universe. Bind to guide thus and also the image thus.

Ambelain: This angel rules over fortune, renown, diplomacy and commerce; he influences voyages, discoveries and maritime expeditions; he protects against tempests and shipwrecks. The person born under this influence will love commerce, be industrious and will distinguish himself through his liberal and philanthropic ideas.

Lenain: Governs fortune, renown, diplomacy, commerce, influence on voyages, discoveries, protection against storms and shipwreck. Loves business, industriousness, liberal and philanthropic ideas.

Attributes: Protection, storms, philanthropy, business acumen, voyages.

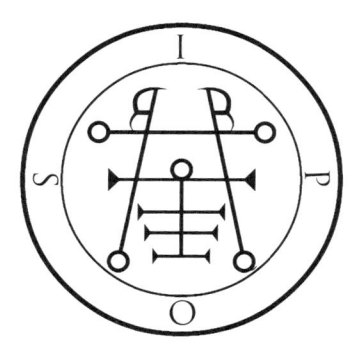

Goetic Demon: IPOS

Hebrew: יפוש

Gematria: 396

Demonic Classifications: Earl and Prince

Planets: Mars and Jupiter

Metals: Copper, silver, and tin

Suffumigations: Cedar and dragon's blood

Description from *Ars Goetia*: The Twenty-second Spirit is lpos. He is an Earl, and a Mighty Prince, and appeareth in the form of an Angel with a Lion's Head, and a Goose's Foot, and Hare's Tail. He knoweth all things Past, Present, and to Come. He maketh men witty and bold.

Attributes: Divination, wit, boldness.

⊰ THE TWENTY-THIRD QUINARY ⊱

Degrees and Sign: 20° 00'–24° 59' Cancer
Equinoctial Hour: 1:20–1:39 p.m.

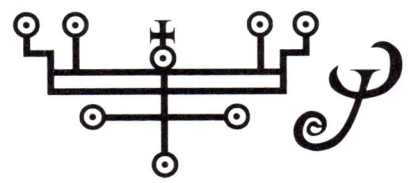

Shem HaMephorash Angel: MELAHEL

Hebrew: מלהאל

Gematria: 106

Ruling Archangel: Zaphkiel

Angelic Choir: Thrones

Invocation: "The Lord shall preserve thy going out and thy coming in from this time forth, and even for evermore." [Psalm 121:8 (KJV)] *Dominus custodiat introilum tuum, et exitum tuum: et ex hoc nunc, et in saeculum.*

Passage from *Sefer Raziel HaMalakh*: Guide by two actions. All the wheel below rises to every one power. Of the unity of one, thus the father. Bind to guide. The image of six powers guides. The daughter becomes the mother.

Ambelain: He serves against arms and to travel in safety. This angel rules water, all products of the earth and principally those plants necessary to the cure of illnesses. The person born under this influence is naturally hardy and capable of undertaking the most perilous expeditions; he distinguishes himself through honorable actions.

Lenain: Against weapons and for safety in travel. Governs water, produce of the earth, and especially plants necessary for the cure of disease. Courageous, accomplishes honorable actions.

Attributes: Against weapons and perils, medicinal herbs, disease, safety, travels, honor.

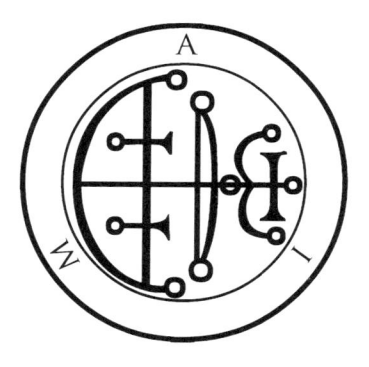

Goetic Demon: AIM

Hebrew: אים

Gematria: 611

Demonic Classification: Duke

Planet: Venus

Metal: Copper

Suffumigation: Sandalwood

Description from *Ars Goetia*: The Twenty-third Spirit is Aim. He is a Great Strong Duke. He appeareth in the form of a very handsome Man in body, but with three Heads, the first, like a Serpent, the second like a Man having two Stars on his Forehead, the third like a Calf. He rideth on a Viper, carrying a Firebrand in his Hand, wherewith he setteth cities, castles, and great Places, on fire. He maketh thee witty in all manner of ways, and giveth true answers unto private matters.

Attributes: Arson, witty, secrets, discreet.

⊰ THE TWENTY-FOURTH QUINARY ⊱

Degrees and Sign: 25° 00'–29° 59' Cancer
Equinoctial Hour: 1:40–1:59 p.m.

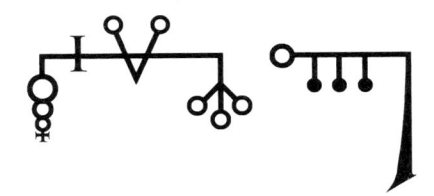

Shem HaMephorash Angel: HAHUIAH or HAIVIAH

Hebrew: ההויה

Gematria: 31

Ruling Archangel: Zaphkiel

Angelic Choir: Thrones

Invocation: "Behold, the eye of the Lord is upon them that fear him, upon them that hope in his mercy." [Psalm 33:18 (KJV)] *Ecce oculi Domini super metuenteseum: et in eis, qui spirant in misericordia ejus.*

Passage from *Sefer Raziel HaMalakh*: Guide by four foundations below the Yod. From the power, התיית עזאבה. From the power of four foundations, bind to guide by measures. Aaron comes near over the hand of the Lord. Follow in beauty. The image of five powers guide by the word, and by all understanding.

Ambelain: He serves to obtain grace and mercy from God. This angel rules over exiles, fugitive prisoners and condemned prisoners; he works against the discovery of secret crimes, and those men who commit them will escape justice provided they do not fall back into the same criminal ways. He protects against harmful beasts and he protects against robbers and assassins. Those born under this influence will love truth and the exact sciences; they will be sincere in their words and their actions.

Lenain: To obtain the grace and mercy of God. Governs exiles, fugitives, defaulters. Protects against harmful animals. Preserves from thieves and assassins. Loves truth, the exact sciences, sincere in word and deed.

Attributes: Grace, exile, against thieves and murderers, protection, truth, sincerity.

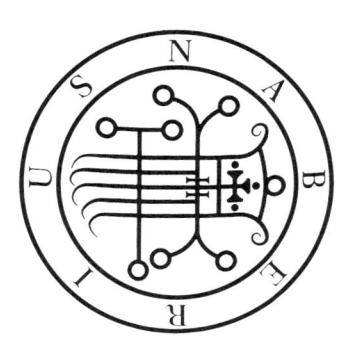

Goetic Demon: NABERIUS or NABERUS

Hebrew: נבריוש

Gematria: 568

Demonic Classification: Marquis

Planet: Luna

Metal: Silver

Suffumigation: Jasmine

Description from *Ars Goetia*: The Twenty-fourth Spirit is Naberius. He is a most valiant Marquis, and showeth in the form of a Black Crane, fluttering about the Circle, and when he speaketh it is with a hoarse voice. He maketh men cunning in all Arts and Sciences, but especially in the Art of Rhetoric. He restoreth lost Dignities and Honours.

Attributes: Cunning, rhetoric, arts and sciences, dignity, honor, hoarse voice.

⊰ THE TWENTY-FIFTH QUINARY ⊱

Degrees and Sign: 0° 00'–4° 59' Leo
Equinoctial Hour: 2:00–2:19 p.m.

Shem HaMephorash Angel: NITHHAIAH

Hebrew: נתהיה

Gematria: 441

Ruling Archangel: Zadkiel

Angelic Choir: Dominions

Invocation: "I will praise thee, O Lord, with my whole heart; I will shew forth all thy marvellous works." [Psalm 9:1 (KJV)] *Confitebortibi Domine in toto corde meo: narrabo omnia mirabilia tua.*

Passage from *Sefer Raziel HaMalakh*: Guide man from the domain of suffering by the strength of Hethokesh. Of the universe, reach in righteousness. In righteousness עזאבה, complete by two measures and bind to guide thus. The image of five powers guides. In secret, the souls go forth from the understanding, in regions in the domain of righteous nations. Speak for the sake of the great strength and bind them with התיית.

Ambelain: He serves to gain wisdom and to discover the truth of hidden secrets. This angel rules over all the occult sciences; he gives revelations in dreams and particularly to those born on the day over which he rules; he influences wise men who love peace and solitude, and upon those who seek truth and practice the magic of the sages, which is that of God.

Lenain: For the acquisition of wisdom and the discovery of the truth of hidden mysteries. Governs occult sciences. Gives revelations in dreams, particularly to those born on the day over which he presides. Influences those who practice the magic of the sages.

Attributes: Wisdom, dreams, occult sciences, revelations, peace, solitude.

Goetic Demon: GLASYA-LABOLAS

Hebrew: גלאסיא לבולש

Gematria: 473

Demonic Classifications: President and earl

Planets: Mercury and Mars

Metals: Quicksilver, copper, and silver

Suffumigations: Storax and dragon's blood

Description from *Ars Goetia*: The Twenty-fifth Spirit is Glasya-Labolas. He is a Mighty President and Earl, and showeth himself in the form of a Dog with Wings like a Gryphon. He teacheth all Arts and Sciences in an instant, and is an Author of Bloodshed and Manslaughter. He teacheth all things Past, and to Come. If desired he causeth the love both of Friends and of Foes. He can make a Man to go Invisible.

Attributes: Arts and sciences, violence, friends, enemies, invisibility.

⊰ THE TWENTY-SIXTH QUINARY ⊱

Degrees and Sign: 5° 00'–9° 59' Leo
Equinoctial Hour: 2:20–2:39 p.m.

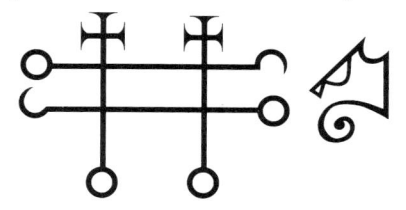

Shem HaMephorash Angel: HAAIAH

Hebrew: האאיה

Gematria: 22

Ruling Archangel: Zadkiel

Angelic Choir: Dominions

Invocation: "I cried with my whole heart; hear me, O Lord: I will keep thy statutes." [Psalm 119:145 (KJV)] *Clamavi in toto corde meo, exaudi me Domine; justifications tuas requiram.*

Passage from *Sefer Raziel HaMalakh*: Guide by three measures. Complete the name אהה. Complete עשאבה by the power of Aleph. Measure one and bind to guide by Vau. Complete them. The image of eight powers guide by the word. All complete by Jacob. Of images of mercy and truth, understand the secret images. Complete the highest, beginning and ending of understanding the secret of the glory.

Ambelain: He serves to win judgments and to render judges favorable. This angel protects all those who seek the truth; he brings men to the contemplation of divine things; he rules over politicians, diplomats, plenipotentiaries, ambassadors, peace treaties and dealings and all pacts in general; he influences couriers, communications, agents and secret expeditions.

Lenain: For the winning of a law suit. Protects those who search after truth. Influences politics, diplomats, secret expeditions and agents.

Attributes: Truth, peace treaties, judgment, divine contemplation, politics, communication.

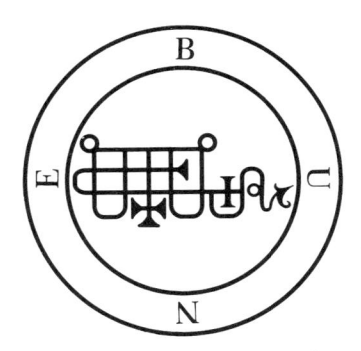

Goetic Demon: BIM or BUNE

Hebrew: בים

Gematria: 612

Demonic Classification: Duke

Planet: Venus

Metal: Copper

Suffumigation: Sandalwood

Description from *Ars Goetia*: The Twenty-sixth Spirit is Bune (or Bim). He is a Strong, Great and Mighty Duke. He appeareth in the form of a Dragon with three heads, one like a Dog, one like a Gryphon, and one like a Man. He speaketh with a high and comely Voice. He changeth the Place of the Dead, and causeth the Spirits which be under him to gather together upon your Sepulchres. He giveth Riches unto a Man, and maketh him Wise and Eloquent. He giveth true Answers unto Demands.

Attributes: Graves, riches, wisdom, eloquence, high, comely voice.

⊰ THE TWENTY-SEVENTH QUINARY ⊱

Degrees and Sign: 10° 00'–14° 59' Leo
Equinoctial Hour: 2:40–2:59 p.m.

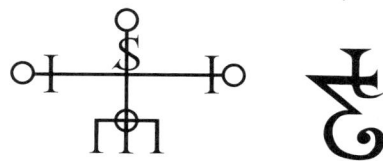

Shem HaMephorash Angel: IERATHEL or JERATHEL

Hebrew: ירתאל

Gematria: 641

Ruling Archangel: Zadkiel

Angelic Choir: Dominions

Invocation: "Deliver me, O Lord, from the evil man: preserve me from the violent man." [Psalm 140:1 (KJV)] *Eripe me Domine ab homine malo, a viro iniquo eripe me.*

Passage from *Sefer Raziel HaMalakh*: Guide by completing the moving. Do not move from the place of victory. עזאבה In unity, establish forever. Bind to guide as 20 measures. Receive this from that until becoming afraid. The image guides all, bound by Yod. Bow down in fear. Do not move from victory.

Ambelain: He serves to confound the wicked and slanderers, and to be delivered from our enemies. This angel protects those who provoke us and unjustly attack us. He rules over the propagation of light, civilization and liberty. The person born under this influence loves peace, justice, sciences and the arts, and he distinguishes himself in literature.

Lenain: To confound wrong-doers and liars and for deliverance from one's enemies. Governs propagation of light, civilization. Love, peace, justice, science and arts; special affinity for literature.

Attributes: Protection from attacks, confounds enemies, liberty, peace, literature.

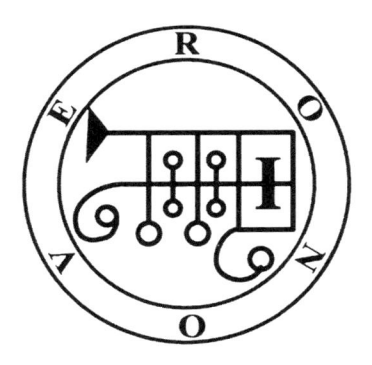

Goetic Demon: RONOVÉ

Hebrew: רונוו

Gematria: 268

Demonic Classifications: Marquis and earl

Planets: Luna and Mars

Metals: Silver and copper

Suffumigations: Jasmine and dragon's blood

Description from *Ars Goetia*: The Twenty-seventh Spirit is Ronové. He appeareth in the Form of a Monster. He teacheth the Art of Rhetoric very well and giveth Good Servants, Knowledge of Tongues, and Favours with Friends or Foes. He is a Marquis and Great Earl.

Attributes: Rhetoric, languages, friends, enemies.

⊰ THE TWENTY-EIGHTH QUINARY ⊱

Degrees and Sign: 15° 00'–19° 59' Leo
Equinoctial Hour: 3:00–3:19 p.m.

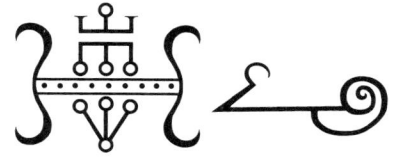

Shem HaMephorash Angel: SEEHIAH, SEEIAH, or SAEEHIAH

Hebrew: שאהיה

Gematria: 321

Ruling Archangel: Zadkiel

Angelic Choir: Dominions

Invocation: "O God, be not far from me: O my God, make haste for my help." [Psalm 71:12 (KJV)] *Deus ne elongeris a me: Deus meus in auxilium meum respice.*

Passage from _Sefer Raziel HaMalakh_: Guide by victory in beauty. By the power of action in Egypt. The middle of degrees עזאבה goes forth to judge in Egypt. The seven bind therein. When passing forth in Egypt, to smite. Bind to guide by the word and image of nine powers. The actions complete in the midst of Egypt. Understand the actions.

Ambelain: He serves against infirmities and thunder. This angel protects against fires, ruined buildings, collapse, maladies, etc. He rules over health and longevity of life. The person born under this influence will be full of good judgment; he will only act with prudence and circumspection.

Lenain: Against infirmities and thunder, protects against fire, the ruin of buildings, falls and illnesses. Governs health, simplicity. Has much judgment.

Attributes: Protection from fire and storms, health, longevity, circumscript, simplicity.

Goetic Demon: BERITH, BEALE, or BOFRY

Hebrew: ברית

Gematria: 612

Demonic Classification: Duke

Planet: Venus

Metal: Copper

Suffumigation: Sandalwood

Description from *Ars Goetia*: The Twenty-eighth Spirit in Order, as Solomon bound them, is named Berith. He is a Mighty, Great, and Terrible Duke. He hath two other Names given unto him by men of later times, viz.: BEALE, or BEAL, and BOFRY or BOLFRY. He appeareth in the Form of a Soldier with Red Clothing, riding upon a Red Horse, and having a Crown of Gold upon his head. He giveth true answers, Past, Present, and to Come. Thou must make use of a Ring in calling him forth, as is before spoken of regarding Beleth. He can turn all metals into Gold. He can give Dignities, and can confirm them unto Man. He speaketh with a, very clear and subtle Voice.

Attributes: Divination, dignity, alchemy and transmutation, honesty, clear, low voice.

⊰ THE TWENTY-NINTH QUINARY ⊱

Degrees and Sign: 20° 00'–24° 59' Leo
Equinoctial Hour: 3:20–3:39 p.m.

Shem HaMephorash Angel: REIIEL or REIAIEL

Hebrew: רייאל

Gematria: 251

Ruling Archangel: Zadkiel

Angelic Choir: Dominions

Invocation: "Behold, God is mine helper: the Lord is with them that uphold my soul." [Psalm 54:4 (KJV)] *Ecce enim Deus adjuvat me: et Dominus susceptor est animae meae.*

Passage from *Sefer Raziel HaMalakh*: Guide by the letters of the sephiroth. Go forth from the star. The understanding of the wisdom of עזאבה is the last wisdom. Bind to guide thus. The image of six powers guides to six ends.

Ambelain: He serves against the impious and the enemies of religion, and to be delivered from all enemies both visible and invisible. This angel rules over all religious sentiment, divine philosophy and meditation. The person born under this influence will be distinguished by his virtues and his zeal to propagate truth; he will make every effort to destroy impiety through his writings and by example.

Lenain: Against the impious and enemies of religion; for deliverance from all enemies both visible and invisible. Virtue and zeal for the propagation of truth, will do his utmost to destroy impiety.

Attributes: Against atheists, theology, truth, mysticism, philosophy.

Goetic Demon: ASTAROTH

Hebrew: אשטארות

Gematria: 917

Demonic Classification: Duke

Planet: Venus

Metal: Copper

Suffumigation: Sandalwood

Description from *Ars Goetia*: The Twenty-ninth Spirit is Astaroth. He is a Mighty, Strong Duke, and appeareth in the Form of an hurtful Angel riding on an Infernal Beast like a Dragon, and carrying in his right hand a Viper. Thou must in no wise let him approach too near unto thee, lest he do thee damage by his Noisome Breath. Wherefore the Magician must hold the Magical Ring near his face, and that will defend him. He giveth true answers of things Past, Present, and to Come, and can discover all Secrets. He will declare wittingly how the Spirits fell, if desired, and the reason of his own fall. He can make men wonderfully knowing in all Liberal Sciences.

Attributes: Truth, arts and sciences, divination.

⊰ THE THIRTIETH QUINARY ⊱

Degrees and Sign: 25° 00'–29° 59' Leo
Equinoctial Hour: 3:40–3:59 p.m.

Shem HaMephorash Angel: OMAEL

Hebrew: ומאאל

Gematria: 78

Ruling Archangel: Zadkiel

Angelic Choir: Dominions

Invocation: "For thou art my hope, O Lord God: thou art my trust from my youth." [Psalm 71:5 (KJV)] *Quoniam tu es patientia mea Domine spes mea a juventute mea.*

Passage from *Sefer Raziel HaMalakh*: Guide by two actions. Proclaim the name of one. The foundation is in the midst. Also, of עזאבה, righteousness is the foundation of the universe. Bind to guide thus. The image of six powers guides to six ends.

Ambelain: He serves against chagrin, despair and to have patience. This angel rules over the animal kingdom; he watches over the generation of beings, in order to see [the] special multiply and races perpetuated; he influences chemists, doctors and surgeons. The person born under this influence will distinguish himself in anatomy and medicine.

Lenain: Against sorrow, despair and for the acquisition of patience. Governs animal kingdom, watches over the generation of beings. Chemists, doctors, surgeons. Affinity for anatomy and medicine.

Attributes: Against depression, generation, anatomy and medicine, animals, patience.

Goetic Demon: FORNEUS

Hebrew: פורנאש

Gematria: 637

Demonic Classification: Marquis

Planet: Luna

Metal: Silver

Suffumigation: Jasmine

Description from *Ars Goetia*: The Thirtieth Spirit is Forneus. He is a Mighty and Great Marquis, and appeareth in the Form of a Great Sea-Monster. He teacheth, and maketh men wonderfully knowing in the Art of Rhetoric. He causeth men to have a Good Name, and to have the knowledge and understanding of Tongues. He maketh one to be beloved of his Foes as well as of his Friends.

Attributes: Rhetoric, reputation, foreign languages, amiable.

⊰ THE THIRTY-FIRST QUINARY ⊱

Degrees and Sign: 0° 00'–4° 59' Virgo
Equinoctial Hour: 4:00–4:19 p.m.

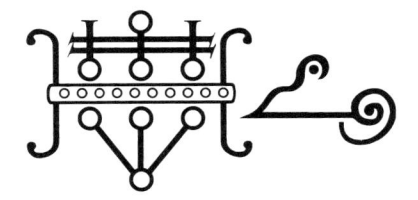

Shem HaMephorash Angel: LECABEL

Hebrew: לכבאל

Gematria: 83

Ruling Archangel: Zadkiel

Angelic Choir: Dominions

Invocation: "I will go in the strength of the Lord God: I will make mention of thy righteousness, even of thine only." [Psalm 71:16 (KJV)] *Quoniam non cognovi literaturam introibo in potentias Domini: Domine memorabor justitiae tuae solius.*

Passage from *Sefer Raziel HaMalakh*: Guide by throne. Of the one throne עזאבה, is the horseman over the fathers. Bind to guide to the crown between wisdom and understanding. The image of five powers reaches to beauty. עחט ברח דפיס .

Ambelain: He rules over vegetation and agriculture. The person born under this influence will love astronomy, mathematics and geometry; he will distinguish himself through his luminous ideas, by resolving the most difficult problems and his talents will make his fortune.

Lenain: For the acquisition of knowledge. Governs vegetation and agriculture. Loves astronomy, mathematics and geometry.

Attributes: Problem-solving, agriculture, astronomy, talents, insight.

Goetic Demon: FORAS

Hebrew: פוראש

Gematria: 587

Demonic Classification: President

Planet: Mercury

Metal: Quicksilver

Suffumigation: Storax

Description from *Ars Goetia*: The Thirty-first Spirit is Foras. He is a Mighty President, and appeareth in the Form of a Strong Man in Human Shape. He can give the understanding to Men how they may know the Virtues of all Herbs and Precious Stones. He teacheth the Arts of Logic and Ethics in all their parts. If desired he maketh men invisible, and to live long, and to be eloquent. He can discover Treasures and recover things Lost.

Attributes: Herbs, stones, logic, ethics, invisibility, longevity, eloquence, lost things.

⊰ THE THIRTY-SECOND QUINARY ⊱

Degrees and Sign: 5° 00'–9° 59' Virgo

Equinoctial Hour: 4:20–4:39 p.m.

Shem HaMephorash Angel: VASARIAH

Hebrew: ושריה

Gematria: 521

Ruling Archangel: Zadkiel

Angelic Choir: Dominions

Invocation: "For the word of the Lord is right; and all his works are done in truth." [Psalm 33:4 (KJV)] *Quia rectum est verbum Domini, et omnia opera ejus in fide.*

Passage from *Sefer Raziel HaMalakh*: Guide by establishing the oath. In the end, reach thus of one. Of the Lord of the qabalah, bind to guide thus. The image of six powers guides by the word.

Ambelain: This angel rules over justice; he influences nobility, legal executives, magistrates and attorneys. The person born under this influence will have a good memory and speak eloquently with ease, and will be amiable, spiritual and modest.

Lenain: Against those who attack us in court. Governs justice. Good memory, articulate.

Attributes: Against false accusations, justice, memory, eloquence, amiable.

Goetic Demon: ASMODAY, ASMODAI, or ASMODEUS

Hebrew: אסמודי

Gematria: 121

Demonic Classification: King

Planet: Sol

Metal: Gold

Suffumigation: Frankincense

Description from *Ars Goetia*: The Thirty-second Spirit is Asmoday, or Asmodai. He is a Great King, Strong, and Powerful. He appeareth with Three Heads, whereof the first is like a Bull, the second like a Man, and the third like a Ram; he hath also the tail of a Serpent, and from his mouth issue Flames of Fire. His Feet are webbed like those of a Goose. He sitteth upon an Infernal Dragon, and beareth in his hand a Lance with a Banner. He is first and choicest under the Power of AMAYMON, he goeth before all other. When the Exorcist hath a mind to call him, let it be abroad, and let him stand on his feet all the time of action, with his Cap or Headdress off; for if it be on, AMAYMON will deceive him and call all his actions to be bewrayed. But as soon as the Exorcist seeth Asmoday in the shape aforesaid, he shall call him by his Name, saying: "Art thou Asmoday?" and he will not deny it, and by-and-by he will bow down unto the ground. He giveth the

Ring of Virtues; he teacheth the Arts of Arithmetic, Astronomy, Geometry, and all handicrafts absolutely. He giveth true and full answers unto thy demands. He maketh one Invincible. He showeth the place where Treasures lie, and guardeth it.

Attributes: Arithmetic, geometry, astronomy, eloquence, invincibility, honesty.

⚜ THE THIRTY-THIRD QUINARY ⚜

Degrees and Sign: 10° 00'–14° 59' Virgo
Equinoctial Hour: 4:40–4:59 p.m.

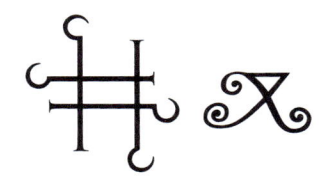

Shem HaMephorash Angel: IEUIAH or IEHUIAH

Hebrew: יהויה

Gematria: 36

Ruling Archangel: Kamael

Angelic Choir: Powers

Invocation: "The Lord knoweth the thoughts of man, that they are vanity." [Psalm 94:11 (KJV)] *Dominus scit cogitationes hominium quoniam vanae sunt.*

Passage from *Sefer Raziel HaMalakh*: Guide by two actions from the six. Of the unity of one, the Lord speaks. Bind to guide thus and in all the dwellings. The image of the four powers guides by two luminaries. Of the secret of two actions, bind by this.

Ambelain: He serves to recognize traitors, to destroy their projects and their machinations. This angel protects all Christian princes; he keeps their subjects in obeisance. The person born under this influence will love to fulfill all the works of his estate.

Lenain: For the identification of traitors.

Attributes: Uncovers plots, protection, loyalty, fidelity.

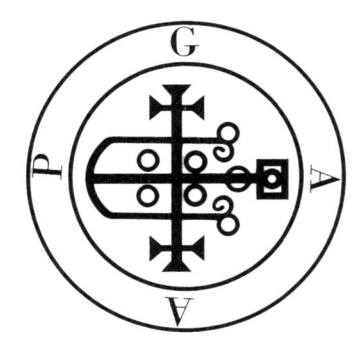

Goetic Demon: GAAPH or GAAP

Hebrew: גאאף

Gematria: 805

Demonic Classifications: President and prince

Planets: Mercury and Jupiter

Metals: Quicksilver and tin

Suffumigations: Storax and cedar

Description from *Ars Goetia*: The Thirty-third Spirit is Gaap. He is a Great President and a Mighty Prince. He appeareth when the Sun is in some of the Southern Signs, in a Human Shape, going before Four Great and Mighty Kings, as if lie were a Guide to conduct them along on their way. His Office is to make men Insensible or Ignorant; as also in Philosophy to make them Knowing, and in all the Liberal Sciences. He can cause Love or Hatred, also he can teach thee to consecrate those things that belong to the Dominion of AMAYMON his King. He can deliver Familiars out of the Custody of other Magicians, and answereth truly and perfectly of things Past, Present, and to Come. He can carry and re-carry men very speedily from one Kingdom to another, at the Will and Pleasure of the Exorcist.

Attributes: Philosophy, arts and sciences, love and hate, transportation, divination.

⊰ THE THIRTY-FOURTH QUINARY ⊱

Degrees and Sign: 15° 00'–19° 59' Virgo
Equinoctial Hour: 5:00–5:19 p.m.

Shem HaMephorash Angel: LEHAHAIAH or LEHAHIAH

Hebrew: לההיה

Gematria: 55

Ruling Archangel: Kamael

Angelic Choir: Powers

Invocation: "Let Israel hope in the Lord from henceforth and forever." [Psalm 131:3 (KJV)] *Speret Israël in Domino; ex hocnunc, et usque in saeculum.*

Passage from *Sefer Raziel HaMalakh*: Guide by two lives. In the place of Chokmah and Binah is abundance by Yod in the place of the highest man. Bind to guide in understanding of abundance by Yod. The image of the powers guide by the word.

Ambelain: This angel rules over crowned heads, princes and nobles; he maintains harmony, understanding and peace between them; he influences the obeisance of subjects towards their princes. The person born under this influence will become famous through his talents and his actions; he will have the confidence and favor of his prince, which he will merit because of his devotion, fidelity and the great service which he will render him.

Lenain: Against anger. Known for his talents and acts, the confidence and fervor of his prayers.

Attributes: International peace, faith, respect, talents, confidence.

Goetic Demon: FURFUR

Hebrew: פהורפההור

Gematria: 582

Demonic Classification: Earl

Planet: Mars

Metal: Copper and silver

Suffumigation: Dragon's blood

Description from *Ars Goetia*: The Thirty-fourth Spirit is Furfur. He is a Great and Mighty Earl, appearing in the Form of an Hart with a Fiery Tail. He never speaketh truth unless he be compelled, or brought up within a triangle. Being therein, he will take upon himself the Form of an Angel. Being bidden, he speaketh with a hoarse voice. Also he will wittingly urge Love between Man and Woman. He can raise Lightnings and Thunders, Blasts, and Great Tempestuous Storms. And he giveth True Answers both of Things Secret and Divine, if commanded.

Attributes: Lies, storms, lust, hoarse voice.

⊰ THE THIRTY-FIFTH QUINARY ⊱

Degrees and Sign: 20° 00'–24° 59' Virgo
Equinoctial Hour: 5:20–5:39 p.m.

Shem HaMephorash Angel: CHAVAKIAH or CHEVAKIAH

Hebrew: כוקיה

Gematria: 141

Ruling Archangel: Kamael

Angelic Choir: Powers

Invocation: "I love the Lord, because he hath heard my voice and my supplications." [Psalm 116:1 (KJV)] *Dilexi quoniam exaudiet Dominus vocem orationis meae.*

Passage from *Sefer Raziel HaMalakh*: Guide by the name of the judgement of the one power. Bind to guide באטרת as Tiphareth and Binah. The image of eight powers guides in the kingdom. Reach the understanding. By two actions, understand the power of the actions.

Ambelain: This angel rules over testaments, successions and all amiable distributions; he supports peace and harmony in families. The person born under this influence will love to live in peace with everybody, even to the cost of his interest; he will make it his duty to repay the fidelity and good offices of those in his service.

Lenain: To regain the favor of those one has offended. Governs testaments, successions and all private financial agreements. Loves to live in peace with everyone. Loves rewarding the loyalty of those in his service.

Attributes: Restores friendship, peace, harmony, selfless, finances, service.

Goetic Demon: MARCHOSIAS

Hebrew: מרחושיאש

Gematria: 865

Demonic Classification: Marquis

Planet: Luna

Metal: Silver

Suffumigation: Jasmine

Description from *Ars Goetia*: The Thirty-fifth Spirit is Marchosias. He is a Great and Mighty Marquis, appearing at first in the Form of a Wolf having Gryphon's Wings, and a Serpent's Tail, and Vomiting Fire out of his mouth. But after a time, at the command of the Exorcist he putteth on the Shape of a Man. And he is a strong fighter. He was of the Order of Dominations. He governeth 30 Legions of Spirits. He told his Chief, who was Solomon, that after 1,200 years he had hopes to return unto the Seventh Throne.

Attributes: Truth, faithful, combative.

⊰ THE THIRTY-SIXTH QUINARY ⊱

Degrees and Sign: 25° 00'–29° 59' Virgo
Equinoctial Hour: 5:40–5:59 p.m.

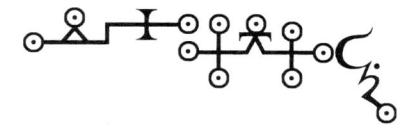

Shem HaMephorash Angel: MENADEL or MANADEL

Hebrew: מנדאל

Gematria: 125

Ruling Archangel: Kamael

Angelic Choir: Powers

Invocation: "Lord, I have loved the habitation of thy house, and the place where thine honour dwelleth." [Psalm 26:8 (KJV)] *Domine dilexi decorum domus tuae: et locum habitationis gloriae tuae.*

Passage from *Sefer Raziel HaMalakh*: Guide as Moses rises up to the heights. Reveal to bind by the image of Binah. Actions of mercy are by two actions of abundance.

Ambelain: This angel gives light to distant people who have received no news for a long time, he brings exiles back to their native land, and uncovers mislaid or disturbed belongings.

Lenain: To retain one's employment and to preserve one's means of livelihood. Against calumny and for the deliverance of prisoners.

Attributes: Against slander, releases prisoners, reparations, livelihood.

Goetic Demon: STOLAS or STOLOS

Hebrew: שטולוש

Gematria: 651

Demonic Classification: Prince

Planet: Jupiter

Metal: Tin

Suffumigation: Cedar

Description from *Ars Goetia*: The Thirty-sixth Spirit is Stolas, or Stolos. He is a Great and Powerful Prince, appearing in the Shape of a Mighty Raven at first before the Exorcist; but after he taketh the image of a Man. He teacheth the Art of Astronomy, and the Virtues of Herbs and Precious Stones.

Attributes: Astronomy, herbs, stones.

⁜ THE THIRTY-SEVENTH QUINARY ⁝

Degrees and Sign: 0° 00'–4° 59' Libra
Equinoctial Hour: 6:00–6:19 p.m.

Shem HaMephorash Angel: ANIEL

Hebrew: אניאל

Gematria: 92

Ruling Archangel: Kamael

Angelic Choir: Powers

Invocation: "Turn us again, O God, and cause thy face to shine; and we shall be saved." [Psalm 80:3 (KJV)] *Deus ad virtutem converte nos: et ostende faciem tuam et salvi erimus.*

Passage from *Sefer Raziel HaMalakh*: Guide by the word. The Yod is of life. Complete the Yod. Of fifty gates עזאבה of the holiness above. Bind by the Tau and the Yod תת עיעד. Reach in understanding. The image of five powers guide by the word.

Ambelain: He serves to give victory and to raise the siege of a town. This angel rules over the sciences and the arts; he reveals the secrets of nature and inspires wise philosophers with their meditations. The person born under this influence will acquire celebrity through his talents and his enlightenment, and he will distinguish himself among the wise.

Lenain: To obtain victory and stop the siege of a city. Governs sciences and arts. Reveals the secrets of nature, inspires philosophers, sages. Distinguished savant.

Attributes: Victory, release from siege, arts and sciences, wisdom, inspirational, fame.

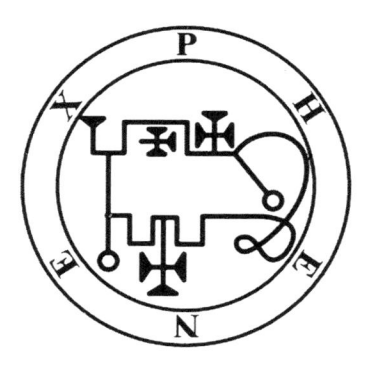

Goetic Demon: PHENEX or PHEYNIX

Hebrew: פאניס

Gematria: 201

Demonic Classification: Marquis

Planet: Luna

Metal: Silver

Suffumigation: Jasmine

Description from *Ars Goetia*: The Thirty-seventh Spirit is Phenex (or Pheynix). He is a great Marquis, and appeareth like the Bird Phoenix, having the Voice of a Child. He singeth many sweet notes before the Exorcist, which he must not regard, but by-and-by he must bid him put on Human Shape. Then he will speak marvellously of all wonderful Sciences if required. He is a Poet, good and excellent. And he will be willing to perform thy requests. He hath hopes also to return to the Seventh Throne after 1,200 years more, as he said unto Solomon.

Attributes: Eloquence, sciences, poetry, high, light voice.

⊰ THE THIRTY-EIGHTH QUINARY ⊱

Degrees and Sign: 5° 00'–9° 59' Libra
Equinoctial Hour: 6:20–6:39 p.m.

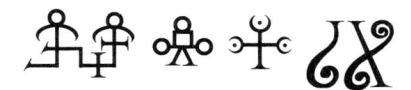

Shem HaMephorash Angel: HAAMIAH

Hebrew: העמיה

Gematria: 130

Ruling Archangel: Kamael

Angelic Choir: Powers

Invocation: "Because thou hast made the Lord, which is my refuge, even the most High, thy habitation." [Psalm 91:9 (KJV)] *Quoniam tu es Domine spes mea: altissimum posuisti refugium tuum.*

Passage from *Sefer Raziel HaMalakh*: Guide by the power of the powers of hosts. The Moon is in twelve tribes of Israel. The Tau התת is between two measures of Aleph. Of עזאבה engrave the name, all from it and therein. Bind to guide by all understanding. The image of seven powers guide by the word.

Ambelain: This angel rules over all religious cults, and above all those which relate to God; it protects all those which seek truth.

Lenain: For the acquisition of all the treasures of heaven and earth. Against fraud, weapons, wild beasts and infernal spirits. Governs all that relates to God.

Attributes: Theology, protection, treasures, against fraud, sects.

Goetic Demon: MALTHOUS, MALTHAS, or HALPHAS

Hebrew: מאלתש

Gematria: 771

Demonic Classification: Earl

Planet: Mars

Metals: Copper and silver

Suffumigation: Dragon's blood

Description from *Ars Goetia*: The Thirty-eighth Spirit is Halphas, or Malthous (or Malthas). He is a Great Earl, and appeareth in the Form of a Stock-Dove. He speaketh with a hoarse Voice. His Office is to build up Towers, and to furnish them with Ammunition and Weapons, and to send Men-of-War to places appointed.

Attributes: Towers, weapons, strategy, hoarse voice.

⊰ THE THIRTY-NINTH QUINARY ⊱

Degrees and Sign: 10° 00'–14° 59' Libra
Equinoctial Hour: 6:40–6:59 p.m.

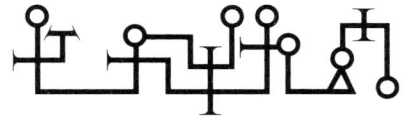

Shem HaMephorash Angel: REHAEL

Hebrew: רהעאל

Gematria: 306

Ruling Archangel: Kamael

Angelic Choir: Powers

Invocation: "Hear, O Lord, and have mercy upon me: Lord, be thou my helper." [Psalm 30:10 (KJV)] *Audivit Dominus, et misertus est mei: Dominus factus est meus adjutor.*

Passage from *Sefer Raziel HaMalakh*: Guide by the Yod. The horseman in the evening is over the Yod. The lives of the Seraphim and A'anephiem are all below and hidden. All Merkabah of Yod and all of Tau. Of עזאבה. The name of four is over all. Bind and the image guides by the word.

Ambelain: He serves as a cure for maladies and to obtain the mercy of God. This angel rules over health and long life; it influences paternal and filial love, and the obeisance and respect of children for their parents.

Lenain: For the healing of the sick. Governs health and longevity. Influences paternal and filial affection.

Attributes: Protection, cures disease, health, longevity, familial.

Goetic Demon: MALPHAS

Hebrew: מאלפש

Gematria: 451

Demonic Classification: President

Planet: Mercury

Metal: Quicksilver

Suffumigation: Storax

Description from *Ars Goetia*: The Thirty-ninth Spirit is Malphas. He appeareth at first like a Crow, but after he will put on Human Shape at the request of the Exorcist, and speak with a hoarse Voice. He is a Mighty President and Powerful. He can build Houses and High Towers, and can bring to thy Knowledge Enemies' Desires and Thoughts, and that which they have done. He giveth Good Familiars. If thou makest a Sacrifice unto him he will receive it kindly and willingly, but he will deceive him that doth it.

Attributes: Buildings, crafts, intelligence, hoarse voice.

⊰ THE FORTIETH QUINARY ⊱

Degrees and Sign: 15° 00'–19° 59' Libra

Equinoctial Hour: 7:00–7:19 p.m.

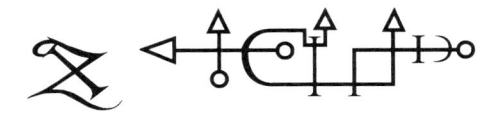

Shem HaMephorash Angel: IEIAZEL

Hebrew: ייזאל

Gematria: 58

Ruling Archangel: Kamael

Angelic Choir: Powers

Invocation: "Lord, why castest thou off my soul? why hidest thou thy face from me?" [Psalm 88:14 (KJV)] *Ut quid Domine repellis orationem meam: avertis faciem tuam a me.*

Passage from *Sefer Raziel HaMalakh*: Guide by twenty-two letters of Merkabah, of one and eight of eight. After, experience the power of עזאבה in eight measures and eight following. Bind two wisdoms by victory. Guide by the word and image thus.

Ambelain: This angel rules over printing and libraries; he influences men of letters and artists. The person born under this influence will love speaking, design, and all sciences in general.

Lenain: For the deliverance of prisoners, for consolation, for deliverance from one's enemies. Governs printing and books. Men of letters and artists.

Attributes: Releases prisoners, literature, the arts, design, eloquence.

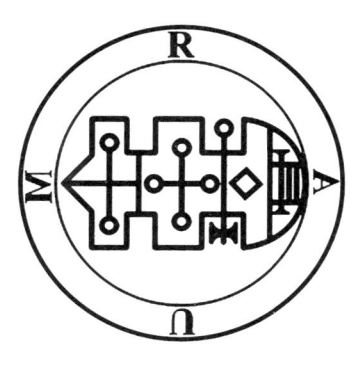

Goetic Demon: RAUM

Hebrew: ראום

Gematria: 807

Demonic Classification: Earl

Planet: Mars

Metals: Copper and silver

Suffumigation: Dragon's blood

Description from *Ars Goetia*: The Fortieth Spirit is Raum. He is a Great Earl; and appeareth at first in the Form of a Crow, but after the Command of the Exorcist he putteth on Human Shape. His office is to steal Treasures out King's Houses, and to carry it whither he is commanded, and to destroy Cities and Dignities of Men, and to tell all things, Past and What Is, and what Will Be; and to cause Love between Friends and Foes. He was of the Order of Thrones.

Attributes: Theft, destruction, divination, love, reconciliation.

⊰ THE FORTY-FIRST QUINARY ⊱

Degrees and Sign: 20° 00'–24° 59' Libra
Equinoctial Hour: 7:20–7:39 p.m.

Shem HaMephorash Angel: HAHAHEL or HAHAEL

Hebrew: הההאל

Gematria: 46

Ruling Archangel: Raphael

Angelic Choir: Virtues

Invocation: "Deliver my soul, O Lord, from lying lips, and from a deceitful tongue." [Psalm 120:2 (KJV)] *Domine libera animam meam a labiis iniquis et a lingua dolosa.*

Passage from *Sefer Raziel HaMalakh*: Guide by Binah, of Geborah and the crown. From the living power of the crown, bind thus. The image guides by Chesed, of the six powers.

Ambelain: He serves against enemies of religion, the impious and slanderers. This angel rules over Christianity; he protects missionaries and all the disciples of Christ, who announce the words of the Scripture to nations; he influences pious souls, prelates, ecclesiastics and all those related to the priesthood. The person born under this influence distinguishes himself by his greatness of soul and his energy; he is completely devoted to the service of God and does not fear martyrdom for Christ.

Lenain: Against the impious, slanderers. Governs Christianity. Greatness of soul, energy. Consecrated to the service of God.

Attributes: Against atheists and slander, Christianity, priests, missionaries.

Goetic Demon: FURCALOR, FORCALOR, or FOCALOR

Hebrew: פהורכלור

Gematria: 547

Demonic Classification: Duke

Planet: Venus

Metal: Copper

Suffumigation: Sandalwood

Description from *Ars Goetia*: The Forty-first Spirit is Focalor, or Forcalor, or Furcalor. He is a Mighty Duke and Strong. He appeareth in the Form of a Man with Gryphon's Wings. His office is to slay Men, and to drown them in the Waters, and to overthrow Ships of War, for he hath Power over both Winds and Seas; but he will not hurt any man or thing if he be commanded to the contrary by the Exorcist. He also hath hopes to return to the Seventh Throne after 1,000 years.

Attributes: Drowning, shipwrecks, seas, wind.

⊰ THE FORTY-SECOND QUINARY ⊱

Degrees and Sign: 25° 00'–29° 59' Libra
Equinoctial Hour: 7:40–7:59 p.m.

Shem HaMephorash Angel: MIKAEL or MICHAEL

Hebrew: מיכאל

Gematria: 101

Ruling Archangel: Raphael

Angelic Choir: Virtues

Invocation: "The Lord shall preserve thee from all evil: he shall preserve thy soul." [Psalm 121:7 (KJV)] *Dominus custodit te ab omni malo; custodiat animam tuam Dominus.*

Passage from *Sefer Raziel HaMalakh*: Guide by three works of the wheel, angel and vestment. Of Yod and the throne of Yod, the power of the A'anephiem is over זאבה. Of the highest, complete all by Yod. Bind the name of the unity over all. The image of four powers guides. Understand the power of the actions.

Ambelain: He serves to travel in safety. This angel rules monarchs, princes and nobles; he keeps their subjects subservient, uncovers conspiracies and all those who seek to destroy their persons and governments. The person born under this influence will become involved in political affairs; he will be curious, and will want to learn the secrets of private offices and foreign news, and he will distinguish himself in affairs of State through his knowledge of diplomacy.

Lenain: For safety in travel. For the discovery of conspiracies. Concerned with political affairs, diplomatic.

Attributes: Safe journeys, curiosity, politics, conspiracies, foreign news.

Goetic Demon: VEPAR or VEPHAR

Hebrew: ופאר

Gematria: 287

Demonic Classification: Duke

Planet: Venus

Metal: Copper

Suffumigation: Sandalwood

Description from _Ars Goetia_: The Forty-second Spirit is Vepar, or Vephar. He is a Duke Great and Strong and appeareth like a Mermaid. His office is to govern the Waters, and to guide Ships laden with Arms, Armour, and Ammunition, etc., thereon. And at the request of the Exorcist he can cause the seas to be right stormy and to appear full of ships. Also he maketh men to die in Three Days by Putrefying Wounds or Sores, and causing Worms to breed in them.

Attributes: Waters, ships, weapons, cargo, storms, parasites.

⊰ THE FORTY-THIRD QUINARY ⊱

Degrees and Sign: 0° 00'–4° 59' Scorpio
Equinoctial Hour: 8:00–8:19 p.m.

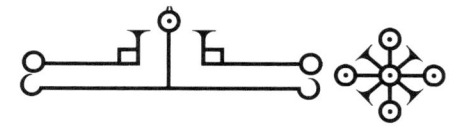

Shem HaMephorash Angel: VEUALIAH

Hebrew: וולית

Gematria: 57

Ruling Archangel: Raphael

Angelic Choir: Virtues

Invocation: "But unto thee have I cried, O Lord; and in the morning shall my prayer prevent thee." [Psalm 88:13 (KJV)] *Et ego ad te Domine clamavi: et mane oratio mea praeveniet te.*

Passage from *Sefer Raziel HaMalakh*: Guide by two actions and the name of 42. Rise in unity. Proclaim the foundation of the universe. The twelve borders are slanted. Of עזאבה, by Yod Heh is the name over the holy temple. Bind the image to guide by the word.

Ambelain: He serves to destroy the enemy and for deliverance from slavery. This angel rules over peace and influences the prosperity of empires; he affirms tottering thrones and kingly power. The person born under this influence will love the military state and glory; he will be continually engaged in those sciences which are in rapport with the angel of war; he will become famous through the means of arms, and will attract the confidence of his prince through the services we renders [*sic*] him.

Lenain: For the destruction of the enemy and deliverance from bondage. Love glory and the military.

Attributes: Destroys enemies, prosperity, bellicose, glory, liberty.

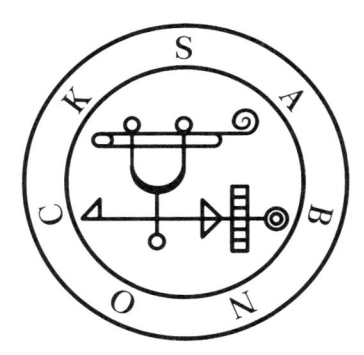

Goetic Demon: SABNOCK or SAVNOK

Hebrew: שבנוך

Gematria: 858

Demonic Classification: Marquis

Planet: Luna

Metal: Silver

Suffumigation: Jasmine

Description from *Ars Goetia*: The Forty-third Spirit, as King Solomon commanded them into the Vessel of Brass, is called Sabnock, or Savnok. He is a Marquis, Mighty, Great and Strong, appearing in the Form of an Armed Soldier with a Lion's Head, riding on a pale-coloured horse. His office is to build high Towers, Castles and Cities, and to furnish them with Armour, etc. Also he can afflict Men for many days with Wounds and with Sores rotten and full of Worms. He giveth Good Familiars at the request of the Exorcist.

Attributes: Buildings, urban, parasites.

⊰ THE FORTY-FOURTH QUINARY ⊱

Degrees and Sign: 5° 00'–9° 59' Scorpio
Equinoctial Hour: 8:20–8:39 p.m.

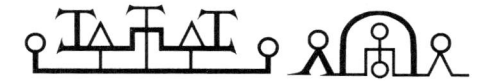

Shem HaMephorash Angel: IELAHIAH

Hebrew: ילהיה

Gemtria: 60

Ruling Archangel: Raphael

Angelic Choir: Virtues

Invocation: "Accept, I beseech thee, the freewill offerings of my mouth, O Lord, and teach me thy judgments." [Psalm 119:108 (KJV)] *Voluntaria oris mei bene placita fac Domine: et judiciatua doce me.*

Passage from *Sefer Raziel HaMalakh*: Guide by rising up. עתתאה. Of wisdom over זאבה, five measures of thirteen measures. Four are of compassion and mercy. The fifth is complete by Heh Yod Vau. Bind thus to guide. Of the image of five powers, five receive to complete.

Ambelain: He is good for getting the protection of magistrates and to win a lawsuit. This angel protects against arms; he gives victory. The person born under this influence will love to travel in order to learn, and will succeed in all his undertakings; he will distinguish himself through his military talents and his bravery, and his name will be famous in the pomp of glory.

Lenain: Success of a useful undertaking. Protection against magistrates. Trials. Protects against armies, gives victory. Fond of travel and learning. All his undertakings are crowned with success; distinguished for military capabilities and courage.

Attributes: Victory in lawsuits, courage, travels, learning.

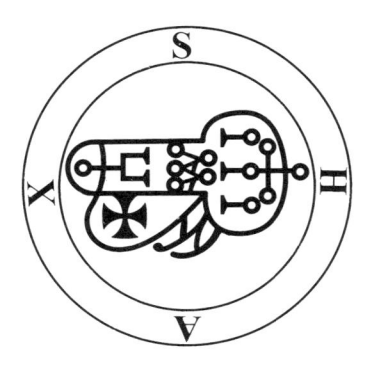

Goetic Demon: SHAZ, SHAX, or SHAN

Hebrew: שאז

Gematria: 308

Demonic Classification: Marquis

Planet: Luna

Metal: Silver

Suffumigation: Jasmine

Description from *Ars Goetia*: The Forty-fourth Spirit is Shax, or Shaz (or Shass). He is a Great Marquis and appeareth in the Form of a Stock-Dove, speaking with a voice hoarse, but yet subtle. His Office is to take away the Sight, Hearing, or Understanding of any Man or Woman at the command of the Exorcist; and to steal money out of the houses of Kings, and to carry it again in 1,200 years. If commanded he will fetch Horses at the request of the Exorcist, or any other thing. But he must first be commanded into a Triangle or else he will deceive him, and tell him many Lies. He can discover all things that are Hidden, and not kept by Wicked Spirits. He giveth good Familiars, sometimes.

Attributes: Blindness, deafness, horses, deceit, theft, hoarse voice.

⊰ THE FORTY-FIFTH QUINARY ⊱

Degrees and Sign: 10° 00'–14° 59' Scorpio
Equinoctial Hour: 8:40–8:59 p.m.

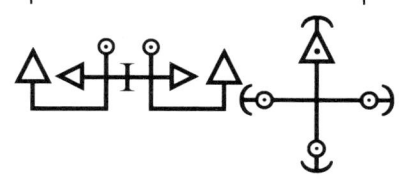

Shem HaMephorash Angel: SEALIAH

Hebrew: סאליה

Gematria: 106

Ruling Archangel: Raphael

Angelic Choir: Virtues

Invocation: "When I said, My foot slippeth; thy mercy, O Lord, held me up." [Psalm 94:18 (KJV)] *Si dicebam, motus est pes meus: misericordia tua Domine, adjuebat me.*

Passage from *Sefer Raziel HaMalakh*: Guide by the Malachim, Asethrial, Aderial, Sandalphon. Of the three palaces in ten sephiroth. Of עזאבה by the power of three letters. Of the chariots of the worlds, the highest power and the highest compassion. The three complete. Bind three times. עתפא. Of the unity of Aleph and the image of seven powers.

Ambelain: He serves to confound the evil and the haughty; he lifts up all those who are humiliated and fallen. This angel rules over vegetation; he bears life and health in all that breathe and influences the principal agents of Nature. The person born under this influence will love to learn; he will have many resources and facilities.

Lenain: To confound the wicked and the proud, to exalt the humiliated and the fallen. Governs vegetation. Loves learning, much aptitude.

Attributes: Confounds evil, vegetation, education, health, learning, resources.

Goetic Demon: VINE or VINEA

Hebrew: וינא

Gematria: 67

Demonic Classification: King and earl

Planets: Sol and Mars

Metals: Gold, copper, and silver

Suffumigations: Frankincense and dragon's blood

Description from *Ars Goetia*: The Forty-fifth Spirit is Vine, or Vinea. He is a Great King, and an Earl; and appeareth in the Form of a Lion, riding upon a Black Horse, and bearing a Viper in his hand. His Office is to discover Things Hidden, Witches, Wizards, and Things Present, Past, and to Come. He, at the command of the Exorcist will build Towers, overthrow Great Stone Walls, and make the Waters rough with Storms.

Attributes: Hidden things, towers, walls, hurricanes, divination, occultism.

⊰ THE FORTY-SIXTH QUINARY ⊱

Degrees and Sign: 15° 00'–19° 59' Scorpio
Equinoctial Hour: 9:00–9:19 p.m.

Shem HaMephorash Angel: ARIEL

Hebrew: עריאל

Gematria: 311

Ruling Archangel: Raphael

Angelic Choir: Virtues

Invocation: "The Lord is good to all: and his tender mercies are over all his works." [Psalm 145:9 (KJV)] *Suavis Dominus universes: et miserationes ejus super omnia opera ejus.*

Passage from *Sefer Raziel HaMalakh*: Guide by the crown of seventy degrees. The powers cast down all the branches. The powers are all cast down until the ten are holy in the name of the glory. Of עזאבה, the Yod is holy. Complete to multiply. The tenth multiply by all and combine. Bind to guide. The image of five powers guides by the word.

Ambelain: He serves to thank God for the gifts He has sent us. This angel discovers hidden treasures; he reveals the greatest secrets of Nature and he shows the objects of one's desires in dreams. The person born under this influence is blessed with a strong and subtle spirit; he will have original ideas and sublime thoughts; he will be able to resolve the most difficult problems; he will be discreet and will act with much circumspection.

Lenain: To procure revelations. To thank God for the good he sends us. Discovers hidden treasure, reveals the greatest secrets of nature; causes the object of one's desire to be seen in dreams.

Strong subtle mind, new and sublime thoughts, discreet, circumspect.

Attributes: Hidden treasures, dreams, imagination, resourceful, circumspect.

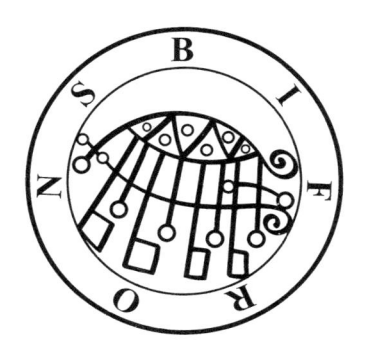

Goetic Demon: BIFRONS, BIFROUS, or BIFROVS

Hebrew: ביפרונש

Gematria: 648

Demonic Classification: Earl

Planet: Mars

Metals: Copper and silver

Suffumigation: Dragon's blood

Description from *Ars Goetia*: The Forty-sixth Spirit is called Bifrons, or Bifrous, or Bifrovs. He is an Earl, and appeareth in the Form of a Monster; but after a while, at the Command of the Exorcist, he putteth on the shape of a Man. His Office is to make one knowing in Astrology, Geometry, and other Arts and Sciences. He teacheth the Virtues of Precious Stones and Woods. He changeth Dead Bodies, and putteth them in another place; also he lighteth seeming Candles upon the Graves of the Dead.

Attributes: Astrology, geometry, arts and sciences, stones, wood, matters of the dead.

⊰ THE FORTY-SEVENTH QUINARY ⊱

Degrees and Sign: 20° 00'–24° 59' Scorpio
Equinoctial Hour: 9:20–9:39 p.m.

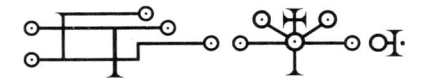

Shem HaMephorash Angel: ASALIAH

Hebrew: עשליה

Gematria: 415

Ruling Archangel: Raphael

Angelic Choir: Virtues

Invocation: "O Lord, how great are thy works! and thy thoughts are very deep." [Psalm 92:5 (KJV)] *Quam magnificata sunt opera tua Domine! Omnia in spientia fecisti: impleta est terra possessione tua.*

Passage from *Sefer Raziel HaMalakh*: Guide by the crown. Establish the oath. The hosts of the Moon in thirteen borders slanted. Of עזאבה, seal the arch. Establish the earth. Bind the image of nine powers; guide by the word in secret.

Ambelain: He serves to praise God and to rise towards Him when he sends us light. This angel rules over justice, men of probity, and over those who raise their spirit to the contemplation of divine things. The person born under this influence will have an agreeable character; he will be passionate to acquire secret light.

Lenain: For the praising of God and the growing towards him when he enlightens us. Governs justice, makes the truth known in legal proceedings. Agreeable character, avid for the acquisition of secret knowledge.

Attributes: Spirituality, justice, contemplation, agreeable, occult learning.

Goetic Demon: UVALL, VUAL, or VOVAL

Hebrew: וואל

Gematria: 43

Demonic Classification: Duke

Planet: Venus

Metal: Copper

Suffumigation: Sandalwood

Description from *Ars Goetia*: The Forty-seventh Spirit is Uvall, or Vual, or Voval. He is a Duke, Great, Mighty, and Strong; and appeareth in the Form of a Mighty Dromedary at the first, but after a while at the Command of the Exorcist he putteth on Human Shape, and speaketh the Egyptian Tongue, but not perfectly. His Office is to procure the Love of Woman, and to tell Things Past, Present, and to Come. He also procureth Friendship between Friends and Foes. He was of the Order of Potestates or Powers.

Attributes: Love, divination, friendship.

⊰ THE FORTY-EIGHTH QUINARY ⊱

Degrees and Sign: 25° 00'–29° 59' Scorpio
Equinoctial Hour: 9:40–9:59 p.m.

Shem HaMephorash Angel: MIHAEL

Hebrew: מיהאל

Gematria: 86

Ruling Archangel: Raphael

Angelic Choir: Virtues

Invocation: "The Lord hath made known his salvation: his righteousness hath he openly shewed in the sight of the heathen." [Psalm 98:2 (KJV)] *Notum fecit Dominus salutare suum: in conspectus gentium revelatit justitiam suam.*

Passage from *Sefer Raziel HaMalakh*: Guide by two actions of one unity. Of עזאבה, do not reveal the hidden name of Moses. Bind Tau of the Yod with the crown. The image of the five powers guides. Receive in secret.

Ambelain: He serves to preserve peace and union between married couples. This angel protects those who have turned to him. They will have presentiments and secret inspiration about all that will happen to them. He rules over the generation of beings and he influences friendship and conjugal fidelity. The person born under this influence will be passionate for love; he will love walking and all pleasure in general.

Lenain: For the preservation of peace and the union of man and wife. Protects those who address themselves to him, gives premonitions and secret inspirations. Governs generation of beings. Avid for love, fond of walks and pleasures in general.

Attributes: Marital harmony, generation, love, protection, fidelity, passionate, pleasure.

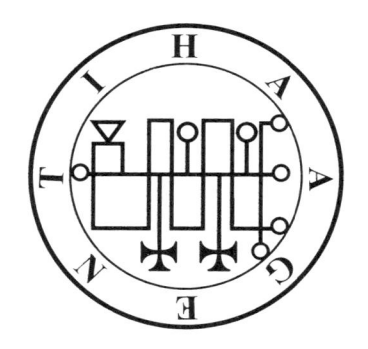

Goetic Demon: HAAGENTI

Hebrew: האגנטי

Gematria: 78

Demonic Classification: President

Planet: Mercury

Metal: Quicksilver

Suffumigation: Storax

Description from *Ars Goetia*: The Forty-eighth Spirit is Haagenti. He is a President, appearing in the Form of a Mighty Bull with Gryphon's Wings. This is at first, but after, at the Command of the Exorcist he putteth on Human Shape. His Office is to make Men wise, and to instruct them in divers things; also to Transmute all Metals into Gold; and to change Wine into Water, and Water into Wine.

Attributes: Knowledge, alchemy, transmutation, transubstantiation.

⊰ THE FORTY-NINTH QUINARY ⊱

Degrees and Sign: 0° 00'–4° 59' Sagittarius
Equinoctial Hour: 10:00–10:19 p.m.

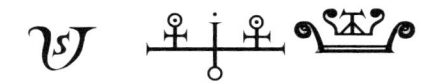

Shem HaMephorash Angel: VEHUEL

Hebrew: והואל

Gematria: 48

Ruling Archangel: Haniel

Angelic Choir: Principalities

Invocation: "Great is the Lord, and greatly to be praised; and his greatness is unsearchable." [Psalm 145:3 (KJV)] *Magnus Dominus et laudabilis nimis et magnitudinia ejus non est finis.*

Passage from *Sefer Raziel HaMalakh*: Guide by three. Divide three. The end is fixed. Begin the unity of one. Of עזאבה, the secret of Heh follows the name. By the division of three following, bind all. Understanding of unity is from the Yod of the crown. The image of four powers guides the word. From that, understand.

Ambelain: He serves to make one enflamed towards God, to bless Him and to glorify Him, when one is touched with admiration. This angel rules over great people and those who raise themselves and distinguish themselves through their talents and virtues. The person born under this influence will have a sensitive and generous nature; he will be held in esteem and will distinguish himself in literature, jurisprudence and diplomacy.

Lenain: Sorrow, contrariness. For the exaltation of oneself for the benediction and glory of God. Sensitive and generous soul. Literature, jurisprudence, diplomacy.

Attributes: Religious, humble, sorrow, contrary, literature, generous, sensitive.

Goetic Demon: CROCELL or CROKEL

Hebrew: כרוכל

Gematria: 276

Demonic Classification: Duke

Planet: Venus

Metal: Copper

Suffumigation: Sandalwood

Description from *Ars Goetia*: The Forty-ninth Spirit is Crocell, or Crokel. He appeareth in the Form of an Angel. He is a Duke Great and Strong, speaking something Mystically of Hidden Things. He teacheth the Art of Geometry and the Liberal Sciences. He, at the Command of the Exorcist, will produce Great Noises like the Rushings of many Waters, although there be none. He warmeth Waters, and discovereth Baths. He was of the Order of Potestates, or Powers, before his fall, as he declared unto the King Solomon.

Attributes: Mysticism, occultism, geometry, baths.

⊰ THE FIFTIETH QUINARY ⊱

Degrees and Sign: 5° 00'–9° 59' Sagittarius
Equinoctial Hour: 10:20–10:39 p.m.

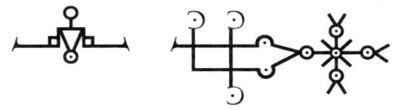

Shem HaMephorash Angel: DANIEL

Hebrew: דניאל

Gematria: 95

Ruling Archangel: Haniel

Angelic Choir: Principalities

Invocation: "The Lord is gracious, and full of compassion; slow to anger, and of great mercy." [Psalm 145:8 (KJV)] *Miserator et misericors Dominus: longanimis et misericors.*

Passage from *Sefer Raziel HaMalakh*: Guide by the root of three names of the crown. Three letters triple. Of עזאבה, the root of the name is Yod Heh Vau. By three holy things, the letters rise up. Bind to guide thus. The image of five powers guide all the unity of Aleph.

Ambelain: He serves to obtain God's mercy, and to receive consolation. This angel rules over justice, counsels, attorneys and magistrates in general. He gives inspiration to those who are encumbered by many things, and do not know how to take decisions. The person born under this influence will be industrious and active in business; he will love literature and will distinguish himself through his eloquence.

Lenain: To obtain the mercy of God and consolation. Governs justice, lawyers, solicitors. Furnishes conclusions to those who hesitate. Industrious and active in business, loves literature and is distinguished for eloquence.

Attributes: Consolation, decisions, justice, merciful, industrious, literature, eloquent.

Goetic Demon: FURCAS

Hebrew: פהורכש

Gematria: 611

Demonic Classification: Knight

Planet: Saturn

Metal: Lead

Suffumigation: Myrrh

Description from *Ars Goetia*: The Fiftieth Spirit is Furcas. He is a Knight, and appeareth in the Form of a Cruel Old Man with a long Beard and a hoary Head, riding upon a pale-coloured Horse, with a Sharp Weapon in his hand. His Office is to teach the Arts of Philosophy, Astrology, Rhetoric, Logic, Cheiromancy, and Pyromancy, in all their parts, and perfectly.

Attributes: Philosophy, astrology, chiromancy, pyromancy, rhetoric.

⊰ THE FIFTY-FIRST QUINARY ⊱

Degrees and Sign: 10° 00'–14° 59' Sagittarius
Equinoctial Hour: 10:40–10:59 p.m.

Shem HaMephorash Angel: HAHASIAH

Hebrew: ההשיה

Gematria: 325

Ruling Archangel: Haniel

Angelic Choir: Principalities

Invocation: "The glory of the Lord shall endure forever: the Lord shall rejoice in his works." [Psalm 104:31 (KJV)] *Sit gloria Domini in saeculum: laetabitur Dominus in operibus suis.*

Passage from *Sefer Raziel HaMalakh*: Guide by the foundation of understanding. By the name, all is complete by Yod. Of עזאבה, the three complete all, in victory rising up. Bind to guide by the word. The image of eight powers guides by all understanding.

Ambelain: He serves to raise the soul to the contemplation of divine things and to uncover the mysteries of wisdom. This angel rules over chemistry and physics; he reveals the greatest of Nature's secrets, notably the Philosopher's Stone and the Universal Physic. The person born under this influence will love abstract sciences; he will be particularly attracted to the knowledge of the properties and virtues attributed to animals, vegetables and minerals; he will be distinguished in medicine through wonderful cures, and he will make many discoveries useful to society.

Lenain: For the elevation of the soul and the discovery of the mysteries of wisdom. Governs chemistry and physics. Reveals the secret of the Philosopher's Stone and universal medicine. Loves abstract science. Devoted to the discovery of the properties of animals, plants and minerals. Distinguished in medicine.

Attributes: Occultism, physics, natural philosophy, medicine, alchemy.

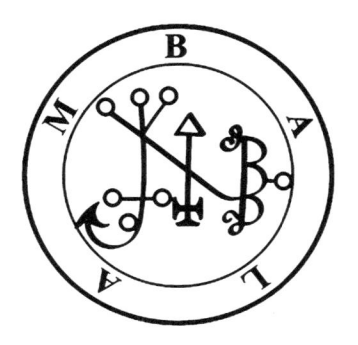

Goetic Demon: BALAM or BALAAM

Hebrew: באלאם

Gematria: 634

Demonic Classification: King

Planet: Sol

Metal: Gold

Suffumigation: Frankincense

Description from *Ars Goetia*: The Fifty-first Spirit is Balam or Balaam. He is a Terrible, Great, and Powerful King. He appeareth with three Heads: the first is like that of a Bull; the second is like that of a Man; the third is like that of a Ram. He hath the Tail of a Serpent, and Flaming Eyes. He rideth upon a furious Bear, and carrieth a Boshawk upon his Fist. He speaketh with a hoarse Voice, giving True Answers of Things Past, Present, and to Come. He maketh men to go Invisible, and also to be Witty.

Attributes: Divination, invisibility, wit, hoarse voice.

⸲ THE FIFTY-SECOND QUINARY ⸲

Degrees and Sign: 15° 00'–19° 59' Sagittarius
Equinoctial Hour: 11:00–11:19 p.m.

Shem HaMephorash Angel: IMAMIAH

Hebrew: עממיה

Gematria: 165

Ruling Archangel: Haniel

Angelic Choir: Principalities

Invocation: "I will praise the Lord according to his righteous-ness: and will sing praise to the name of the Lord most high." [Psalm 7:17 (KJV)] *Confitebor Domino secundum justitiam ejus: et psallam nomini Domini altissimi.*

Passage from *Sefer Raziel HaMalakh*: Guide by the branch of the tree, from the Yod and from the five powers of all. Of עזאבה, the branches of the tree, the power of wheels and planets are from the power of the keys. Bind to rise up. Bind one in the foundation. The image of seven powers guides by the word.

Ambelain: He is good for destroying the power of enemies and to humiliate them. This angel rules over all travel in general; he protects prisoners who call upon him; and inspires in them the means to obtain their liberty; he influences all those who seek the truth of good faith, and turn away from their mistakes by making a truly sincere return to God. The person born under this influence will have a strong and vigorous temperament; he will bear adversity with much patience and courage; he will love work and will complete everything he wishes with ease.

Lenain: Destroys the power of enemies and humbles them. Governs voyages in general, protects prisoners who turn to him and gives them the means of obtaining their freedom. Forceful, vigorous temperament, bears adversity with patience and courage. Fond of work.

Attributes: Destroys enemies, vigor, research, voyages, protection, liberty, stoic.

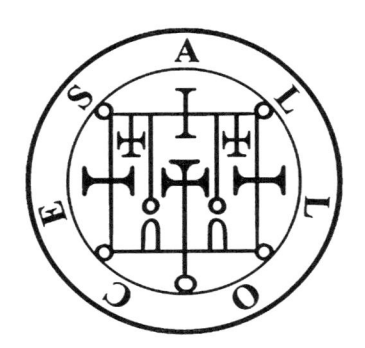

Goetic Demon: ALLOCES, ALLOCER, or ALOCAS

Hebrew: אלוכאס

Gematria: 118

Demonic Classification: Duke

Planet: Venus

Metal: Copper

Suffumigation: Sandalwood

Description from *Ars Goetia*: The Fifty-second Spirit is Alloces, or Alocas. He is a Duke, Great, Mighty, and Strong, appearing in the Form of a Soldier riding upon a Great Horse. His Face is like that of a Lion, very Red, and having Flaming Eyes. His Speech is hoarse and very big. His Office is to teach the Art of Astronomy, and all the Liberal Sciences. He bringeth unto thee Good Familiars.

Attributes: Arts and sciences, astronomy, loud, hoarse voice.

⊰ THE FIFTY-THIRD QUINARY ⊱

Degrees and Sign: 20° 00'–24° 59' Sagittarius
Equinoctial Hour: 11:20–11:39 p.m.

Shem HaMephorash Angel: NANAEL

Hebrew: ננאאל

Gematria: 132

Ruling Archangel: Haniel

Angelic Choir: Principalities

Invocation: "I know, O Lord, that thy judgments are right, and that thou in faithfulness hast afflicted me." [Psalm 119:75 (KJV)] *Cognovi Domine quia aequitas judicia tua: et in veritate tua humiliasti me.*

Passage from *Sefer Raziel HaMalakh*: Guide by the foundation. The secret of four powers is the power of the living blessings. The powers of marvelous deeds go forth from the motion after the wisdom. All is made known by wisdom in 100 days of the highest glory and unity of one, therefore concealed and unknown as עזאבה. Of the highest powers, praised is the name. Of every day, by 100 kinds of powers, establish 100 blessings of Israel. Bind and the image of the five powers guides by the word.

Ambelain: This angel rules over the high sciences; he influences religious men, teachers, magistrates and men of law. The person born under this influence will possess a melancholic demeanor; he will pursue a private life, rest and meditation, and he will distinguish himself through his knowledge of the abstract sciences.

Lenain: Governs the high sciences. Melancholy humor, avoids rest, meditation, well-versed in the abstract sciences.

Attributes: Enlightenment, higher sciences, law, melancholy humor, private, retired.

Goetic Demon: CAMIO or CAIM

Hebrew: כאמיו

Gematria: 77

Demonic Classification: President

Planet: Mercury

Metal: Quicksilver

Suffumigation: Storax

Description from *Ars Goetia*: The Fifty-third Spirit is Camio, or Caim. He is a Great President, and appeareth in the Form of the Bird called a Thrush at first, but afterwards he putteth on the Shape of a Man carrying in his Hand a Sharp Sword. He seemeth to answer in Burning Ashes, or in Coals of Fire. He is a Good Disputer. His Office is to give unto Men the Understanding of all Birds, Lowing of Bullocks, Barking of Dogs, and other Creatures; and also of the Voice of the Waters. He giveth True Answers of Things to Come. He was of the Order of Angels, but now ruleth over 30 Legions of Spirits Infernal.

Attributes: Animals, clairvoyance, disputation, dogs, birds.

⁂ THE FIFTY-FOURTH QUINARY ⁂

Degrees and Sign: 25° 00'–29° 59' Sagittarius
Equinoctial Hour: 11:40–11:59 p.m.

Shem HaMephorash Angel: NITHAEL

Hebrew: ניתאל

Gematria: 491

Ruling Archangel: Haniel

Angelic Choir: Principalities

Invocation: "The Lord hath prepared his throne in the heavens; and his kingdom ruleth over all." [Psalm 103:19 (KJV)] *Dominus in coelo paravit sedem suam: et regnum ipsius omnibus dominabitur.*

Passage from *Sefer Raziel HaMalakh*: Guide by the secret of התיע. The dominion is destroyed. Of the blessing over Israel of עזאבה, of Tzaddiq, by the power of Yod, reveal the eternal name. All is sealed as one. Bind to guide thus. The image of four powers guides. The unity is complete.

Ambelain: He serves to obtain the mercy of God, and to obtain long life. This angel rules over emperors, kings, princes and all civilian and ecclesiastical dignitaries. He watches over all legitimate dynasties and over the stability of empires; he gives a long and peaceful reign to princes who have recourse to him, and protects all those who wish to remain in their employ. The person born under this influence will become famous through his writings and his eloquence; he will have a strong reputation among the wise, and will distinguish himself through his virtues and will merit the confidence of his prince.

Lenain: To obtain the mercy of God and live long. Emperor, king, and prince. Renowned for writings and eloquence, of great reputation among the learned.

Attributes: Mercy, longevity, stability, writer, eloquent, learned.

Goetic Demon: MURMUS, MURMUX, or MURMUR

Hebrew: מורמוס

Gematria: 352

Demonic Classification: Duke and earl

Planets: Venus and Mars

Metals: Copper and silver

Suffumigations: Sandalwood and dragon's blood

Description from *Ars Goetia*: The Fifty-fourth Spirit is called Murmur, or Murmus, or Murmux. He is a Great Duke, and an Earl; and appeareth in the Form of a Warrior riding upon a Gryphon, with a Ducal Crown upon his Head. There do go before him those his Ministers, with great Trumpets sounding. His Office is to teach Philosophy perfectly, and to constrain Souls Deceased to come before the Exorcist to answer those questions which he may wish to put to them, if desired. He was partly of the Order of Thrones, and partly of that of Angels.

Attributes: Philosophy, necromancy.

⊰ The Fifty-fifth Quinary ⊱

Degrees and Sign: 0° 00'–4° 59' Capricorn
Equinoctial Hour: 12:00–12:19 a.m.

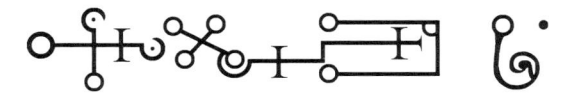

Shem HaMephorash Angel: MABAIAH or MEBAHAIAH

Hebrew: מבהיה

Gematria: 62

Ruling Archangel: Haniel

Angelic Choir: Principalities

Invocation: "But thou, O Lord, shall endure forever; and thy remembrance unto all generations." [Psalm 102:12 (KJV)] *Tu autem Domine in aeternum permanes: et memoriale tuum in generationem.*

Passage from *Sefer Raziel HaMalakh*: Guide by the power of the crown with the hosts of the Lord. All from the images of man. עזאבה commands to descend in the midst of man. The universe is diminished. Bind to guide by all unity of one. The image of six powers guides the Yod and completes the Heh.

Ambelain: He is good for obtaining consolation and for those who wish to have children. This angel rules over morality and religion; he influences those who protect them with all their power and spread them by all possible means. The person born under this influence will be distinguished by his good works, his piety and his zeal for completing his duties before God and man.

Lenain: Beneficial for obtaining consolation and compensations. Governs morality and religion. Distinguished by good deeds and piety.

Attributes: Consolation, fertility, religion, piety, morality.

Goetic Demon: OROBAS

Hebrew: ורובש

Gematria: 514

Demonic Classification: Prince

Planet: Jupiter

Metal: Tin

Suffumigation: Cedar

Description from *Ars Goetia*: The Fifty-fifth Spirit is Orobas. He is a great and Mighty Prince, appearing at first like a Horse; but after the command of the Exorcist he putteth on the Image of a Man. His Office is to discover all things Past, Present, and to Come; also to give Dignities, and Prelacies, and the Favour of Friends and of Foes. He giveth True Answers of Divinity, and of the Creation of the World. He is very faithful unto the Exorcist, and will not suffer him to be tempted of any Spirit.

Attributes: Divination, honors, amiable, faithful.

⊰ THE FIFTY-SIXTH QUINARY ⊱

Degrees and Sign: 5° 00'–9° 59' Capricorn
Equinoctial Hour: 12:20–12:39 a.m.

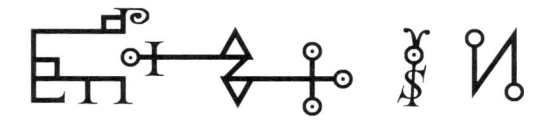

Shem HaMephorash Angel: POIEL

Hebrew: פויאל

Gematria: 127

Ruling Archangel: Haniel

Angelic Choir: Principalities

Invocation: "The Lord upholdeth all that fall, and raiseth up all those that be bowed down." [Psalm 145:14 (KJV)] *Allevat Dominus omnes qui corrunt: et origit omnes elisos.*

Passage from *Sefer Raziel HaMalakh*: Guide by the strength and glory of the action in Egypt. Of עזאבה, consider the ten plagues as ten commandments. Bind in the midst of the temple. Bind two actions. The image of four powers guides the word. Extend the powers to understand the actions.

Ambelain: He serves to obtain what one wants. This angel rules fame, fortune and philosophy. The person born under this influence will be held in esteem by all for his modesty, moderation and agreeable humor; he will only make his fortune by talents and his conduct.

Lenain: For the fulfillment of one's request. Governs renown, fortune and philosophy. Well esteemed by everyone for his modesty and agreeable humor.

Attributes: Wishes, fame, fortune, modest, agreeable, funny, talented.

Goetic Demon: GREMORY or GAMORI

Hebrew: גמורי

Gematria: 259

Demonic Classification: Duke

Planet: Venus

Metal: Copper

Suffumigation: Sandalwood

Description from *Ars Goetia*: The Fifty-sixth Spirit is Gremory, or Gamori. He is a Duke Strong and Powerful, and appeareth in the Form of a Beautiful Woman, with a Duchess's Crown tied about her waist, and riding on a Great Camel. His Office is to tell of all Things Past, Present, and to Come; and of Treasures Hid, and what they lie in; and to procure the Love of Women both Young and Old.

Attributes: Divination, treasures, love.

⊰ THE FIFTY-SEVENTH QUINARY ⊱

Degrees and Sign: 10° 00'–14° 59' Capricorn
Equinoctial Hour: 12:40–12:59 a.m.

Shem HaMephorash Angel: NEMAMIAH

Hebrew: נממיה

Gematria: 145

Ruling Archangel: Michael

Angelic Choir: Archangels

Invocation: "Ye that fear the Lord, trust in the Lord: he is their help and their shield." [Psalm 115:11 (KJV)] *Qui timet Dominum speraverunt in Domino: adjutor eorum et protector eorum est.*

Passage from *Sefer Raziel HaMalakh*: Guide by the light of the Moon and by the warmth of the Sun. Two reach by Nun. Thus the Shekinah exists. Appoint the rows and release Israel. By the ram's horn, reach the unity above. Speak of the holy, the Nun of the holy crown. Bind to guide by two luminaries. Bind by the ram's horn. The image of eight powers guides. In the end, release the ram's horn.

Ambelain: He serves to bring prosperity in all things and to deliver prisoners. This angel rules over great captains, admirals, generals and all those who fight in a just cause. The person born under this influence loves the military state; and he will distinguish himself through his actions, bravery, and greatness of spirit, and he will endure hardship with great courage.

Lenain: For general prosperity and the deliverance of prisoners. Governs great captains. Drawn to the military; distinguished for activity and the courageous bearing of fatigue.

Attributes: Prosperity, warfare, delivers prisoners, active, brave, stoic.

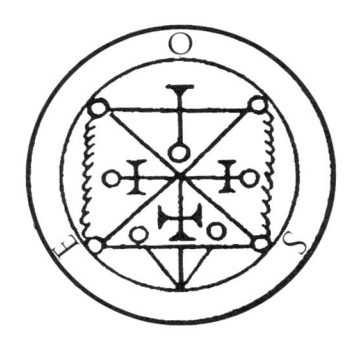

Goetic Demon: OSO, OSÉ, or VOSO

Hebrew: ושז

Gematria: 313

Demonic Classification: President

Planet: Mercury

Metal: Quicksilver

Suffumigation: Storax

Description from *Ars Goetia*: The Fifty-seventh Spirit is Oso, Ose, or Voso. He is a Great President, and appeareth like a Leopard at the first, but after a little time he putteth on the Shape of a Man. His Office is to make one cunning in the Liberal Sciences, and to give True Answers of Divine and Secret Things; also to change a Man into any Shape that the Exorcist pleaseth, so that he that is so changed will not think any other thing than that he is in verity that Creature or Thing he is changed into.

Attributes: Arts and sciences, occultism, shape-shifting.

⊰ THE FIFTY-EIGHTH QUINARY ⊱

Degrees and Sign: 15° 00'–19° 59' Capricorn
Equinoctial Hour: 1:00–1:19 a.m.

Shem HaMephorash Angel: IEIALEL

Hebrew: יילאל

Gematria: 85

Ruling Archangel: Michael

Angelic Choir: Archangels

Invocation: "My soul is also sore vexed: but thou, O Lord, how long?" [Psalm 6:3 (KJV)] *Et anima turbata est valde: sed tu Domine usque quo?*

Passage from *Sefer Raziel HaMalakh*: Guide by raising up the Yod over all created. Of עזאבה, rise up the sign of power over all. Bind to guide over the understanding. Conceal the unity of one. The image of four powers guides by the word.

Ambelain: He serves against chagrins and cures illnesses, principally problems with the eyes. This angel rules over fire; he influences armourers, metal-workers, cutlers and those involved in commerce; he confounds the evil and those who bear false witness. The person born under this influence will be distinguished by his bravery and boldness, and he will be passionate for Venus.

Lenain: Protects against sorrow and care and heals the sick, especially afflictions of the eyes. Influences iron and those in commerce. Brave, frank, affinity for Venus.

Attributes: Against troubles, eyesight, iron, locksmiths, bravery, bold, commerce.

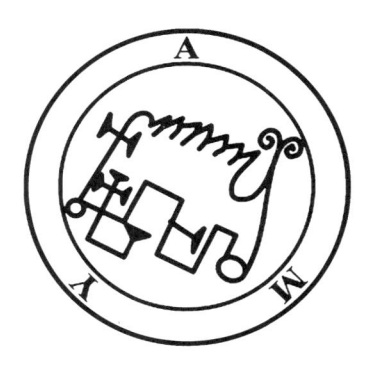

Goetic Demon: AVNAS, AUNS, or AMY

Hebrew: אונש

Gematria: 357

Demonic Classification: President

Planet: Mercury

Metal: Quicksilver

Suffumigation: Storax

Description from *Ars Goetia*: The Fifty-eighth Spirit is Amy, or Avnas. He is a Great President, and appeareth at first in the Form of a Flaming Fire; but after a while he putteth on the Shape of a Man. His office is to make one Wonderful Knowing in Astrology and all the Liberal Sciences. He giveth Good Familiars, and can bewray Treasure that is kept by Spirits.

Attributes: Astrology, arts and sciences, treasures.

⊰ THE FIFTY-NINTH QUINARY ⊱

Degrees and Sign: 20° 00'–24° 59' Capricorn
Equinoctial Hour: 1:20–1:39 a.m.

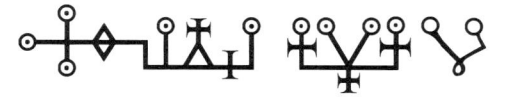

Shem HaMephorash Angel: HARAEL or HARAHEL

Hebrew: הרהאל

Gematria: 241

Ruling Archangel: Michael

Angelic Choir: Archangels

Invocation: "From the rising of the sun unto the going down of the same the Lord's name is to be praised." [Psalm 113:3 (KJV)] *A solis ortu usque ad occasum, laudabile nomen Domini.*

Passage from *Sefer Raziel HaMalakh*: Guide by unity. Thus אבה bind to guide the living Earth. Complete the understanding. The image of five powers is complete by all.

Ambelain: He serves against the sterility of women and to make children subservient and respectful towards their parents. This angel rules over treasures, agents of change, public funds, archives, libraries and all rare and precious closets; he influences printing, the book trade and all those involved in this business. The person born under this influence will love to be instructed in all sciences in general; he will be busy in business, will follow the activities of the Stock Exchange, will speculate successfully and be distinguished by his probity, talents and fortune.

Lenain: Against the sterility of women and to make children obedient to their parents. Governs treasure and banks. Printing, books. Love of learning, successful in business, money.

Attributes: Fertility, helps with problem children, treasures, business acumen, talented.

Goetic Demon: ORIAS or ORIAX

Hebrew: וריאס

Gematria: 277

Demonic Classification: Marquis

Planet: Luna

Metal: Silver

Suffumigation: Jasmine

Description from *Ars Goetia*: The Fifty-ninth Spirit is Oriax, or Orias. He is a Great Marquis, and appeareth in the Form of a Lion, riding upon a Horse Mighty and Strong, with a Serpent's Tail; and he holdeth in his Right Hand two Great Serpents hissing. His Office is to teach the Virtues of the Stars, and to know the Mansions of the Planets, and how to understand their Virtues. He also transformeth Men, and he giveth Dignities, Prelacies, and Confirmation thereof; also Favour with Friends and with Foes.

Attributes: Stars, planets, talismans, transformation, amiable.

⊰ THE SIXTIETH QUINARY ⊱

Degrees and Sign: 25° 00'–29° 59' Capricorn
Equinoctial Hour: 1:40–1:59 a.m.

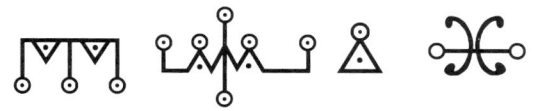

Shem HaMephorash Angel: MITZRAEL or MIZRAEL

Hebrew: מצראל

Gematria: 361

Ruling Archangel: Michael

Angelic Choir: Archangels

Invocation: "The Lord is righteous in all his ways, and holy in all his works." [Psalm 145:17 (KJV)] *Justus Dominus in omnibus viis suis: et sanctus in omnibus operibus suis.*

Passage from *Sefer Raziel HaMalakh*: Guide as these two names. Change the actions before the place. The name goes forth. Of the image in the secret time of עזאבה, of every one, do not change any and diminish. Guide thus by the beauty of the crown by Binah. The image of five powers is of the abundance. Complete by Yod.

Ambelain: He serves to heal spiritual ills and to be delivered from those who persecute one; he rules over illustrious people who are distinguished by their talents and virtues; he influences the fidelity and obeisance of subordinates towards their superiors. The person born under this influence will unite all the fine qualities of body and soul; he will distinguish himself through his virtues, spirit, agreeable humor and will have a long life.

Lenain: For the cure of mental illness and deliverance from those who persecute us. Virtuous, longevity.

Attributes: Spiritual and mental health, against persecution, virtue, talents, humor, longevity.

Goetic Demon: NAPHULA or VAPULA

Hebrew: נפולא

Gematria: 167

Demonic Classification: Duke

Planet: Venus

Metal: Copper

Suffumigation: Sandalwood

Description from *Ars Goetia*: The Sixtieth Spirit is Vapula, or Naphula. He is a Duke Great, Mighty, and Strong; appearing in the Form of a Lion with Gryphon's Wings. His Office is to make Men Knowing in all Handcrafts and Professions, also in Philosophy, and other Sciences.

Attributes: Crafts, professions, philosophy.

⊰ THE SIXTY-FIRST QUINARY ⊱

Degrees and Sign: 0° 00'–4° 59' Aquarius
Equinoctial Hour: 2:00–2:19 a.m.

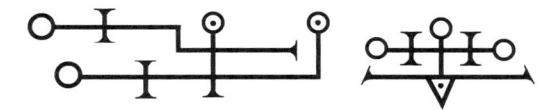

Shem HaMephorash Angel: UMABEL or VMABEL

Hebrew: ומבאל

Gematria: 79

Ruling Archangel: Michael

Angelic Choir: Archangels

Invocation: "Blessed be the name of the Lord from this time forth and for evermore." [Psalm 113:2 (KJV)] *Sit nomen Domini benedictum, ex hoc nunc et usque in saeculum.*

Passage from *Sefer Raziel HaMalakh*: Guide by four powers of the name, by 22 boundaries around the day of the illumination and the night. עזאבה leads from east to west. Of the unity of one, bind to guide thus. Of the image of five powers, all is secret. The Yod completes.

Ambelain: He serves to obtain a person's friendship. This angel rules over astronomy and physics; he influences all those who distinguish themselves in these fields. The person born under this influence will love travel and all honest pleasures; he will have a sensitive heart and love will cause him grief.

Lenain: To obtain the friendship of a given person. Fond of travel and honest pleasures; sensitive heart.

Attributes: Friendship, astronomy, physics, sensitive heart in love, travels, pleasures.

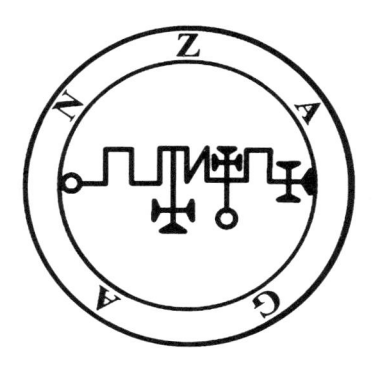

Goetic Demon: ZAGAN

Hebrew: זאגאן

Gematria: 712

Demonic Classification: King and president

Planet: Mercury

Metal: Quicksilver

Suffumigation: Storax

Description from *Ars Goetia*: The Sixty-first Spirit is Zagan. He is a Great King and President, appearing at first in the Form of a Bull with Gryphon's Wings; but after a while he putteth on Human Shape. He maketh Men Witty. He can turn Wine into Water, and Blood into Wine, also Water into Wine. He can turn all Metals into Coin of the Dominion that Metal is of. He can even make Fools wise.

Attributes: Witty, transubstantiation, transmutation, alchemy, makes fools wise.

⊰ THE SIXTY-SECOND QUINARY ⊱

Degrees and Sign: 5° 00'–9° 59' Aquarius
Equinoctial Hour: 2:20–2:39 a.m.

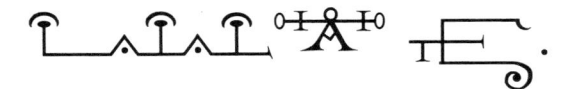

Shem HaMephorash Angel: IAHHEL or IAHHAEL

Hebrew: יההאל

Gematria: 51

Ruling Archangel: Michael

Angelic Choir: Archangels

Invocation: "Consider how I love thy precepts: quicken me, O Lord, according to thy lovingkindness." [Psalm 119:159 (KJV)] *Vide quoniam mandata tua dilexi Domine, in misericordia tua vivifica me.*

Passage from *Sefer Raziel HaMalakh*: Guide by the unity. The unity is with the crown. Of עזאבה, the secret is the Heh. Take the universe from what is received. Bind to guide thus. The image of five powers guides all by the Yod.

Ambelain: He serves to acquire wisdom. This angel rules philosophers, enlightened ones and all those who wish to retire from the world. The person born under this influence will love tranquility and solitude; he will precisely fulfill the duties of his state and will be distinguished by his modesty and virtues.

Lenain: For the acquisition of wisdom. Governs philosophers, illuminati. Loves tranquility and solitude, modest, virtuous.

Attributes: Wisdom, knowledge, philosophy, tranquility, solitude, modest, virtuous.

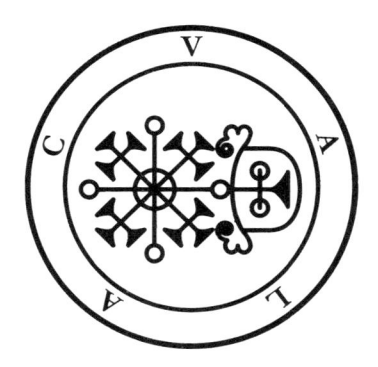

Goetic Demon: VALU, VALAK, VALAC, or VOLAC

Hebrew: ואלו

Gematria: 43

Demonic Classification: President

Planet: Mercury

Metal: Quicksilver

Suffumigation: Storax

Description from *Ars Goetia*: The Sixty-second Spirit is Volac, or Valak, or Valu. He is a President Mighty and Great, and appeareth like a Child with Angel's Wings, riding on a Two-headed Dragon. His Office is to give True Answers of Hidden Treasures, and to tell where Serpents may be seen. The which he will bring unto the Exorciser without any Force or Strength being by him employed.

Attributes: Treasures, serpents, childlike.

⊰ THE SIXTY-THIRD QUINARY ⊱

Degrees and Sign: 10° 00'–14° 59' Aquarius
Equinoctial Hour: 2:40–2:59 a.m.

Shem HaMephorash Angel: ANAVEL

Hebrew: עֲנוּאֵל

Gematria: 157

Ruling Archangel: Michael

Angelic Choir: Archangels

Invocation: "Serve the Lord with gladness: come before his presence with singing." [Psalm 100:2 (KJV)] *Servite Domino in timore: et exultate ei cum tremore.*

Passage from *Sefer Raziel HaMalakh*: Guide the sound of the highest assembly in Israel. From the rest, those also unite the lives. Reach and complete the highest and also the lowest. The outer branches extend. Of עזאבה, guide by scattering the languages. Bind to guide by the word and image of five powers. All is complete by the crown בעטרה. In the midst, understand the power of the actions.

Ambelain: He serves to convert nations to Christianity and to confound those who are its enemies. This angel protects against accidents, he preserves health and cures illnesses; he rules over commerce, bankers, businessmen and clerks. The person born under this influence will have a subtle and ingenious spirit; he will distinguish himself through his industry and his actions.

Lenain: For the conversion of nations to Christianity. Protects against accidents, heals the sick. Governs commerce, banking. Subtle and ingenious, industrious and active.

Attributes: Against accidents, health, trade and business, banks, ingenious, industrious.

Goetic Demon: ANDRAS

Hebrew: אנדראש

Gematria: 556

Demonic Classification: Marquis

Planet: Luna

Metal: Silver

Suffumigation: Jasmine

Description from *Ars Goetia*: The Sixty-third Spirit is Andras. He is a Great Marquis, appearing in the Form of an Angel with a Head like a Black Night Raven, riding upon a strong Black Wolf, and having a Sharp and Bright Sword flourished aloft in his hand. His Office is to sow Discords. If the Exorcist have not a care, he will slay both him and his fellows.

Attributes: Discord, murderous, chaos.

⊰ THE SIXTY-FOURTH QUINARY ⊱

Degrees and Sign: 15° 00'–19° 59' Aquarius
Equinoctial Hour: 3:00–3:19 a.m.

Shem HaMephorash Angel: MEHIEL

Hebrew: מהיאל

Gematria: 86

Ruling Archangel: Michael

Angelic Choir: Archangels

Invocation: "Behold, the eye of the Lord is upon them that fear him, upon them that hope in his mercy." [Psalm 33:18 (KJV)] *Ecce oculi Domini super metuentes eum: et in eis, qui sperant super misericordiam ejus.*

Passage from *Sefer Raziel HaMalakh*: Guide the two most holy assemblies of Israel. Reach to the highest in unity. Of unity, Aleph is the highest. In the lowlands, bind the tabernacle of עזאבה. In order to be darkened by one power, bind one. Bind to guide the secret of two actions. Of all understanding, the image of five powers guides. All is complete by the strength of desire.

Ambelain: This angel protects against rabies and ferocious animals; he rules over the wise, teachers, orators and authors; he influences printing and bookshops and all those who engage in this type of business. The person born under this influence will distinguish himself in literature.

Lenain: Against adversities. Protects against rabies and wild beasts. Governs savants, professors, orators and others. Distinguished in literature.

Attributes: Against rabies and dangerous animals, oration, teacher, author, literature.

Goetic Demon: HAURES, HAURAS, HAVRES, or FLAUROS

Hebrew: האוראש

Gematria: 513

Demonic Classification: Duke

Planet: Venus

Metal: Copper

Suffumigation: Sandalwood

Description from *Ars Goetia*: The Sixty-fourth Spirit is Haures, or Hauras, or Havres, or Flauros. He is a Great Duke, and appeareth at first like a Leopard, Mighty, Terrible, and Strong, but after a while, at the Command of the Exorcist, he putteth on Human Shape with Eyes Flaming and Fiery, and a most Terrible Countenance. He giveth True Answers of all things, Present, Past, and to Come. But if he be not commanded into a Triangle he will Lie in all these Things, and deceive and beguile the Exorcist in these things, or in such and such business. He will, lastly, talk of the Creation of the World, and of Divinity, and of how he and other Spirits fell. He destroyeth and burneth up those who be the Enemies of the Exorcist should he so desire it; also he will not suffer him to be tempted by any other Spirit or otherwise.

Attributes: Divination, deceit, destruction, divinity, cosmogony.

⊰ THE SIXTY-FIFTH QUINARY ⊱

Degrees and Sign: 20° 00'–24° 59' Aquarius
Equinoctial Hour: 3:20–3:39 a.m.

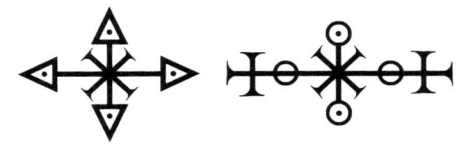

Shem HaMephorash Angel: DAMABIAH

Hebrew: דמביה

Gematria: 61

Ruling Archangel: Gabriel

Angelic Choir: Angels

Invocation: "Return, O Lord, how long? and let it repent thee concerning thy servants." [Psalm 90:13 (KJV)] *Convertere Domine, et usque qua? Et deprecabilis esto super savos tuos.*

Passage from *Sefer Raziel HaMalakh*: Guide seven lamps from the beauty. Of seven by the crown עזאבה. The name illuminates seven above and thus below seven. Of the righteous seven, bind thus to guide. The image of five powers guides. All is complete by Yod.

Ambelain: He serves against sorcery and to obtain wisdom and success in useful enterprises. This angel rules overseas, rivers, springs, maritime expeditions and naval construction; he influences sailors, pilots, fishing and all those for work in this line of commerce. The person born under this influence will distinguish himself in marine affairs through his expeditions and discoveries, and he will amass a considerable fortune.

Lenain: Against magic spells and for the obtainment of wisdom and the undertaking of successful ventures. Governs seas, rivers, springs, sailors. Sailor; amasses a considerable fortune.

Attributes: Against sorcery, wisdom, sailors, water, expeditions, wealth.

Goetic Demon: ANDREALPHUS

Hebrew: אנדראלפוש

Gematria: 672

Demonic Classification: Marquis

Planet: Luna

Metal: Silver

Suffumigation: Jasmine

Description from *Ars Goetia*: The Sixty-fifth Spirit is Andrealphus. He is a Mighty Marquis, appearing at first in the form of a Peacock, with great Noises. But after a time he putteth on Human shape. He can teach Geometry perfectly. He maketh Men very subtle therein; and in all Things pertaining unto Mensuration or Astronomy. He can transform a Man into the Likeness of a Bird.

Attributes: Geometry, astronomy, birds.

⊰ THE SIXTY-SIXTH QUINARY ⊱

Degrees and Sign: 25° 00'–29° 59' Aquarius
Equinoctial Hour: 3:40–3:59 a.m.

Shem HaMephorash Angel: MANAKEL

Hebrew: מנקאל

Gematria: 221

Ruling Archangel: Gabriel

Angelic Choir: Angels

Invocation: "Forsake me not, O Lord: O my God, be not far from me." [Psalm 38:21 (KJV)] *Ne derelinquas me Domine Deus maus; ne discesseris a me.*

Passage from *Sefer Raziel HaMalakh*: Guide by the name of four that measures two around. Of beauty, thus two classes of Malachim. Of power around the crown, proclaim the Tree of Life grows in Jerusalem. Reveal עזאבה. Of the abundance in the Garden of Eden, the highest power binds to guide. By understanding, complete this by that of one power. The image of five powers guides. All is complete by the crown.

Ambelain: He serves to appease God's anger and to cure epilepsy. He rules over vegetation and aquatic animals; he influences sleep and dreams. The person born under this influence will unite all the good qualities of body and soul; he will bring about friendship and goodwill among all good people through his pleasantness and the sweetness of his character.

Lenain: For the appeasement of the anger of God and for the healing of epilepsy. Governs vegetation, aquatic animals. Influences dreams. Gentleness of character.

Attributes: Against leprosy and anger, vegetation, dreams, sweet, pleasant.

Goetic Demon: KIMARIS, CIMERIES, CIMEJES, or CIMEIES

Hebrew: כימאריש

Gematria: 581

Demonic Classification: Marquis

Planet: Luna

Metal: Silver

Suffumigation: Jasmine

Description from *Ars Goetia*: The Sixty-sixth Spirit is Cimejes, or Cimeies, or Kimaris. He is a Marquis, Mighty, Great, Strong and Powerful, appearing like a Valiant Warrior riding upon a goodly Black Horse. He ruleth over all Spirits in the parts of Africa. His Office is to teach perfectly Grammar, Logic, Rhetoric, and to discover things Lost or Hidden, and Treasures.

Attributes: Grammar, logic, rhetoric, treasures, valiant.

⊰ THE SIXTY-SEVENTH QUINARY ⊱

Degrees and Sign: 0° 00'–4° 59' Pisces
Equinoctial Hour: 4:00–4:19 a.m.

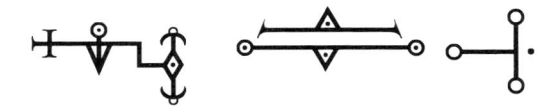

Shem HaMephorash Angel: EIAEL

Hebrew: איעאל

Gematria: 112

Ruling Archangel: Gabriel

Angelic Choir: Angels

Invocation: "Delight thyself also in the Lord: and he shall give thee the desires of thine heart." [Psalm 37:4 (KJV)] *Delectare in Domino et dabit tibi petitiones cordis tui.*

Passage from *Sefer Raziel HaMalakh*: Guide by two actions. Change Moses in the secret image alone. Do not see the Nephesh in highest Jerusalem and in lowest Jerusalem. Seek after from the highest to highest. See the highest, and receive. Do not receive for the sake of the highest and sublime secret of עזאבה. By the name, petition to come to Earth. Do not listen. Bind to guide by beauty. The crown over 70 judgements is the secret of the sublime mysteries. Do not come to Earth. The image of six powers guides by the word.

Ambelain: He serves to receive consolation in adversity and to acquire wisdom. This angel rules over change, the preservation of monuments and long life; he influences the occult sciences; he reveals truth to those who have recourse to him in their works. The person born under this influence will become illuminated by the spirit of God; he will love solitude and will be distinguished in the high sciences, principally astronomy, physics and philosophy.

Lenain: To obtain consolation in adversity and for the acquisition of wisdom. Influences occult science. Makes the truth known to those who call on him in their work. Enlightened requirements of the spirit of God. Fond of solitude, distinguished in higher sciences.

Attributes: Against adversity, wisdom, change, occultism, solitude, mysticism.

Goetic Demon: AMDUKIAS, AMDUSCIAS, or AMDUSIAS

Hebrew: אמדוכיאש

Gematria: 382

Demonic Classification: Duke

Planet: Venus

Metal: Copper

Suffumigation: Sandalwood

Description from *Ars Goetia*: The Sixty-seventh Spirit is Amdusias, or Amdukias. He is a Duke Great and Strong, appearing at first like a Unicorn, but at the request of the Exorcist he standeth before him in Human Shape, causing Trumpets, and all manner of Musical Instruments to be heard, but not soon or immediately. Also he can cause Trees to bend and incline according to the Exorcist's Will. He giveth Excellent Familiars.

Attributes: Music, trees.

⚜ THE SIXTY-EIGHTH QUINARY ⚜

Degrees and Sign: 5° 00'–9° 59' Pisces
Equinoctial Hour: 4:20–4:39 a.m.

Shem HaMephorash Angel: CHABUIAH, HABUIAH, or HAHNIAH

Hebrew: חבויה

Gematria: 31

Ruling Archangel: Gabriel

Angelic Choir: Angels

Invocation: "Praise ye the Lord. O give thanks unto the Lord; for he is good: for his mercy endureth forever." [Psalm 106:1 (KJV)] *Confitemini Domino, quoniam bonus: quoniam in saeculum misericordia ejus.*

Passage from *Sefer Raziel HaMalakh*: Guide in unity complete. Of עזאבה, also bind to one. The image of five powers guides by the word.

Ambelain: He serves to preserve health and to cure diseases. This angel rules agriculture and fertility. The person born under this influence will love the countryside, hunting, gardens and all things connected with agriculture.

Lenain: For the preservation of health and the healing of the sick. Governs agriculture and fecundity. Fond of the countryside, hunting, gardens and all that is related to agriculture.

Attributes: Cures disease, health, fertility, agriculture, rural.

Goetic Demon: BELIAL

Hebrew: בליאל

Gematria: 73

Demonic Classification: King

Planet: Sol

Metal: Gold

Suffumigation: Frankincense

Description from *Ars Goetia*: The Sixty-eighth Spirit is Belial. He is a Mighty and a Powerful King, and was created next after LUCIFER. He appeareth in the Form of Two Beautiful Angels sitting in a Chariot of Fire. He speaketh with a Comely Voice, and declareth that he fell first from among the worthier sort, that were before Michael, and other Heavenly Angels. His Office is to distribute Presentations and Senatorships, etc.; and to cause favour of Friends and of Foes. He giveth excellent Familiars, and governeth 50 Legions of Spirits. Note well that this King Belial must have Offerings, Sacrifices and Gifts presented unto him by the Exorcist, or else he will not give True Answers unto his Demands. But then he tarrieth not one hour in the Truth, unless he be constrained by Divine Power.

Attributes: Politics, favor, offerings, comely voice.

⊰ THE SIXTY-NINTH QUINARY ⊱

Degrees and Sign: 10° 00'–14° 59' Pisces
Equinoctial Hour: 4:40–4:59 a.m.

Shem HaMephorash Angel: ROEHEL

Hebrew: ראהאל

Gematria: 237

Ruling Archangel: Gabriel

Angelic Choir: Angels

Invocation: "The Lord is the portion of mine inheritance and of my cup: thou maintainest my lot." [Psalm 16:5 (KJV)] *Dominus pars haereditatis meae, et calicis mei: tu es, qui restitues haereditatem meam mihi.*

Passage from *Sefer Raziel HaMalakh*: Guide over eight names. The seven release to indicate correspondence to seven names. Of the name of 42, by the Heh complete all by the ram's horn. Of עזאבה, calculate the eight sephiroth. Bring forth in the period of the Sabbath. Thus bind this to that until the beginning place. Bind to guide thus. The image of six powers guides to complete the ends.

Ambelain: He serves to find lost or hidden objects, and to know the person who has removed them. This angel rules renown, fortune and succession; he influences jurisconsults, magistrates, attorneys, solicitors and notaries. The person born under this influence will be distinguished at the bar, by his knowledge of morality, custom and the spirit of the laws of all people.

Lenain: To find lost or stolen objects and discover the person responsible. Distinguished in the judiciary, morals and customs of all peoples.

Attributes: Finds stolen goods, law, fame, morality, customs.

Goetic Demon: DECARABIA

Hebrew: דכאארביא

Gematria: 238

Demonic Classification: Marquis

Planet: Luna

Metal: Silver

Suffumigation: Jasmine

Description from *Ars Goetia*: The Sixty-ninth Spirit is Decarabia. He appeareth in the Form of a Star in a Pentacle, at first; but after, at the command of the Exorcist, he putteth on the image of a Man. His Office is to discover the Virtues of Birds and Precious Stones, and to make the Similitude of all kinds of Birds to fly before the Exorcist, singing and drinking as natural Birds do.

Attributes: Birds, stones, illusions, singing, drinking.

⊰ THE SEVENTIETH QUINARY ⊱

Degrees and Sign: 15° 00'–19° 59' Pisces
Equinoctial Hour: 5:00–5:19 a.m.

Shem HaMephorash Angel: IABAMIAH or JABAMIAH

Hebrew: יבמיה

Gematria: 67

Ruling Archangel: Gabriel

Angelic Choir: Angels

Invocation: "In the beginning God created the heaven and the earth." [Genesis 1:1 (KJV)]

בראשית ברא אלהים את השמים ואת הארץ

Passage from *Sefer Raziel HaMalakh*: Guide by the crown. By the power of the beauty, reach to the power after. עזאבה indicates the measure following to complete all. Bind to guide by the word. The image of five powers guide by the word. All is complete by Yod.

Ambelain: This angel rules over the generation of beings and phenomena of Nature; he protects those who desire to regenerate themselves, and to reestablish in themselves that harmony which was broken by the disobedience of Adam, which they will accomplish by raising themselves before God and purifying those parts which constitute the nature of man through the elements: thus they will regain their rights and their original dignity. They will be once more become the masters of nature and will enjoy all the prerogatives which God gave them at their creation. The person born under this influence will be distinguished by his genius; he will be considered one of the great luminaries of philosophy.

Lenain: Governs the generation of beings and phenomena of nature. Protects those who wish to progress spiritually. Distinguished by genius; one of the great lights of philosophy.

Attributes: Regeneration, inner harmony, philosophy, genius, spiritual protection.

Goetic Demon: SEERE, SEAR, or SEIR

Hebrew: שאר

Gematria: 501

Demonic Classification: Prince

Planet: Jupiter

Metal: Tin

Suffumigation: Cedar

Description from *Ars Goetia*: The Seventieth Spirit is Seere, Sear, or Seir. He is a Mighty Prince, and Powerful, under AMAYMON, King of the East. He appeareth in the Form of a Beautiful Man, riding upon a Winged Horse. His Office is to go and come; and to bring abundance of things to pass on a sudden, and to carry or recarry anything whither thou wouldest have it to go, or whence thou wouldest have it from. He can pass over the whole Earth in the twinkling of an Eye. He giveth a True relation of all sorts of Theft, and of Treasure hid, and of many other things. He is of an indifferent Good Nature, and is willing to do anything which the Exorcist desireth.

Attributes: Travel, manifestation, theft, hidden things.

⊰ THE SEVENTY-FIRST QUINARY ⊱

Degrees and Sign: 20° 00'–24° 59' Pisces
Equinoctial Hour: 5:20–5:39 a.m.

Shem HaMephorash Angel: HAIAIEL or HAIEL

Hebrew: הייאל

Gematria: 56

Ruling Archangel: Gabriel

Angelic Choir: Angels

Invocation: "I will greatly praise the Lord with my mouth; yea, I will praise him among the multitude." [Psalm 109:30 (KJV)] *Confitebor Domino nimis in ore meo: et in medio multorum laudabo eum.*

Passage from *Sefer Raziel HaMalakh*: Guide to indicate every secret of creation and the secret of ten sephiroth. By the secret of the three most holy, every one guides ten. Consider the resemblance to the house of the Lord. In the temple, speak Yod is over Yod and Yod. Three complete. Consider the secret of the sephiroth, of the divine emanations and three highest mediums. Of three mediums, it is indicated in the Torah, three follow every commandment. Of every commandment and every Sabbath, complete all. Go forth on every secret path of the names. It is decreed, go forth and complete in the foundation. At that time, proclaim the foundation of Binah. All dwell on the Earth. Proclaim to go forth from Egypt, the highest in night and day. The lives reach to the strength. Complete by Aleph in secret in three days. From the name of three is the highest and most sublime secret. Every secret reveals עזאבה. Speak of the God of the children of Israel. The secret name is remembered from generation to generation, all the written name. Bind to guide on the path. The image of the four most glorious powers guides by the most holy and by all understanding.

Ambelain: He serves to confound the evil and to be delivered from all those who wish to oppress one. This angel protects all those who have need of him; he gives victory and peace; he influences weapons, arsenals, fortresses and all connected with the military genius. The person born under this influence will have a lot of energy; he will love the military state and will be distinguished by his bravery, talents and actions.

Lenain: To confound the wicked and for deliverance from those who seek to oppress us. Protects those who call upon him. Influences fire. Brave.

Attributes: Confounds evil, victory, weapons, iron, bravery, protection, fire.

Goetic Demon: DANTALION

Hebrew: דאנטאליון

Gematria: 811

Demonic Classification: Duke

Planet: Venus

Metal: Copper

Suffumigation: Sandalwood

Description from *Ars Goetia*: The Seventy-first Spirit is Dantalion.

He is a Duke Great and Mighty, appearing in the Form of a Man with many Countenances, all Men's and Women's Faces; and he hath a Book in his right hand. His Office is to teach all Arts and Sciences unto any; and to declare the Secret Counsel of any one; for he knoweth the Thoughts of all Men and Women, and can change them at his Will. He can cause Love, and show the Similitude of any person, and show the same by a Vision, let them be in what part of the World they Will.

Attributes: Arts and sciences, love, similitude, visionary, telepathic.

⊰ THE SEVENTY-SECOND QUINARY ⊱

Degrees and Sign: 25° 00'–29° 59' Pisces
Equinoctial Hour: 5:40–5:59 a.m.

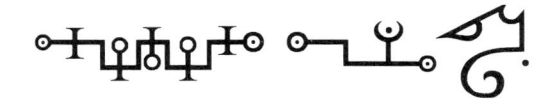

Shem HaMephorash Angel: MUMIAH

Hebrew: מומיה

Gematria: 101

Ruling Archangel: Gabriel

Angelic Choir: Angels

Invocation: "Return unto thy rest, O my soul; for the Lord hath dealt bountifully with thee." [Psalm 116:7 (KJV)] *Convertere anima mea in requiem tuam: quia Dominus beneficit tibi.*

Passage from *Sefer Raziel HaMalakh*: Guide by completing two actions. By all of them עזאבה is the beginning. End by the power of compassion. Every one is combined by six ends of the everlasting temples and the two actions of power. Speak, you are in the highest heavens and you are in the highest Earth. Bind to guide thus. By the image of Moses, complete therein all and all therein.

Ambelain: This angel protects in mysterious operations; he brings success in all things and brings all things to their conclusion; he rules over chemistry, physics and medicine; he influences health and longevity. The person born under this influence will be distinguished in medicine; he will become famous through his marvelous cures, will unveil many secrets of nature which will lead to the prosperity of the children of earth, and he will devote his labors and his care to; ease the poor and the sick.

Lenain: A divine talisman should be prepared under favorable influences with the name of the spirit on the reverse side. Protects in mysterious operations, brings success in all things. Governs chemistry, physics and medicine. Influences health and longevity.

Attributes: Happy conclusions, medicine, longevity, success, helps the poor and infirm.

Goetic Demon: ANDROMALIUS

Hebrew: אנדרומליוש

Gematria: 647

Demonic Classification: Earl

Planet: Mars

Metals: Copper and silver

Suffumigation: Dragon's blood

Description from *Ars Goetia*: The Seventy-second Spirit in Order is named Andromalius. He is an Earl, Great and Mighty, appearing in the Form of a Man holding a Great Serpent in his Hand. His Office is to bring back both a Thief, and the Goods which be stolen; and to discover all Wickedness, and Underhand Dealing; and to punish all Thieves and other Wicked People and also to discover Treasures that be Hid.

Attributes: Retrieve stolen goods, discovers wickedness, punishment.

5
The Quinaries in
Natal Astrology

ARMED WITH THE ANGELIC AND DEMONIC significations, correspondences, and attributes, along with other information from the reference entries in the preceding chapter, we now apply this perspective to the art of *genethlialogy* or natal astrology and show how these factors may be applied to chart delineation. In the examples given in this chapter, I work within the conventions of traditional Western tropical astrology, which fixes 0 degree Aries at the vernal equinox, and use the whole-sign house system, in which sign and house cusps are shared.[1] Bear in mind, however, that the quinaries may also be used in sidereal astrology and with any house system, providing theoretical adjustments are made where necessary.

Before moving on to the examples using the quinaries in chart delineation, we will first discuss the scope of natal astrology. While the present study presumes the reader has some knowledge of astrological fundamentals, it is necessary to place the art in the context of traditional astrology, as it differs from the modern form in a few key technical and philosophical areas.

NATAL ASTROLOGY

Natal astrology is centered upon the artful interpretation of a *nativity* or natal chart. The subject of a nativity is referred to as its *native*, the owner of the natal figure. The nativity is an astrological figure erected for the moment the native became an independent entity. This moment is generally regarded as when the native was separated from the mother and began breathing on their own. It is at this moment that the native begins to participate in the *pneuma* (ancient Greek meaning "breath"), which is the animating spirit or life force. This view is metaphysically supported by the Platonic philosophies (Hermetism, Gnosticism, Neoplatonism, etc.) current at the time of astrology's inception in Hellenistic Alexandria, Egypt, at the dawn of the Common Era. In the past, conception charts were sometimes consulted, but this is no longer a common practice. It is important that the moment of birth be accurately recorded down to the minute because this yields the degrees of the angles, parts, and house cusps. If the birth time is unobtainable for some reason, the native may consult an astrologer skilled in *chart rectification*, a process by which the birth time is determined through a chronological examination of the native's lived experience.

The nativity is a snapshot of the cosmos showing the planets as they were arrayed against the signs of the zodiac at the moment of birth. The *ascendant* denotes the exact degree of the zodiac that was on the eastern horizon at that time. Anciently, the ascendant was called the *horoskopos*, meaning "hour watcher," which is why nativities are sometimes referred to as horoscopes.[2] The *rising sign* is the sign containing the ascendant. The angle opposite the ascendant is the *descendant*, which is the zodiacal degree on the western horizon. The *midheaven* (*medium coeli*) denotes the local meridian at the place of birth. It is opposite the *imum coeli*. Traditional forms of astrology use the seven visible planets exclusively; these are the sun, moon, Mercury, Venus, Mars, Jupiter, and Saturn. There are also a variety of Arabic parts or lots, which are theoretically sensitive points, usually based on the distance between two planets, which is then cast from the ascendant.

A causal cycle is engaged at birth—the nativity is an astrological diagram of that cycle. Astrology addresses both *internal* and *external* causation. Internal causation is driven by the native's character because, in any given situation, people tend to act within the confines of their character. The nature of one's character may be assessed through astrology. This is accomplished by determining the condition and placement of the seven visible planets in a nativity—a process revealing the native's unique *schematic of character*.[3] External causation is driven by the introduction of events and circumstances from without. The navigation of such obstacles and opportunities may also be made clear through astrology; particularly by the application of timing techniques such as *transits* and *profections*. The causal aggregate of internal and external forces is reflected in the nativity. Based on such data, a skilled natal astrologer may make inferences as to how the native might navigate life's events and phenomena. *The assessment of these modes of causation is the basis of natal astrology's predictivity.*

Natal astrology is predicated on the notion that the cosmos is inherently meaningful and that the macrocosmic universe is symbolically reflected in the microcosmic human. This idea is supported by the oft-quoted Hermetic axiom: "That which is above is like that which is below."[4] The three Hermetic arts of astrology, alchemy, and theurgy (magic) are extensions of this worldview. A *genethlialogist* (natal astrologer) is one who has studied how to derive meaning from the placements and configurations of the planets, parts, and angles, as they are distributed among the zodiacal signs at the time of birth.

In this book, I am highlighting the effects and influence of the Shem angels and the goetic demons, as their influences are emanated through the 72 quinaries of the zodiac. Every planet in a nativity is placed in one quinary or another; and every quinary is ruled by an angel and a demon; ergo, every planet is subject to angelic and demonic influence. This influence may be assessed and interpreted genethlialogically.

USING THE QUINARIES IN CHART DELINEATION

Commonly, in a natal consultation, the astrologer assesses the condition and influence of the native's "big three," which refers to the ascendant, sun, and moon. This usually yields a good, baseline idea of the native's character and personality. Assessing prominent features such as these is a fine way to begin to *find* the native in the nativity, particularly if the subject's chronology and biography are unknown to the astrologer.

The ascendant, and the rising sign in which it is found, symbolizes the native's physique and temperament. It was anciently referred to as the helm, because it is the point from which the life's vessel is steered. The planet that rules the ascendant (traditional ruler of the rising sign) is called the helmsman and is the planet that most represents the native in the nativity.[5] The ascendant is commonly equated with the *ego* (not in the modern pejorative sense of the word), since this is the part of the psyche that evaluates, plans, and interfaces with the external world. The ego is the center of consciousness and the condition of the native's ascendant, as well as the ruler of their rising sign, can tell us a lot about the subject.

Astrologically, the sun signifies the native's inner sense of self. The sun is the will, the intellect, and the central organizing principle of the native's personality. On the psychological plane, if the ascendant is the ego, the sun is the *self*. As the sun is the center of our solar system, so is the self simultaneously the center and circumference of personality. This is symbolized in the planetary glyph for the sun: the *circumpunct* or point within a circle. The sun is also the natural significator of the father.

The moon signifies the physical body, the emotions, and the irrational mind. According to the Aristotelian physics, she is the nexus between Earth and the six planets beyond her sphere. She serves a similar purpose, astrologically. Psychologically, the moon corresponds to the *id*, which is the most primitive part of the psyche, largely instinctual and unconscious, primarily directed toward fulfilling basic needs and comforts. The mother is naturally signified by the moon.

Another common consultation strategy is to take a house-based approach to delineation. This works particularly well if the native has questions about specific areas of their life. To gain some clarity and insight on financial matters, for example, the astrologer would look to the second house and its lord; for health concerns, examine the sixth and its lord; for relationships, assess the seventh house; and so on, based on the standard body of house significations. As the astrologer makes their way around the houses, the various planets are engaged, either by residency, by rulership, or by aspect, and a holistic picture of the nativity begins to emerge.

Good astrology is multifactorial. The astrologer should look for agreeing testimonies from several technical perspectives. The influence of the quinaries is another factor to be considered *in addition to* what the astrologer finds from the common delineation techniques. Whatever approach the astrologer chooses to employ—interpreting the big three, reading by houses, viewing the planets as natural significators—a consideration of the quinaries will add further detail and nuance, as we shall see in the following examples.

EXAMPLE NATIVITIES

In the first example (see fig. 5.1), we will delineate the native's ascendant. This is a common way to develop a general idea of the native's character, temperament, and physique. We begin with the standard practice of assessing the qualities of the rising sign—such as its *polarity*, *triplicity*, and *quadruplicity*—as well as the placement and condition of its lord or lady, that is, the planetary ruler of the sign. Then, we will synthesize these findings with the significations and attributes of the angel and demon governing the rising quinary. The technical delineation will be given first, then an interpretation of the placement.

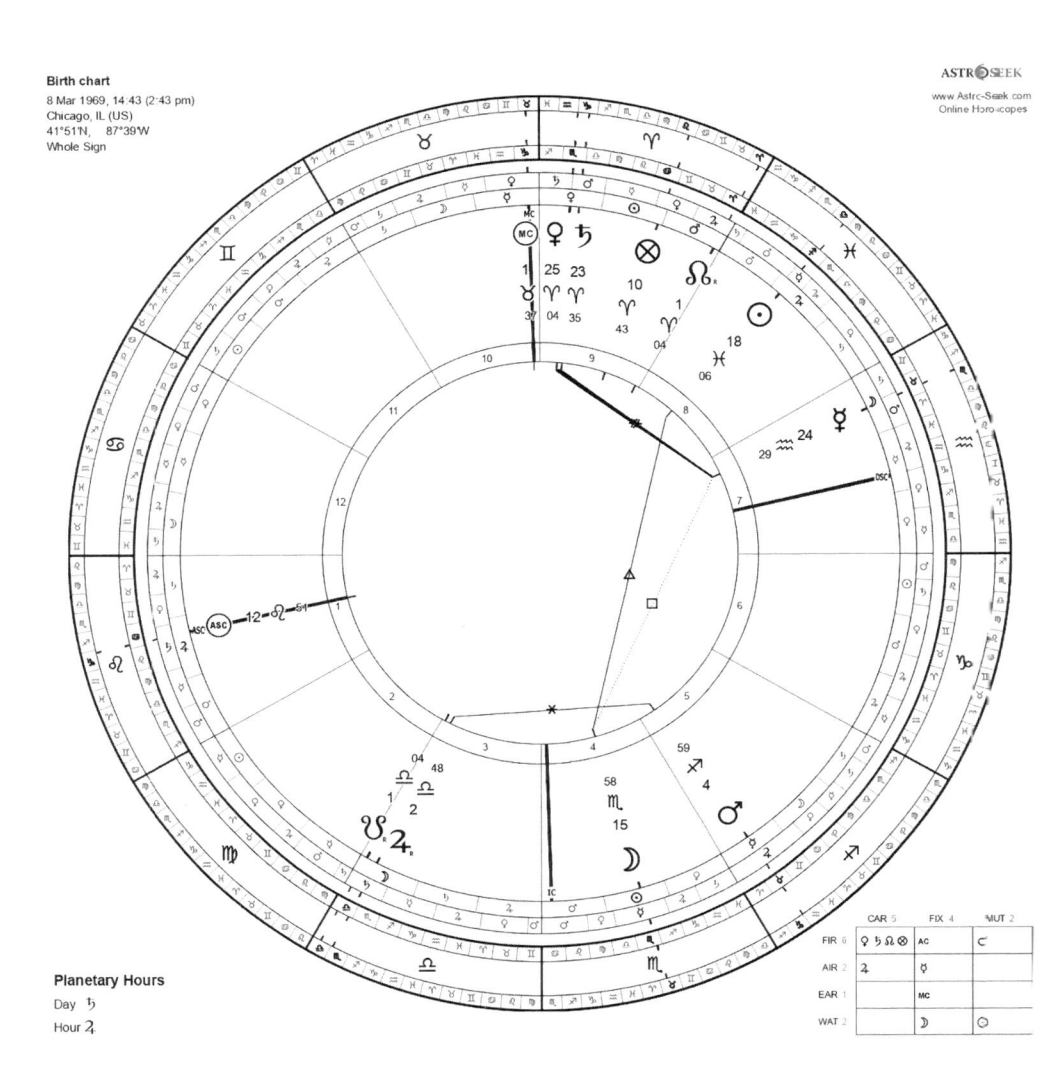

Fig. 5.1. March 8, 1969, 14:43, Chicago, Illinois.
Astro-Seek

Leo is rising in this figure. It is an active, fixed, and fiery sign, which tends toward a choleric temperament. The sun—lord of the rising sign—is in Pisces on the eighth house. Turning to the quinarian data, we note that the degree of the ascendant is 12° 51' Leo, which is in the twenty-seventh quinary (10° 00'–14° 59' Leo). The governing angel of this quinary is Ierathel. Of this angel, Ambelain says, "The person born under this influence loves peace, justice, sciences and the arts, and he distinguishes himself in literature."[6] The presiding demon of this quinary is Ronové, who teaches rhetoric and languages.[7]

When this information is synthesized, we arrive at a body of characteristics and proclivities with which we may begin to paint a portrait of the native. By the intuitive application of the *interpretive art* of astrology, we might conclude that the native is rather tall with longish blond or red hair. They are well spoken and well read and possess a natural talent for writing. The native is motivated and driven—perhaps a little arrogant—and likely destined to be successful. Professionally, they may be in banking, investments, or law. They may also be the recipient of a large inheritance (probably bequeathed in their thirty-first or forty-third year of life). Of course, there are many other factors to consider, but this is a good start toward building a holistic character profile.

In the next example (see fig. 5.2), we will assess the native's overall financial circumstances using standard delineation techniques in conjunction with the angelic and demonic influences of the quinaries. As before, we begin by noting the qualities of the sign on the second house and then assess the condition and placement of the lord of that sign. From there, we will consider how the significations and attributes of the quinary hosting the Lord of the second house influence the native's financial sphere. Again, we will synthesize that information into a composite picture of the native's second house of finances and movable goods.

Beginning with the technical delineation, we note that Aquarius is on the second whole sign house in this chart. This is an active, fixed, airy sign, ruled by the planet Saturn. Bodily, Saturn is exalted in Libra on the tenth house. Libra is an active, cardinal, and airy sign, in a harmonious trine configuration with Aquarius on the second house. At 29° 43' Libra, Saturn is in the forty-second quinary (25° 00'–29° 59' Libra), which is governed by the Shem angel Mikael. Of Mikael's quinary, Ambelain says, "The person born under this influence will become

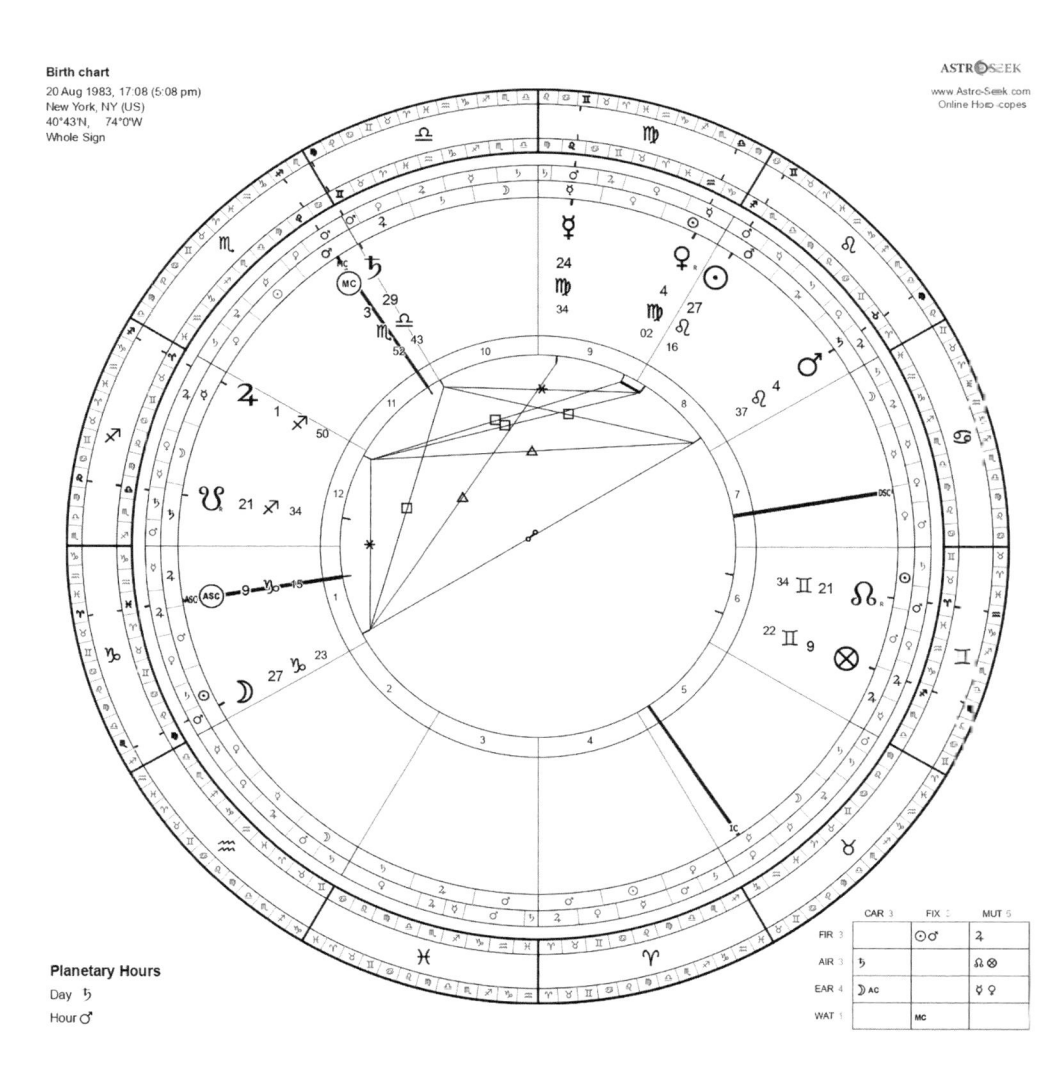

Fig. 5.2. August 20, 1983, 17:08, New York City, New York.
Astro-Seek

involved in political affairs; he will be curious, and will want to learn the secrets of private offices and foreign news, and he will distinguish himself in affairs of State through his knowledge of diplomacy."[8] The complementary goetic demon of the forty-second quinary is the Duke Vepar, who is said to govern the waters and to guide warships.[9]

Again, it is at this point that intuition and intellect must artfully meet. Based on what we see in the technical delineation, we might say that the native is a highly intelligent, well-to-do, and disciplined leader in their field. This is a person of influence, an authority, wielding considerable power in the socioeconomic spheres of others, perhaps internationally. They may trade in foreign commodities—a volatile market, subject to the vicissitudes of global politics. Despite having more resources than they need, they are exceedingly tight and frugal. Their financial sphere is closely linked with their career, which may be in the tech industry. We would also expect this native to trade in cryptocurrency.

QUINARIAN TRANSITS

Transits are an astrological timing method that analyzes the configurations made by present or future planetary placements in reference to those on a *radical* (root) chart, such as a nativity or inception chart.[10] For instance, suppose a given nativity shows Jupiter at 17 degrees Cancer while transiting Mercury is currently at 17 degrees Libra. In this case, transiting Mercury is said to be *squaring* natal Jupiter. Transits are consulted when one wishes to *consider*, in the literal sense (i.e., *con*, meaning "with," and *sideri*, meaning "the stars"), the auspices of current or future astrological conditions. Suppose someone were to schedule a first date with a new prospective partner; depending on the desired outcome of the meeting, they may elect to meet under a favorable aspect, such as transiting Venus applying a trine to natal Mars. Minding the transits to their natal placements is an astrologically conscious way of averting potential *disaster*, also in the literal sense (i.e., *dis*, meaning "bad," and *astrum*, meaning "stars").

It is also important to consider the effect of transiting planets on the houses through which they pass. The topics associated with the twelve terrestrial domains may be activated and/or modified by the significations of transiting planets. In their zodiacal journeys, the planets spend time in each of the houses, and it is during these periods that the planets express themselves in the domestic context. For example, suppose Saturn were transiting the native's seventh house. This means that, for the next two to three years, Saturn's significations will have an influence on seventh house matters. Depending on a variety of factors, this transit could symbolize a number of possible scenarios, such as the development of an exclusive relationship, a period of celibacy, or a relationship with an older partner.

Similarly, significations mingle when planets transit the 72 quinaries. As we have seen, the angels and demons of the quinaries use the planets to express their agendas in the sublunar context of the houses. On average, Saturn transits each quinary for approximately five months. During this period, Saturnian significations mingle with those of the planet's host quinary and find expression in the area of the native's life dictated by the house. Suppose transiting Saturn has *ingressed* the seventieth quinary on the ninth house. The angel Iabamiah[11] and the demon Seere[12] govern this quinary. For a period of about five months in the native's life, we may expect Saturnian themes such as structure and discipline to be mingled with Iabamiah's philosophical introspection and Seere's wanderlust in the context of the ninth house's religiosity and foreign travel. Accordingly, the native ends up taking an extended trip to India to study meditation with an aged guru of renown.

THE RISING QUINARY AND
THE ANGEL OF THE NATIVITY

The zodiacal sign that hosts the ascendant in a nativity is called the *rising sign*. Traditionally, this sign and its planetary ruler are most representative of the native—*certainly more so than the sun sign*.[13] The rising sign gives us information relative to the native's character, personality, and physique. Suppose Aries is rising in a nativity. Aries, being an active, cardinal, fire sign, is ruled by Mars, who signifies anger, courage, and the choleric temperament. We might expect the native to be an assertive self-starter. They may have a lean, athletic build, red hair, and a ruddy complexion. Perhaps they can be argumentative or have a fiercely competitive nature. Obviously, there are other factors at play, but the native's Ariean and martial traits are likely to find expression in their outward form and character.

Similarly, the rising quinary and its angelic ruler also provide information relative to the ascendant, and thereby to the native's character, physique, and personality. We begin by observing which 5-degree arc segment hosts the ascendant. From there, we note the significations of the angelic and demonic ruler of that quinary (see chapter 4 for significations and attributes). Suppose the ascendant is 13° 44' Capricorn. This degree of the zodiac is in the fifty-seventh quinary, which is governed by the angel Nemamiah[14] and the demon Osé.[15] Nemamiah brings prosperity, bravery, courage, and rules over generals and admirals. Osé makes the native proficient in the liberal arts and allows them to change their outward appearance at will. These significations are then synthesized into the astrologer's interpretation. Perhaps the native is strategic in intellect, martial in character, and protean in appearance, able to blend in with the crowd. They may have a commanding demeanor, with clear, gray eyes, reminiscent of gray-eyed Athena, goddess of bellicose strategy.

From antiquity to the modern era, special attention has been paid to the planetary ruler of the rising sign and ascendant. In some traditions, this planet has been considered the general chart ruler, due to its influence over the ascendant and first house—both natural significators of the native. From the perspective of quinarian astrology, the angelic ruler of the rising quinary has the distinction of being the Angel of the Nativity. This entity exerts an especially powerful influence pertaining to the native's physical body, temperament, and character. The Angel of the Nativity should not be confused with the Kyrios Geneseos (Lord of the Nativity), as encountered in certain Hellenistic astrological traditions.[16]

Suppose the ascendant is 7° 16' Virgo in a given nativity. This degree of the zodiac is in the thirty-second quinary, which is ruled by the Shem angel Vasariah.[17] Ergo, Vasariah is the Angel of the Nativity. Vasariah brings good memory, eloquence in speech, modesty, and a sense of justice. This angel governs lawyers and judges, particularly. Clearly, these significations imply a career in the court system, but may also be interpreted abstractly; perhaps the native's powers of discernment are particularly developed, and they frequently find themselves mediating arguments, defending some and prosecuting others. The inverse may also occur; perhaps these qualities are absent or underdeveloped. In which case, the development of such abilities may become the central project in the native's life. Whatever the circumstances, the native's connection to Vasariah, the Angel of their Nativity, is an existential imperative in quinarian astrology and may aid in this sort of character development. In this capacity, the angel of the quinary hosting the ascendant is somewhat akin to the native's personal daimōn— their tutelary guide and mystagogue; an ally in the lifelong project of self-realization.[18]

Establishing a connection with the Angel of the Nativity can be as simple as reciting their invocatory Psalm (e.g., for Vasariah: *"Quia rectum est verbum Domini, et omnia opera ejus in fide."*) during their quinarian week and hour, or as complex as following the various modes of invocation and conjuration prescribed in the Solomonic grimoire tradition, upon which this book is based. Obviously, there are several centuries' worth of grimoires detailing these processes; reiterating them here is unnecessary—particularly since our focus is the application of the angelic and demonic significations to astrology. Suffice it to say that the angel governing the rising quinary (i.e., the quinary hosting the ascendant) is the single most important angel in the figure, and the native should make a concerted effort to develop a working relationship with that entity.

6
The Quinaries in Electional Astrology

ELECTIONAL ASTROLOGY INVOLVES the deliberate consideration of timing to maximize and engage cosmic momentum. Some moments have the very motion of the cosmos propelling them, whereas others are cosmically doomed. Electional astrology is, by far, the most common branch of the art encountered in the magical context. Most grimoires make some reference to calculating the best time to perform an operation, such as an invocation or a talisman consecration. Observation of the days and hours ruled by the seven visible planets is crucial to the success of such operations.

Electional or *katarchic* astrology is probably the second-oldest branch of the art, as we see no evidence of natal astrology before the fifth century BCE.[1] The oldest form is *mundane astrology*, which deals with politics and the fortunes of cities and nations. As early as 1800 BCE, Mesopotamian astrologers made note of the positions of the planets against the canopy of stars and how these celestial configurations were reflected on the terrestrial sphere.[2] After centuries of documenting fortunate and unfortunate terrestrial events and phenomena along with their corresponding celestial reflections, they had built up a body of *omenic* significations, primarily in reference to warfare. It was only a short conceptual leap to theorize that they could *elect* to engage auspicious cosmic cycles, and that some moments were better suited to certain objectives than others. This is the foundation of electional astrology.[3]

Electional astrology continued to evolve throughout the Hellenistic era when the introduction of horoscopy allowed astrologers to put a much finer temporal point on their elections. This branch of astrology reached its apex in the medieval Islamic world when the Persian astrologer Masha'allah (740–815 CE) was tasked by the Caliph al-Manṣūr to devise an election for the founding of Baghdad.[4] Ultimately, July 31, 762, was elected, when Jupiter—the significator of kingdoms, wealth, and peace—was in Sagittarius, his domicile, and conjunct the ascendant. The sun was in Leo, also dignified by domicile, and rejoicing in the ninth whole sign house of religion and higher learning. In the election, malefic Mars, planet of war, was descending, among other notable features. Masha'allah's election was indeed auspicious as it marked the inception of the Islamic golden age, which would last half a millennium, and established Baghdad and its *Bayt al-Ḥikmah* (House of Wisdom) as the global center of intellectual, economic, and cultural advancement.

The timing of magical operations typically adheres to the conditions of electional astrology. For example, an invocation of Tzadkiel, archangel of Jupiter, might be performed on a Thursday and during a Jupiterian hour. Elections such as these are ubiquitous in the grimoire tradition because they are of preliminary importance. As we have seen in the literature, planetary hours and days are the first levels of election, but if we really want to concentrate the occult virtues of a star or planet in the sublunary sphere, we would do well to consider hitting other points of essential and accidental dignity. Agrippa explains the importance of considering other features from the chart in a strong election—not merely the day and hour.

> Also in every work there are to be observed, the situation, motion, and aspect of the Stars, and Planets, in Signs and Degrees, and how all these stand in reference to the length and latitude of the Climate;

for by this are varied the qualities of the angles, which the rays of Celestial bodies upon the figure of the thing describe, according to which Celestial vertues are infused. So when thou art working any thing which belongs to any Planet, thou must place it in its dignities, fortunate, and powerful, and ruling in the day, hour, and in the Figure of the Heaven.[5]

The first consideration when composing an election is to decide which planet governs the intention of the operation. If the operation were for love or relationships, we might use Venus or the Lord of the seventh house. If the operation were for business opportunities, we might use Mercury or the ruler of the second or tenth house, depending on the particulars. Then we place that planet not only in its day and hour, but also in as many of its essential and accidental dignities as possible. This is what Agrippa means by consulting the "Figure of the Heaven," which is simply the electional chart.[6] The more points of dignity engaged, the higher the concentration of planetary virtue; ergo, the more cosmic momentum propelling the operation. In addition to the primary significator, the elector must also pay particular attention to the moon.

> FIRST, thou shalt know and observe the Moon's Age for thy working. The best days be when the Moon Luna is 2, 4, 6, 8, 10, 12, or 14 days old, as Solomon saith; and no other days be profitable.[7]

In electional astrology, the moon signifies the operation in general. Cosmologically, the moon (symbolized by Hecate, in this capacity) is the distributor of stellar and planetary influence to the sublunary sphere, as she governs the liminal space between the terrestrial and celestial realms. Because of this role, the moon's placement is crucial and must always be considered in every election. A poorly placed moon can ruin an otherwise auspicious election. We will want to keep an eye on the lunar phase, aspects, sign, and house placement. The moon's applying aspects are generally considered to represent future events, while separating aspects represent the past.[8]

While no election is perfect, we want to do our best to find the moment that will best support and project the intention. So, to use Jupiter as our example again, the operator might elect to perform their invocation of the archangel Tzadkiel not only in Jupiter's day and hour, but also when the planet is in either Sagittarius or Pisces, in the planet's own face and term, of the *sect* in favor (in a day chart), well-aspected by Venus and the luminaries, unaspected by the malefics (Saturn and Mars), in direct motion, and conjunct either the ascendant or midheaven. Granted, it is unreasonable to expect to meet *all* these criteria *every* time, due to the rarity of such placements, but care should be taken to utilize the best election within reason. The ability of a planet to bring about its constructive significations is proportionate to its condition and placement, which is gauged by its essential and accidental dignity.

USING THE QUINARIES IN ELECTIONAL ASTROLOGY

In a typical election, we would first choose the planet that best signifies the theme of the operation. This might be through the natural significations of the planets—Venus for love, Jupiter for wealth, and so on—or by fortifying the Lord of the house whose topics best signify the objective. We would then look for a time when the given planet is fortunately placed, essentially and accidentally. For instance, if one were emailing an offer on a new home, one might send the email when the ruler of the fourth house (real estate) was on the ascendant or conjunct the midheaven. Of course, there are other factors to be considered, but this is the basic idea.

As we have said, each quinary is associated with a certain body of significations and a scope of influence. Utilizing the quinaries in astrological elections is very similar to how we use the significations of the planets and houses. Suppose one were electing to foster a friendship with some important figure. Normally, one might call, email, or schedule a meeting with the prospective friend when, say, the ruler of the first house (significator of the elector) was conjunct the ruler of the eleventh house of friends (significator of the prospective friend), providing each planet were in good condition and under an unafflicted, waxing moon. Using the quinaries, we find that Haziel, the angel of the ninth quinary, assists in fostering friendships with important people.[9] The astrologer-elector may then choose to call, email, or schedule a meeting with their prospective friend while the ninth quinary was either rising at the ascendant or culminating at the midheaven, or when either the ascendant or midheaven were within 10° 00'–14° 59' Taurus. Another option is to use the quinarian hour; Haziel rules the equinoctial hour of 8:40–8:59 a.m. each day—perhaps a breakfast meeting could be scheduled to commence during that interval.

A quinarian election such as that above may be magically enhanced by the invocation of the angel of the quinarian hour in question, or by the construction and consecration of a talisman dedicated to this purpose. We will be going into more detail on this sort of magical praxis in chapter 8, which deals specifically with quinarian magic and talismans.

Electional astrology is a useful way of engaging and capitalizing on cosmic momentum. All the standard methods of election may be repurposed in a quinarian setting. Whereas planetary and house significations are typically the primary fodder for composing effective elections, the significations and attributions of the Shem angels and the goetic demons may also be used in this context. Magical elements are also introduced by using the quinaries, if the elector chooses to employ their attributes, sigils, and seals in the accompanying ritualism and talismanic projects.

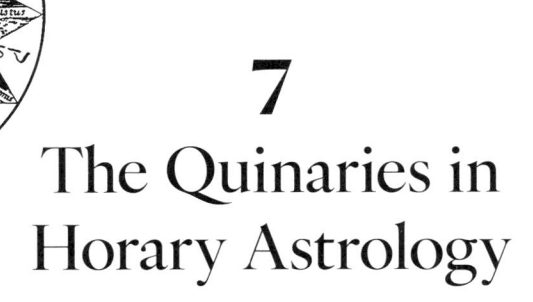

7

The Quinaries in
Horary Astrology

THE LAST BRANCH OF ASTROLOGY to which we will apply the quinarian technique is *horary astrology*. Also known as interrogational astrology, horary is a question-based form of astrological divination. As the name suggests, it is the astrology "of the hour." The querent (the subject posing the question) will frame their query in such a way that it is answerable by consulting a horary figure—using phraseology such as "will I?" as opposed to "should I?" A figure is then cast for the moment the question is understood by the astrologer. The horary astrologer then uses a specialized set of significations and delineation techniques to arrive at the answer.

Suppose the querent asks, "Will I get the job?" The astrologer will erect a figure for the moment the question is fully formed in their mind. They will then make sure the chart is *radical* (a root question that is fit to be judged) by subjecting it to certain criteria, such as William Lilly's *considerations before judgment*.[1] The significators of the querent and the *quesited* (the object of the horary) are then assigned. The querent is represented by the lord* of the first house and cosignified by the moon.[2] The quesited is signified by the planet ruling the house under

---

*The lord (for the masculine planets) and lady (for the moon and Venus) are the respective rulers of the signs (sun in Leo, moon in Cancer, etc.) and, thereby, the house cusps.

which the topic falls; in this case, the lord of the tenth house of careers and profession.[3] The astrologer then assesses the quality of the aspect relationship between the querent and the quesited—easy or hard, applying or separating. At this point, other features from the chart, such as resident planets, sign, and house placement, may come into play. These factors add further nuance to the horary delineation, often telling the whole story in striking detail. The placement and condition of the moon should be taken into consideration, as it usually says something about the flow of the narrative. Timing techniques may also be applied to discern the temporal sequence of events. For example, if the planetary significator of the querent is applying to perfect a trine aspect with the significator of the quesited in 4 degrees, the astrologer may expect contact between the two significators in four days, weeks, or months, depending on certain factors.

There is a legendary account[4] of the development of horary astrology from the medieval Perso-Arabic astrological tradition that, while it is almost certainly not historical, illustrates how the art may have developed over time. According to one version of the legend, a loved one had run away. The jilted lover goes to the astrologer to find out where the beloved may have gone. The astrologer asks if the querent knew what time the quesited had slipped away, with the intention of casting a figure for that moment. Alas, the querent does not know. The astrologer then asks what time the abandoned lover became aware of the missing loved one, thinking that moment might serve as the ascendant of a radical chart. Sadly, they are unable to recall with sufficient accuracy. Frustrated but undaunted, the astrologer says, "Then I shall raise a figure for the moment the question became clear in *my* mind." The rationale being that, if all knowledge is fractally diffused throughout the cosmos, then the casting of a figure will serve to *condense* the answer out of the *æther* (in the Aristotelian sense), similarly to how humidity condenses out of the warm, moist air onto the surface of a cold glass. Clearly, horary engages a different cosmic mechanism than that which is at play in natal or electional astrology.

As in elections, the moon plays a significant role in horary astrology. It is the cosignificator of the querent and its placement and aspects symbolize the actions of the parties involved. The moon's separating aspects symbolize past events and her applying aspects symbolize things to come.[5] The querent is primarily signified by the planetary ruler of the rising sign. Assigning the quesited's planetary significator is a little more involved, as it is based on the house topics and their planetary rulers. For example, the querent's sibling is the lord of the third house; their parent is the lord of the fourth house; their child is the lord of the fifth house; their dog is the lord of the sixth house; and so on, based on the traditional house significations. Everything can be assigned to an astrological house, sign, or planet. This includes all people, places, things, colors, numbers, emotions, and thoughts. Everything in the sublunary terrestrial sphere has its sympathetic correspondence in the superlunary celestial sphere.

Horary, like the other branches of astrology, is predicated on the concept of a *great chain of being*, which descends from the primum movens, through the stellar and planetary spheres, and into the sublunary sphere of the elements. All terrestrial animals, vegetables, and minerals are hierarchically suspended from their ruling planets, angels, and demons. The implication is that the answers to our questions may be divined and communicated through this cosmic network.

USING THE QUINARIES IN HORARY ASTROLOGY

The Shem angels and the goetic demons may also be fitted into this great schema of Hermetic gnosis. Since each quinarian angel and demon has its own body of significations, attributes, and scope of influence, we might begin by noting the *rising quinary* at the time the question is understood by the astrologer. The very nature of this particular angel or demon could tell us something about the question's foundation, such as whether the figure is qualitatively radical. The rising quinary may also reveal other information relative to the nature of the question. From there, we may consider assessing the quinaries in which the natural significators of the querent and quesited are found. Do these angels and demons tell us any pertinent information regarding the subject and object of the question, respectively? Finally, the quinarian pair governing the moon may reveal information relevant to the narrative flow of events.

Suppose the querent asks, "Will I win my court case?" First, a chart is cast for the moment the question becomes clear in the astrologer's mind. The ascendant is at 28 degrees Gemini, which is in the eighteenth quinary. This quinary is ruled by the angel Caliel, whose attributes include truth, integrity, and trials. This obviously has a bearing on the question, ergo, the figure is fit to be judged. The defendant-querent is signified by Mercury, lord of Gemini, the rising sign. Mercury is at 11 degrees Leo, in the twenty-seventh quinary, which is ruled by the angel Ierathel and the demon Ronové. Things are looking pretty good for the defendant because Ierathel defends against unjust attacks and confounds enemies; and Ronové bestows rhetorical skill, which probably couldn't hurt in court. Plus, Mercury naturally governs oration and argumentation, which may come in handy. The plaintiff-quesited is signified by the lord of the seventh house cusp (signifying legal opponents), which in this case is Jupiter, lord of Sagittarius. Things are getting interesting because Jupiter signifies morality and justice, he rules courtrooms, and he is the natural significator of judges. But what is his condition? Jupiter is retrograde at 13 degrees Aries, in the third quinary, which is ruled by the angel Sitael and the demon Vassago. Sitael grants magnanimity and nobility; Vassago aids in divination and finding lost items. The astrologer would also note that Mercury and Jupiter are mutually applying to a conjunction in one degree's time.

Considering these quinarian factors alongside those gained from standard horary technique, one of a few potential outcomes emerges. The defendant speaks eloquently and appropriately (Ronové's rhetorical gift) and is insulated from potential slander and libel (Ierathel's defense against unjust attacks). The plaintiff, retracing his steps (symbolized by Jupiter's retrograde motion), remembers a crucial piece of information (the lost "items" of Vassago) and suddenly drops the charges (Sitael's magnanimity). In the end, the plaintiff and the defendant come to an amicable agreement (both are applying to trine). Certainly, there are many other factors to consider, such as house placement and the condition of the moon, but this simple example serves to illustrate how the angels and demons of the quinaries may be applied to horary delineation.

Horary is a vast and complicated branch of astrology. It is certainly a specialized corner of the astrological world. As such, we can only provide a rudimentary account of the practice here. Suffice it to say that the significations of the Shem angels and goetic demons may offer pertinent information in the context of horary interrogation. They are certainly worth consulting, as the quinaries add a significant amount of detail, which could prove to be meaningful in horary astrology.

8
Quinarian Magic and Talismans

THOUGH WE MOST COMMONLY encounter the quinaries in the context of qabalistic lore and the Solomonic grimoire tradition, the primary purpose of this book has been to establish them as a practicable delineation technique. The quinaries are, after all, an astrological device—they are 5-degree arc segments of the zodiac bearing an influence on any planet, angle, or part found within their cusps. As such, they lend themselves to chart interpretation since every planet in a figure is in one quinary or another at any given time. However, the quinaries—having been kept for centuries by grimoire writers and practitioners—have developed a decidedly magical patina as well as a body of occult significations, thus rendering them particularly suited to magical operations such as ritualized invocation and the talismanic arts.

The use of the quinarian angels and demons in conjuration is obviously well documented. We need not reiterate the contents of the *Ars Goetia* or the *Sefer Raziel HaMalakh* here. If the reader is interested in the invocation and binding of these spirits, we direct them to the Solomonic grimoire cycle (see chapter 3). We might also recommend that, following Vigenère and Rudd, they consider insulating themselves against the potentially chaotic influence of the goetic demons by employing the assistance of the corresponding Shem angels. As we have seen, the angels may be used to bind the demons and thereby minimize the possibility of demonic mischief and other adverse effects.[1]

In this chapter, we will discuss how the quinaries may be used in talisman composition, construction, and consecration. This area merits our attention as it is underdeveloped in the European grimoire tradition. There are a few notable medieval resources—*Picatrix*[2] (eleventh century CE) and Thābit ibn Qurra's *De Imaginibus*[3] (ninth century CE) being chief among them—readily available to those wishing to make talismans based on the images of the individual planets, the thirty-six decans, or the twenty-eight lunar mansions. However, to my knowledge, there is no such resource for those wishing to create *quinarian* talismans specifically.

In the following, we will discuss the nature and use of talismans and how the Shem angels and the goetic demons may be utilized in this way. Before we discuss the production and use of quinarian talismans, we will first provide context relating to the state of the magical worldview in the modern era. We will also address some of the factors that led to the abandonment of the enchanted paradigm as it existed before the advent of the Enlightenment and the Scientific Revolution.

THE DISENCHANTMENT OF THE COSMOS

The *Ars Goetia* defines magic thus:

> MAGIC is the Highest, most Absolute, and most Divine Knowledge of Natural Philosophy, advanced in its works and wonderful operations by a right understanding of the inward and occult virtue of things.[4]

This dovetails nicely with the usage we encounter in, say, Agrippa's *Three Books of Occult Philosophy* or Francis Barrett's *The Magus* (1801). It neatly reflects the Renaissance and early modern perspective of the art. To be thorough, we must also square this understanding of magic with that of antiquity. To accomplish this, we will consider the range and scope of the concept from the perspective of the ancient Greek language because the terms constellated around the subject are clearer here than in English. There is a peculiar precision and clarity to *koiné*, the ancient Greek language; that aspect along with it being adopted as the lingua franca helped create an environment in which philosophy could flourish. For instance, instead of the somewhat vague and slippery English word *love*, which could mean a number of things in a variety of contexts, the Greek language had several words to describe varieties of love, such as *storgē* (familial love), *agápē* (divine love), *philia* (love between friends), or *erōs* (erotic love). In English, the single term *time* is used to express a range of concepts, whereas the Greeks had recourse to a variety of words, such as *aion*, *kairos*, and *chronos*—each denoting a specific facet of time. Similarly, the English word *magic* is used to signify a host of disparate concepts and practices—from pulling a rabbit out of a hat to communicating with the dead. Clearly, a single word is incapable of capturing the scope and nuance of the idea in its totality. In ancient Greek, however, we encounter an intricate taxonomy of words representing the notion of magic in its various specialized applications: *manteíā*, *pharmaka*, *goeteia*, *theourgía*, *thaumatourgía*, and *telestiké*, being a few of the most prominent.

Of particular interest to the present study are goetia, theurgy, thaumaturgy, and telestiké. Goetia, at least initially, connoted a lower magic we might associate with sorcery. This concept would eventually expand to encompass the *nigromantic* or demonic magic used by Solomon to build the First Temple. Theurgy, somewhat conversely, is a divine magic. Its morphology refers to a "god-working" or *microcosmogony*, a terrestrial imitation of the divine cosmogenesis. Theurgy is often ritualized and typically involves the invocation of celestial intelligences or intellectual entities such as angels. Thaumaturgy, as we have discussed, denotes the working of wonders, such as Moses's parting of the Red Sea—a miraculous event from the book of Exodus, which qabalists directly associate with the angels of the Shem HaMephorash. Telestiké refers to the ensoulment of images, such as statues and talismans, and is also used in reference to initiation. In the context of the present study, we may associate theurgy and thaumaturgy with the Shem angels; goetia with the demons; and telestiké with talismans.

In his *De mysteriis*, Iamblichus describes theurgy as a sort of ritualized cosmogony—a ceremonialized creative fiat in miniature.[5] The theurgist, like the *dēmiurgós* or Platonic "craftsman," creates and preserves a sympathetic model of the very cosmos. The Neoplatonists also make use of *synthemata*, which are signatures or tokens in the sublunary sphere, organized in *seira* (often understood as chains) suspended from the Platonic *ideas* in the intelligible, noetic realm. These very mechanisms and motifs are present in the Solomonic magic of the *Ars Goetia*. The exorcist stands in the elemental center of the magic circle, which is a *microcosmos*, a little world. The magician is surrounded by the seven planetary spheres, which are themselves enveloped by the Ogdoad, or sphere of the fixed stars and zodiac. Signatures and tokens such as sigils, seals of the spirits, and suffumigations serve to anchor the entities on the material plane, whereupon the magician enacts the ritualized microcosmogony—itself, an imitation of the divine cosmogony.

Notions such as these supported magical praxis for millennia; a protracted period during which the occult causality was a matter of course. The other two Hermetic arts—alchemy and astrology—were also accepted parts of the natural philosophical landscape. They were components of a *mosaic of meaning*, which comprised the enchanted understanding of the world. To the ancient as well as the Renaissance mind, it was not considered ludicrous to think of the cosmos as being animated and meaningful. Occult forces and entities permeated all of life's events and phenomena. This was the *magical worldview*.[6]

This supernaturalistic understanding of the world quietly but precipitously faded with the advance of the Enlightenment. The idea of an ensouled cosmos, replete with its own inherent sense of meaning and purpose, gave way to the positivistic secularism, nihilism, and hubris that accompanied the Scientific Revolution. Banished were the angels, demons, and djinn who inhabited the world from prehistory through antiquity and into the Renaissance. The very *anima mundi* (world soul) herself was exorcised from the world, leaving only a disenchanted carcass of weights, measures, and materialistic quantifiability.

In time, magic resurfaced, but it had been psychologized. Disincarnate entities and their numinous workings became compartmentalized aspects of the psyche emerging through various complexes. As we mentioned previously, Johann Weyer may have hammered the first nail into the coffin of the magical worldview by his psychologization of witchcraft, albeit in defense of witches. He framed their species of spirit contact as a sort of mental illness. More recently, in his introduction to Mathers's translation of the *Goetia*, British occultist Aleister Crowley proposed that the goetic demons were merely figments of the operator's imagination.[7] The project of mystical subjectification was further advanced and concretized in the work of C. G. Jung, reaching its apotheosis in his analytical psychology. The numinous had ostensibly been recuperated, but only after undergoing the processes of scientific sanitization and secular justification. This, largely, reflects the current state of magical affairs.

It is difficult for the modern mind to fathom a time when the Hermetic arts of astrology, alchemy, and magic were a natural component of the common philosophical mosaic. They were not considered esoteric arts before the Scientific Revolution; they *became* esoteric upon being swept into the "dustbin of rejected knowledge."[8] Astrology became astronomy, which is merely the quantification of a dead universe. Alchemy, stripped of its Hermetic resonance, became chemistry. And all forms of magic—the enchanted technologies of the ancients— were deemed pseudoscience. The Hermetic arts were now simply the laughable vestiges of a primitive and superstitious world. No astronomer today would publicly admit to believing that each of the seven classical planets has its own agenda to actualize, as the ancients understood these visible gods. Similarly, the modern chemist does not believe that the external processes of transformation occurring in their Erlenmeyer flasks mirror corresponding internal processes in the body, mind, and spirit of the chemist. These arts were disenchanted with the separation of the qualitative and the quantitative. The current academic position is that only an idiot or a crackpot would entertain such backward delusions as to believe in the objectivity of supernatural entities and phenomena.

Today, we have reached somewhat of an impasse, as science, in its myopic empiricism, struggles to adequately explain life's more mysterious features, such as those arising in the world of modern theoretical physics. A collective quest for meaning is clearly underway, as the West slowly warms up to traditions such as neopaganism, witchcraft, and nature religions. The Hermetic arts of astrology, alchemy, and magic are also enjoying a recent surge in popularity. A critique of this slow, collective paradigm shift is beyond the scope of this book, but some of the major contributors seem to be the general malaise, meaninglessness, and deep uncertainty with which modern humankind grapples. Hence, the renewed interest in divinatory systems such as astrology and tarot. We are clearly in the midst of a collective existential crisis. And the modern mind has become increasingly dissatisfied with accepting the quantitative at the expense of the qualitative. Could it be that nihilistic materialism is finally falling out of fashion?

TALISMANS

Talismans are magically enchanted objects that have been imbued with elemental, planetary, and stellar virtues, or those of a particular angelic or demonic entity. They are classically referred to as *images*[9] (particularly if they incorporate the astrological pictographs associated with the thirty-six faces or the twenty-eight lunar mansions) and may take the form of anything from a ring, an amulet, or a piece of parchment to a statue, a temple, or even a whole city, such as the fabled Adocentyn of the *Picatrix*.[10] Talismans usually bear some sort of magical engraving or inscription such as illustrations, texts, glyphs, or sigils, often pertaining to the object's purpose. They may be produced for a variety of purposes, such as for personal protection, professional advancement or relationships, and fertility.

> So great is the extent, power and efficacy of the Celestiall bodies, that not only naturall things, but also artificiall when they are rightly esposed to those above, do presently suffer by that most potent agent, and obtain a wondefull life, which oftentimes gives them an admirable Celestiall virtue [. . .] even garments, buildings and other artificiall works whatsoever, do receive a certain qualification from the Stars; so the Magicians affirm, that not only by the mixture and application of naturall things, but also in Images, Seals, Rings, Glasses, and some other Instruments, being opportunely framed under a certain constellation, some Celestiall Illustration may be taken, and some wonderfull thing may be received; for the beams of the Celestiall bodies being animated, living, sensuall, and bringing along with them admirable gifts, and a most violent power, do, even in a moment, and at the first touch, imprint wonderfull powers in the Images [. . .] Yet they bestow more powerfull vertues on the Images, if they be framed not of any, but of a certain matter, namely whose naturall, and also specificall vertue is agreeable with the work, and the figure of the image is like to the Celestial; for such an Image, both in regard of the matter naturally congruous to the operation and Celestiall influence, and also for its figure being like to the Heavenly one, is best prepared to receive the operations and powers of the Celestiall bodies and figures, and instantly receiveth the Heavenly gift into it self.[11]

Appropriately constructed talismans and pentacles may be used to capture and retain the planet's concentrated influence in the terrestrial sphere of the elements. Telestic and theurgic rituals are also used to create connections between the stellar or planetary spheres and the sublunary sphere. As mentioned previously, tokens and signatures, called *synthemata* in the Neoplatonic tradition, act as resonant links in a cosmic chain connecting the sublunar talisman to its corresponding noetic idea. For the purposes of the present work, I will break the process of talisman production into three stages: composition, construction, and consecration.

The first consideration when composing a talisman is its intention or the purpose that it is meant to serve. Normally, the operator or astrological magician chooses a planet, house, fixed star, face, or lunar mansion whose significations match the desired intention, and its influence is concentrated in the form of a talisman. For instance, if the intention is to protect a traveler during a long, international journey, the magician may choose to fortify the ninth house in an electional chart. If the intention is to win the affection of a potential partner, the magician may choose to accentuate the planet Venus in their election. The fixed stars, faces, and lunar mansions also each possess a particular scope of activity and influence, lending themselves to talismanic production. For example, the fixed star Regulus may be used in a king-making talisman to secure a lofty position. Similarly, the second face of Taurus deals with nobility and power. The fifteenth lunar mansion, Algafra, signifies the acquisition of friendship and may be fortified and concentrated in a talisman for that purpose.[12] Often, the astrological magician will place the planet, star, face, or lunar mansion at the ascendant or midheaven of the electional chart for the talisman.

After choosing the planet, house, star, face, or lunar mansion whose significations fit the intention and purpose of the talisman, the magician may begin to assemble the images, glyphs, sigils, seals and other compositional design motifs representing the operation. The corresponding materials, colors, numbers, and suffumigations are also collected before the construction stage begins.

The construction of the talisman must be performed at an elected time. For instance, if the planet Jupiter (signifying wealth, children, religion, and wisdom) figures prominently in the intention of the talisman, the construction might take place on a Thursday during a Jupiterian hour with a dignified Jupiter at either the ascendant or midheaven and under an unafflicted, waxing moon. Providing a minimum of astrological provisions are met, the magician may choose to inscribe the glyph for Jupiter on a blue, tin disc. Blue is one of the colors associated with Jupiter, as is the metal tin. Other materials—such as parchment paper or wood—may be used, but the idea is to make a terrestrial object that is attractive to the celestial and intellectual influences that will animate it. *The more synthemata that can be combined in the sublunar object, the greater the concentration of superlunar influences.*

Once the composition and construction stages are complete, the talisman must be consecrated. This involves supporting ritualization, which must also be performed at an elected time. The operator may choose to recite an Orphic Hymn to Jupiter while passing the completed talisman through the smoke of, say, a storax suffumigation. Tzadkiel, the archangel of Jupiter, may also be invoked at this time. Appropriately corresponding music may be played or performed, such as the jovial Lydian mode of the major scale. Each planet has a set of magically resonant numbers; for Jupiter, these numbers are 4, 16, 34, and 136. These numbers may be fitted into the symbolism and ritual accompanying the production of the talisman, such as in the number of candles or circumambulations around the magical working space.

QUINARIAN TALISMAN PRODUCTION

Talisman production using the quinaries is similar in practice to other forms of talisman production. First, the intention of the talisman is identified; the compositional materials are assembled; the talisman is manufactured at an elected time; and finally, the talisman is consecrated. We will go through each of these stages in a start-to-finish example of a quinarian talisman.

Suppose you desire a talisman for love and marital fidelity. You may begin by consulting the quinarian catalog in this book, scanning the descriptions and attributes for qualities corresponding to the intention.

Find that the angel and demon of the thirteenth quinary have significations that satisfy your intention. The Shem angel Iezazel[13] aids in marital fidelity and Beleth,[14] the corresponding goetic demon, assists in romantic matters. Since we are utilizing the talents of the pair, you may blend their correspondences into one talisman. This works to the operator's benefit because, as we have discussed, the angel binds the demon, thereby insulating the operator from the demon's potentially chaotic influences.

Begin by making a list of some of the symbolic components to be used in the composition and consecration of the talisman. Iezalel's gematriac value is 78, his ruling archangel is Jophiel, and he is of the cherubic choir. The demon Beleth is a great king: his planet is Sol (the sun), his metal is gold, and his suffumigation is frankincense. You may also incorporate solar symbolism, such as the color yellow and the numbers 6, 36, 111, and 666, when working with this entity. The Psalm 98:4 may be used in the invocation, as well as an invocation of Jophiel. These are among the elements that can be used to construct the talisman.

A good election must be chosen for the construction stage.[15] You might elect to have the sun in the thirteenth quinary (0° 00'–4° 59' Gemini) and place that quinary on either the ascendant or the midheaven. This operation may be performed at a solar hour or within the equinoctial quinarian "hour" ruled by the thirteenth quinary (10:00–10:19 a.m.). A Sunday would be ideal, but as noted earlier, no election is perfect. However, you should always do your best to wait for the strongest election, within reason. This often requires patience. As always, mind the condition of the moon. During this interval, assemble the talisman. Anything may be used for the body, from a piece of parchment to an actual golden coin. For this example, use a small, flat piece of wood about two inches square and one-quarter inch thick. Spraypaint the object either yellow or gold. Using a violet or purple marker, the complementary color of yellow, draw the sigil of Iezalel on one side and the seal of Beleth on the other. Iezalel's name in Hebrew may be drawn on his side of the talisman, or the number 78, which is the gematriac value of his name. On the Beleth side, draw a solar glyph or one of the solar numbers listed above. By bringing together as many signatures and tokens as possible, the object is rendered a more fitting telestic receptacle, one capable of receiving noetic influence.

After constructing the talisman, it must be consecrated. This may be done immediately after the construction, providing the election is still valid, that is still during the quinarian "hour" or during a solar hour. The suffumigation is frankincense, and the talisman should be passed through the smoke. The Shem angel Iezalel may be invoked by reciting Psalm 98:4 ("Make a joyful noise unto the Lord, all the earth: make a loud noise, and rejoice, and sing praise"). The pertinent passages from the *Ars Goetia* may also be consulted for invoking Beleth.

A consecrated talisman may be worn or carried about until the objective is fulfilled and then should be decommissioned. Talismans may also be periodically reconsecrated during a suitable later election with accompanying ritual.

9
Astrology beyond the Ogdoad

UNTIL NOW, practical access to the Shem angels and the goetic demons has been exclusively limited to specialized angel magicians and exorcists applying them in the context of invocation and conjuration. Despite the angels and demons being neatly fitted to the 72 quinaries, the gates to their rarified celestial and intellectual realms have remained closed to the astrologer for centuries. For one reason or another, the leap had not been made to apply their significations in the context of astrological delineation—or, if anyone had, they left no record of the practice. This book is an attempt to remedy the matter. Additionally, the angels and demons have their own body of correspondences and attributions making them particularly suited to chart interpretation. All the components of a workable system are present—all one must do is observe which angel and demon govern their planetary placements. This would provide an understanding not accessible by merely assessing a planet configured in a sign and house. The quinaries are the mechanism by whose application we may access the angelic and demonic dimensions of astrology—domains that were hitherto inaccessible. The modern astrologer now has recourse to this fascinating body of occult significations, revealing an angelic and demonic astrology.

Beyond the quinaries' applications in the several domains of established astrological inquiry, the use of the quinaries gives the astrologer access to at least three new areas in which to astrologize: the *qabalistic*, the *Solomonic*, and the *noetic*. Qabalistic astrology uses the quinaries to access the angels and their significations. Solomonic astrology uses them to access the significations of the goetic demons. But perhaps most intriguingly, the quinaries make it possible for the astrologer to apply terrestrial and celestial astrological methodology to delineation on the noetic plane, or the *intellectual world*.

NOETIC ASTROLOGY

As we illustrated in chapter 1, the art and science of astrology is predicated on an enchanted view of the world built upon a foundation of the Aristotelian physics and Ptolemaic cosmology. This model situates Earth at the center of the cosmos. We realize this is not the case according to modern cosmology, which is why we posit a *georeferential* model—one that envisions Earth as the locus of human consciousness and the central point of observation. The movement of all other celestial bodies stays the same; we simply view Earth—not the sun—as the relatively stationary object (ultimately, it does not matter because *both* are moving through space). We live in the sublunar realm of the classical elements, which are simply the states of matter: earth is solid; water is liquid; air is gas; fire is plasma. All matter is in a state of Heraclitean flux and becoming; of generation and corruption. The elements are acted upon by the planets. This planetary action is observable through the astrological houses, which are the terrestrial domains of human affairs. This is the *natural world*.[1]

Above, or rather around, this natural or elemental region are the seven visible planets, enveloping us in their concentric, crystalline spheres. The planets are unchanging, ætheric bodies whose movements are perfect and eternal. The canopy of the fixed stars and zodiac, sometimes called the *firmament* or the Ogdoad, lies beyond the planets.

Astrology is primarily concerned with this celestial region—the planets, the fixed stars, and the zodiac. Astrologers interpret the cosmic expressions of the planets as they are configured against the zodiacal signs. This is also the domain of demons, such as the stellar and decanal entities described in the *Testament of Solomon*[2] and elsewhere in the grimoire tradition. This is the *celestial world*.[3]

The Source of all emanations and expressions has many names, although Aristotle's *prime mover* or Aquinas's *first cause* function rather nicely in the context of astrological causality. This divine entity resides in the supercelestial realm beyond the Ogdoad. The archetypal plane corresponding to Plato's forms. This final cosmological domain, outside both the natural and celestial worlds, contains the hierarchy of the angelic choirs, which was codified by the Christian Neoplatonist and theologian Pseudo-Dionysius the Areopagite (fifth to sixth century). Angels, being supercelestial beings, are perhaps best understood as mathematical entities, as Iamblichus, Agrippa, Dee, and others envisioned them. They exist beyond the confines of space-time in the abstract, noetic realm of incorporeal *ideas*. This is the *intellectual world*.[4]

The angels of the Shem HaMephorash are *intellectual* entities. Ergo, they inhabit the noetic realm, which is better imagined as an abstract or metaphysical *category* than a place, per se. Whereas the houses and triplicities of astrology correspond to the elemental plane of humanity, and the planets, stars, and aspects correspond to the celestial realm of the demons, the quinaries and their associated angels correspond to the intellectual world of the unmoved mover. As the stellar faces are 10-degree segments of the Ogdoadic celestial eighth sphere, the noetic quinaries are 5-degree segments of the supercelestial ninth sphere or Ennead. They thus give us a glimpse into the *precausal* cosmic mechanism—that which is not yet subject to the perturbations of the stars and planets. In this sense, the angels truly are the *messengers* (from the Greek word ἄγγελος or *ángelos,* which means "messenger") of supernal communications, operating within the liminal space between the first cause and the stars.

Fig. 9.1. The anima mundi from Robert Fludd's
Utriusque Cosmi Historia (1617).

The practice of this new quinarian astrology clearly carries with it formidable philosophical implications relative to the science of the stars. By engaging the rarified angelic dimension, we are pointing to an undiscovered plane in astrological inquiry. For the first time in the history of the art, we are practicing a *noetic* astrology. This is an ange-lological astrology, above and beyond the astral plane of the planets and stars. Quinarian astrology is an *intellectual* astrology.

Throughout the history of the art thus far, astrology has been confined to the natural (houses, elemental triplicity, etc.) and celes-tial (planets, signs, fixed stars, etc.) worlds. Quinarian astrology, being concerned with delineating demonic and angelic significations, allows us—*for the first time in the two-thousand-plus-year history of the art*—to astrologize on the intellectual plane. We now have unprecedented access to an astrology beyond the Ogdoad: that is, above the fixed stars and the zodiac. This potentially poses significant philosophical and even theological problems.

According to the astrological and metaphysical doctrines we have examined in this book, causality begins *beneath* the Ogdoad. The noetic realm *above* the firmament is abstract and atemporal—it is not subject to the necessities and impositions of space-time. Clearly, there can be no causality in the absence of space and time. It is the stars and planets, then, that weave the fortunes of humankind—a central astro-logical notion. We see this feature symbolized by the three Fates who attend the great Spindle of Necessity in Plato's "Myth of Er" (*Republic*, Book X).

Since the quinaries make noetic astrology possible, and the intel-lectual plane is not subject to the fates and fortunes of the stars and planets, we are now confronted with a precausal astrology. This is, to some extent, absurd because time and causality are the media and sub-stance of astrology. Yet, here we are. Having stormed the zodiacal gates and torn back the celestial curtains of the firmament, we stand before the cosmic maw of eternity—the First Time[5] upon which all subsequent eternal recurrences have been patterned—with angels as our guides.

Glossary

æther: In Aristotle's physics and cosmology, the unchangeable and incorruptible quintessence or fifth element of which the stars and planets, along with their crystalline spheres, are composed.

Almuten Figuris: "Winner of the Figure"; the planet with the most essential and accidental dignity in the chart; often associated with the Kyrios Geneseos or Lord of the Nativity.

angel: "Messenger"; an entity in the intellectual world who communicates the divine will; "thwarting" angels bind their associated demons enabling man to control them.

Angel of the Nativity: The Shem angel who rules the rising quinary in a nativity.

angles: The degrees of the ascendant, midheaven, descendant, and imum coeli.

anima mundi: "World soul"; the primarily Platonic notion of an astral being through which every living thing is connected.

ascendant: The zodiacal sign and/or degree of the eastern horizon at any given time; opposite the descendant.

aspect: A geometrical configuration made between planets, parts, angles, or cusps on the ecliptic. The Ptolemaic aspects recognized in traditional astrology are: 60 degrees sextile, 90 degrees square, 120 degrees trine, and 180 degrees opposition. Technically, 0 degree conjunction is not an aspect because it does not inscribe a regular polygon in the ecliptical circle.

astrology: The study of kaironic, qualitative time, as opposed to chronic, quantitative time; a predictive art, predicated on the notion that macrocosmic celestial events and phenomena are mirrored in microcosmic terrestrial events and phenomena.

astromythology: Allegorical personae and narratives based on celestial objects and phenomena.

astrotheology: Religious personae and themes based on celestial objects and phenomena.

astrotheurgy: Astrological magic, typically involving entities associated with celestial objects.

bounds: *See* "terms."

cast: To erect or raise a figure.

celestial world: In the enchanted cosmology of classical occultism, it is the domain between and including the sphere of the moon and the sphere of the fixed stars and zodiac (Ogdoad).

cosmogony: The study of the birth, creation, and/or formation of the universe.

cosmology: The study of the form, structure, and/or contents of the universe.

cusps: The borders separating signs or houses.

decans: *See* "faces."

demon: *Also,* daimon (Greek) and dæmon (Latin); an entity in the fiery sublunar and celestial world; intermediary stellar or decanal beings.

descendant: The zodiacal degree on the western horizon at any given time; opposite the ascendant.

Eighth sphere: *See* "Ogdoad."

election: An astrologically significant time, deliberately chosen; usually meant to engage cosmic momentum.

empyrean: The highest heavenly sphere; usually associated with the first cause.

Ennead: The ninth heavenly sphere, beyond the fixed stars and zodiac; usually associated with the *primum mobile* or first moved.

faces: *Also*, decans; thirty-six 10-degree arc segments of the zodiac; usually associated with decanal demons, each governed by one of the seven visible planets; one point of essential dignity.

figure: An astrological chart.

gematria: Hebrew alphanumerology; the numerical value of each Hebrew letter.

genethlialogy: Natal astrology; the study of nativities.

georeferentiality: An astrological worldview in which Earth, while not being the center of the solar system or the cosmos, is recognized as the locus of human consciousness and the central point of astrological observation.

goetia: Sorcery, in general; a type of magic usually dealing with demonic entities; one of the five books of the *Lesser Key of Solomon*.

grimoire: A magical textbook, usually dealing with spells, invocations, and the making of magical objects such as talismans.

Hermetism (antiquity to the Middle Ages); also, Hermeticism (Renaissance to today): The philosophical tradition associated with Hermes Trismegistus, dealing primarily with the Hermetic arts (astrology, alchemy, and magic), as outlined in a body of technical and philosophical "wisdom literature" collectively known as *Hermetica*.

horary: Interrogational astrology; the astrology of questions, wherein a figure is cast for the moment the question is understood by the astrologer and delineated by specialized techniques.

horoscope: The ascendant; an astrological figure, in general.

houses: The twelve terrestrial domains of human action and activity, wherein zodiacally conditioned, planetary expressions play out.

imum coeli: IC; the antimeridional degree opposite that of the midheaven; the lowest possible point on the ecliptic.

ingress: The moment a planet enters a sign.

intellectual world: In the enchanted cosmology of classical occultism, it is the domain above the Ogdoad, consisting of the angelic hierarchy, *primum mobile* and *primum movens*; the archetypal realm of Platonic forms.

lady or lord: The planet ruling the sign and/or house under consideration.

medium coeli: MC or midheaven; the degree of the local meridian in an astrological figure; opposite the IC.

midheaven: *See* "medium coeli."

native: The subject of a nativity; the owner of a natal figure.

nativity: A natal figure or chart.

natural world: In the enchanted cosmology of classical occultism, it is the domain below the sphere of the moon (sublunar), wherein the four classical Empedoclean elements (earth, water, air, and fire) are in a constant state of generation and corruption.

necromancy: A form of divination involving communication with the dead.

Neoplatonism: A modern term denoting a philosophical tradition rooted in the works of Plato, dealing with mystical concepts such as theurgy and *henosis*, meaning "oneness," "unity," or "union with the One."

nigromancy: Demonic magic; a form of divination involving the invocation, binding, and interrogation of demons.

ninth heavenly sphere: *See* "Ennead."

noetic: Intellectual, abstract; usually pertaining to the realm beyond the Ogdoad.

Ogdoad: The Eighth; the sphere of the fixed stars and zodiac.

parts: *Also* lots; in astrology, an Arabic part is a mathematical point derived by casting the distance between two planets, parts, or angles from a third point (usually the ascendant).

pinax: An astrologer's board, presumably used in ancient consultation as a visual aid.

placement: The situation of a planet, part, or angle in signs and houses.

polarity: The binary expression of the signs: positive/negative, masculine/feminine, active/passive. Fire and air signs are active; water and earth signs are passive.

primum mobile: The first moved, associated with the Enneadic or ninth heavenly sphere.

primum movens: The prime mover or first cause, associated with the empyrean.

profections: An ancient "time lord" or astrological timing technique that assigns a house to each year, month, day, or hour.

Qabalah: A medieval Jewish mystical and exegetical tradition, including a system of cryptographical techniques.

quadruplicity: Quality, modality; three groups (cardinal, fixed, and mutable) each consisting of four astrological signs, having a qualitative bearing on the signs.

querent: The person asking the question in a horary; usually signified by the ruler of the ascendant.

quesited: The object of a horary, the thing sought; usually signified by the ruler of the topically appropriate house.

quinary: Seventy-two 5-degree arc segments of the zodiac, usually associated with the angels of the Shem HaMephorash and the demons of the *Ars Goetia*.

radical: Generally, relating to the root chart, such as a nativity in relation to subsequent transits; in horary, when a figure has met certain conditions and is fit to be judged.

Sephirot: "Emanations"; qabalistic spheres on the Tree of Life, corresponding to the Ptolemaic spheres; archetypal concentrations.

Shem HaMephorash: "The Explicit Name"; the 72-fold name of God and source of the Shem angels.

signs: Twelve 30-degree arc segments; zodiacal sectors of space-time; separate from, but named after, the zodiacal constellations.

sublunar: "Below the moon"; terrestrial, natural, elemental.

suffumigation: The use of fumes or smoke from burning resins, aromatic woods, and herbs, either as incense or inhaled during a magical ritual.

synthemata: Terrestrial signatures or tokens imbued with occult celestial and/or intellectual virtues.

talisman: An object that has been animated or ensouled with celestial or intellectual virtues; usually at an elected time.

terms: *Also*, bounds; five uneven arc segments of each zodiacal sign, each corresponding to one of the five nonluminary classical planets; two points of essential dignity.

tetragrammaton: יהוה. YHVH; the four-letter name of God.

tetraktys: A emanationist cosmogonical model, held sacred by the Pythagoreans.

theurgy: "God working"; divine magic or ritualized microcosmogony, typically involving invocation.

transits: Current or future planets examined in relation to a natal or other radical figure.

triplicity: Four elemental groups (earth, water, air, and fire) each composed of three astrological signs; the elemental correspondences of the signs, having a qualitative bearing on them.

Notes

INTRODUCTION: ILLUMINATING THE QUINARIES

1. Skinner and Rankine, *Goetia of Dr Rudd*, 71.
2. Lamb, "72 Quinaries."
3. Lenain, *Science of the Kabbalah*, 55–97.
4. Mathers, *Goetia*, 27–65.
5. Ambelain, *Practical Kabbalah*, 155.
6. Mathers, *Goetia*, 58.
7. Lenain, *Science of the Kabbalah*, 67.
8. Mathers, *Goetia*, 37.
9. Lamb, "72 Quinaries."
10. Brennan, *Hellenistic Astrology*, xix.
11. Lamb, "72 Quinaries," 18–21.

1. THE 72 QUINARIES

1. Ptolemy, *Ptolemy's Almagest*, 41–42.
2. Lamb, "Developing an Astrological Worldview."
3. Aristotle, *Physics*, 8.4, 255b13–17.
4. Hahm, "Fifth Element," 62.
5. Goldstein, "Arabic version of Ptolemy's Planetary Hypothesis," 6.
6. Litwa, *Hermetica II*, 314.
7. Ptolemy, *Tetrabiblos*, I:4.
8. Brennan, *Hellenistic Astrology*, 103.

9. Holden, *History of Horoscopic Astrology*, 16.

10. Tester, *History of Western Astrology*, 161–62.

11. Gleadow, *Origin of the Zodiac*, 15–26.

12. Ma'shur and al-Qabisi, *Introductions to Traditional Astrology*, 48.

13. "Quinary," Etymologeek.

14. "Quinance," Wiki Golden Dawn Online Resource.

15. Crowley, *Complete Astrological Writings*, 24.

16. Aaboe, "Culture of Babylonia."

17. Tester, *History of Western Astrology*, 22.

18. Boll, "Hephaestio of Thebes."

19. Brennan, *Hellenistic Astrology*, 72–77.

20. DeConick and Adamson, *Histories of the Hidden God*, 65.

21. DeConick and Adamson, *Histories of the Hidden God*, 65.

22. DeConick and Adamson, *Histories of the Hidden God*, 65.

23. Tester, *History of Western Astrology*, 22.

24. Ptolemy, *Ptolemy's Almagest*, 45–47.

25. Neugebauer, "Alleged Babylonian Discovery."

26. Hart, *Egyptian Myths*, 40–41.

27. Mathers, "Shem HaMephorash."

28. Hall, "Stone Horoscope," 18.

29. Jastrow et al., "Breastplate of the High Priest."

30. Agrippa, *Three Books of Occult Philosophy*, II:15.

2. THE ANGELS OF THE SHEM HAMEPHORASH

1. Agrippa, *Three Books of Occult Philosophy*, 285.

2. Dan, *Kabbalah*, chaps. 5 and 9.

3. Mathers, *Kabbalah Denudata*, 6.

4. Mathers, *Kabbalah Denudata*, 10.

5. Mathers, *Kabbalah Denudata*, 16–18.

6. Aristotle, *Physics*, 8.4, 255b13–17.

7. Reuchlin, *De art cabalistica*, 21.

8. Maimonides, *Mishneh Torah, Oaths*, chap. 12.

9. Bacher, "Shem Ha-Meforash."

10. Hayyim, "Ben Yehoyada on Kiddushin," 71a:2.

11. Maimonides, *Guide for the Perplexed*, pt. 1, 62:3.

12. Trachtenberg, *Jewish Magic and Superstition*, 92.

13. Reuchlin, *De art cabalistica*, 273.

14. McLaughlin and Eisenstein, "Names of God."

15. Kaplan, *Bahir*, 42.

16. Reuchlin, *De art cabalistica*, 267.

17. Reuchlin, *De art cabalistica*, 267.

18. Mackey, *Encyclopedia*, 780.

19. Reuchlin, *De art cabalistica*, 261.

20. Burton and Grandy, *Magic, Mystery, and Science*, 69.

3. THE DEMONS OF THE *ARS GOETIA*

1. Greenbaum, *Daimon in Hellenistic Astrology*, 4.

2. Nilsson, *History of Greek Religion*, 283.

3. Lamb, "Daimonic Astrology," 40–43.

4. Greenbaum, *Daimon in Hellenistic Astrology*, 255–66.

5. Mathers, *Book of the Sacred Magic of Abramelin*, xxvi.

6. Charlesworth, *Old Testament Pseudepigrapha*, 952.

7. Charlesworth, *Old Testament Pseudepigrapha*, 935–59.

8. Davies, *Grimoires*, 1.

9. Agrippa, *Three Books of Occult Philosophy*, II:34.

10. Kaplan, *Bahir*, 42.

11. Gager, *Curse Tablets and Binding Spells*, 106.

12. Margalioth, *Sepher Ha-Razim*, xx.

13. Torijano, *Solomon*, 170–71.

14. Marathakis, *Hygromanteia*, 12–14.

15. Skinner and Rankine, *Goetia of Dr Rudd*, 32–33.

16. Peterson, *Lemegeton Clavicula Salomonis*, xiii.

17. Skinner and Rankine, *Goetia of Dr Rudd*, 14–19.

18. Peterson, *Lemegeton Clavicula Salomonis*, xi–xvii.

19. Skinner and Rankine, *Goetia of Dr Rudd*, 31, 82.

20. Skinner and Rankine, *Goetia of Dr Rudd*, 14–19.

21. Charlesworth, *Old Testament Pseudepigrapha*, 935–36.

4. THE SIGNIFICATIONS OF THE QUINARIES

1. Skinner and Rankine, *Goetia of Dr Rudd*, 103–75.

2. Savedow, *Sepher Rezial Hemelach*.

3. Ambelain, *Practical Kabbalah*.

4. Lenain, *Science of the Kabbalah*.

5. Mathers, *Goetia*.

5. THE QUINARIES IN NATAL ASTROLOGY

1. Ma'shur and al-Qabisi, *Introductions to Traditional Astrology*, 11.

2. Brennan, *Hellenistic Astrology*, 17–18.

3. Lamb, "Daimonic Astrology," 40–43.

4. Litwa, *Hermetica II*, 314.

5. George, *Ancient Astrology*, 645–46.

6. Ambelain, *Practical Kabbalah*, 142.

7. Mathers, *Goetia*, 40.

8. Ambelain, *Practical Kabbalah*, 148.

9. Mathers, *Goetia*, 50.

10. Brennan, *Hellenistic Astrology*, 545–49.

11. Lenain, *Science of the Kabbalah*, 95–96.

12. Mathers, *Goetia*, 64–65.

13. George, *Ancient Astrology*, 645–46.

14. Lenain, *Science of the Kabbalah*, 88.

15. Mathers, *Goetia*, 58.

16. George, *Ancient Astrology*, 1085–97.

17. Lenain, *Science of the Kabbalah*, 72–73.

18. Lamb, "Daimonic Astrology," 40–43.

6. THE QUINARIES IN ELECTIONAL ASTROLOGY

1. Rochberg, *Babylonian Horoscopes*, x.

2. Rochberg, *Babylonian Horoscopes*, x.

3. Tester, *History of Western Astrology*, 88–92.

4. Bishr and Masha'allah, *Works of Sahl and Masha'allah*, vii.

5. Agrippa, *Three Books of Occult Philosophy*, II:29.

6. Agrippa, *Three Books of Occult Philosophy*, II:29.

7. Mathers, *Goetia*, 67.

8. Lilly, *Christian Astrology*, 110.

9. Lenain, *Science of the Kabbalah*, 60.

7. THE QUINARIES IN HORARY ASTROLOGY

1. Lilly, *Christian Astrology*, 121.
2. Lilly, *Christian Astrology*, 123–24.
3. Lilly, *Christian Astrology*, 123.
4. László, "Origins of Horary Astrology."
5. Lilly, *Christian Astrology*, 110.

8. QUINARIAN MAGIC AND TALISMANS

1. Skinner and Rankine, *Goetia of Dr Rudd*, 14–15.
2. Greer and Warnock, *Complete Picatrix*.
3. Greer, *Astral High Magic*.
4. Mathers, *Goetia*, 21.
5. Shaw, "Theurgy."
6. Greer, "Sources of Power," 99–125.
7. Mathers, *Goetia*, 17.
8. Hanegraaff, *Western Esotericism*, 13.
9. Greer, *Astral High Magic*, 2.
10. Greer and Warnock, *Complete Picatrix*, 243.
11. Agrippa, *Three Books of Occult Philosophy*, II:35.
12. Greer and Warnock, *Complete Picatrix*, 35.
13. Lenain, *Science of the Kabbalah*, 62.
14. Mathers, *Goetia*, 34.
15. Greer and Warnock, *Complete Picatrix*, 94.

9. ASTROLOGY BEYOND THE OGDOAD

1. Agrippa, *Three Books of Occult Philosophy*, I.
2. Charlesworth, *Pseudepigrapha Old Testament*, 952.
3. Agrippa, *Three Books of Occult Philosophy*, II.
4. Agrippa, *Three Books of Occult Philosophy*, III.
5. Naydler, *Temple of the Cosmos*, 91–93.

Bibliography

Aaboe, Asger. "Babylonian Mathematics, Astrology, and Astronomy." In *The Assyrian and Babylonian Empires and Other States of the Near East, from the Eighth to the Sixth Centuries B.C.*, edited by John Boardman, I. E. S. Edwards, N. G. L. Hammond, and E. Solberger, 276–92. Vol. 3, pt. 2 of *The Cambridge Ancient History*. Cambridge, UK: Cambridge University Press, 1991.

Agrippa, Heinrich Cornelius. *Three Books of Occult Philosophy*. Edited and annotated by Donald Tyson. Translated by James Freake. Woodbury, MN: Llewellyn, 1992. First published in English in 1651.

Ambelain, Robert. *The Practical Kabbalah*. Translated by Piers Vaughan. Bayonne, NJ: Rose Circle Books, 2020. First published in French in 1951.

Aristotle. *Physics*. Translated by R. P. Hardie and R. K. Gaye. Internet Classics Archive.

Bacher, Wilhelm. "Shem Ha-Meforash." In *The Jewish Encyclopedia*, edited by Isidore Singer, 262–64. New York: Funk and Wagnalls, 1901.

Bishr, Shal ibn, and Masha'allah. *Works of Sahl and Masha'allah*. Translated by Benjamin N. Dykes. Minneapolis, MN: Cazimi Press, 2008.

Boll, Franz, trans. "Hephaestion of Thebes." In *Catalogus Codicum Astrologorum Graecorum*, vol. 7, edited by Franz Cumont and Franz Boll, 129–51. Brussels, Belgium: H. Lamertin, 1908.

Brennan, Chris. *Hellenistic Astrology: The Study of Fate and Fortune*. Denver, CO: Amor Fati, 2017.

Burton, Dan, and David Grandy. *Magic, Mystery, and Science: The Occult in Western Civilization*. Bloomington: Indiana University Press, 2004.

Campion, Nicholas. *Astrology and Cosmology in the World's Religions.* New York: New York University Press, 2012.

Charlesworth, James H. *The Old Testament Pseudepigrapha: Apocalyptic Literature and Testaments.* Vol. 1. Peabody, MA.: Hendrickson Academic, 2010.

Copenhaver, Brian P., trans. *Hermetica.* Cambridge, UK: Cambridge University Press, 1992.

Crowley, Aleister. *The Complete Astrological Writings Containing a Treatise on Astrology.* Liber 536. London: Duckworth, 1974.

Crowley, Aleister, and Evangeline Adams. *The General Principles of Astrology.* Liber 536. Boston: Weiser Books, 2002.

Dan, Joseph. *Kabbalah: A Very Short Introduction.* Oxford, UK: Oxford University Press, 2007.

Davies, Owen. *Grimoires: A History of Magic Books.* Oxford, UK: Oxford University Press, 2009.

DeConick, April D., and Grant Adamson. *Histories of the Hidden God: Concealment and Revelation in Western Gnostic, Esoteric, and Mystical Traditions.* London: Routledge, 2014.

DuQuette, Lon Milo. *The Key to Solomon's Key: Secrets of Magic and Masonry.* San Francisco, CA: CCC Publishing, 2006.

Eliade, Mircea. *The Sacred and the Profane: The Nature of Religion.* Boston: Mariner Books, 1968.

Gager, John G. *Curse Tablets and Binding Spells from the Ancient World.* Oxford, UK: Oxford University Press, 1999.

George, Demetra. *Ancient Astrology in Theory and Practice: A Manual of Traditional Techniques.* Vols. 1 and 2. Auckland, NZ: Rubedo Press, 2019.

Gleadow, Rupert. *The Origin of the Zodiac.* Garden City, NY: Dover, 2011.

Goldstein, Bernard R. "The Arabic Version of Ptolemy's Planetary Hypothesis." *Transactions of the American Philosophical Society* 57, no. 4 (1967): 3–55.

Greenbaum, Dorian Gieseler. *The Daimon in Hellenistic Astrology.* Leiden, Netherlands: Brill, 2016.

Greer, John Michael, trans. *Astral High Magic: De Imaginibus of Thabit Ibn Qurra.* Commentary by Christopher Warnock. Renaissance Astrology, 2011.

———. "Sources of Power in Medieval and Modern Magic." In *The Celestial Art*, edited by Austin Coppock, 99–125. Hercules, CA: Three Hands Press. 2018.

Greer, John Michael, and Christopher Warnock, trans. *The Complete Picatrix: The Occult Classic of Astrological Magic*. Liber Atratus Edition. Annotated by Greer and Warnock. Renaissance Astrology/Adocentyn Press, 2011.

Hahm, David E. "The Fifth Element in Aristotle's De Philosophia: A Critical Re-Examination." *Journal of Hellenic Studies* 102 (1982): 60–74.

Hall, Judy. "The Stone Horoscope: Evidence for Continuity of Ancient Esoteric Tradition and Practice." Master's thesis, Bath Spa University, Bath, UK, 2007.

Hanegraaff, Wouter. *Western Esotericism: A Guide for the Perplexed*. London: Bloomsbury Academic, 2013.

Hart, George. *Egyptian Myths*. Austin: University of Texas Press, 1990.

Hayyim, Yosef. "Ben Yehoyada on Kiddushin." *William Davidson Talmud*. Sefaria, 2017.

Holden, James Herschel. *A History of Horoscopic Astrology*. Tempe, AZ: American Federation of Astrologers, 1996.

Jastrow, Morris, Ira Maurice Price, Marcus Jastrow, and Louis Ginzberg. "Breastplate of the High Priest." In *The Jewish Encyclopedia*, edited by Isidore Singer, 366–67. New York: Funk and Wagnalls, 1901.

Kaplan, Aryeh. *The Bahir: Illumination*. Newburyport, MA: Red Wheel/Weiser, 1989.

Lamb, Jaime Paul. "Daimōnic Astrology and the Cosmic Return." *Mountain Astrologer*. Cancer Sol, no. 227 (June–August 2023): 40–43.

———. "Developing an Astrological Worldview." Jaime Paul Lamb (website), November 16, 2022.

———. "The 72 Quinaries." *Mountain Astrologer*. 2023 Yearbook, no. 225, vol. 2022, issue 5 (2023): 18–21.

László, Levente. "The Origins of Horary Astrology." *The Astrology Podcast*, episode 145. Interview by Chris Brennan, February 21, 2018.

Lenain, Lazare. *The Science of the Kabbalah*. Translated by Piers Vaughan. Bayonne, NJ: Rose Circle, 2020. First published 1823.

Lilly, William. *Christian Astrology*. New York: Cosimo Classics, 2011. First published 1647.

Litwa, M. David, trans. *Hermetica II*. Cambridge, UK: Cambridge University Press, 2018.

Mackey, Albert M. *An Encyclopedia of Freemasonry and Its Kindred Sciences*. New York: Masonic History Company, 1916. First published 1873.

Maimonides, Moses. *The Guide for the Perplexed*. Translated by M. Friedlander. New York: E. P. Dutton, 1904.

———. *Mishneh Torah, Oaths*. Translated by Eliyahu Touger. New York: Moznaim, n.d.

Majercik, Ruth, trans. *The Chaldean Oracles*. 2nd ed. Gloucestershire, UK: The Prometheus Trust, 2013.

Marathakis, Ioannis, trans. *The Magical Treatise of Solomon, or Hygromanteia*. Singapore: Golden Hoard Press, 2011.

Margalioth, Mordecai. *Sepher Ha-Razim: A Newly Recovered Book of Magic from the Talmudic Period*. Jerusalem: Yediot Achronot, 1966.

Ma'shur, Abu, and al-Qabisi. *Introductions to Traditional Astrology*. Translated and edited by Benjamin N. Dykes. Minneapolis, MN: Cazimi Press, 2010.

Mathers, Samuel Liddell MacGregor, trans. *The Book of the Sacred Magic of Abramelin the Mage*. Garden City, NY: Dover, 1975. First published 1458.

———. *The Goetia: The Lesser Key of Solomon the King; Clavicula Salomonis Regis*. Newburyport, MA: Red Wheel/Weiser, 1995. First published 1904.

———. *Kabbalah Denudata: The Kabbalah Unveiled*. London: KB Classics, 2017.

———. "Shem HaMephorash: The 72-Fold Name." Golden Dawn Lectures. Available online at tarrdaniel.com, n.d.

McLaughlin, J. F., and Judah David Eisenstein. "Names of God." In *The Jewish Encyclopedia*, edited by Isidore Singer, 160–65. New York: Funk and Wagnalls, 1901.

Naydler, Jeremy. *Temple of the Cosmos: The Ancient Egyptian Experience of the Sacred*. Rochester, VT: Inner Traditions, 1996.

Neugebauer, Otto. "The Alleged Babylonian Discovery of the Precession of the Equinoxes." *Journal of the American Oriental Society* 70, no. 1 (1950): 1–8.

Nilsson, Martin Persson. *A History of Greek Religion*. Oxford, UK: Oxford University Press, 1925.

Peterson, Joseph H., trans. *Lemegeton Clavicula Salomonis: The Lesser Key of Solomon, Detailing the Ceremonial Art of Commanding Spirits Both Good and Evil*. Cape Neddick, ME: Weiser Antiquarian Books, 2001.

Porphyry of Tyre. *An Introduction to the Tetrabiblos of Ptolemy*. Translated by Andrea Laurel Gehrz. Portland, OR: Moira Press, 2010.

Ptolemy, Claudius. *Ptolemy's Almagest*. Translated by G. J. Toomer. London: Duckworth, 1984.

———. *Tetrabiblos*. Translated by J. M. Ashmand. Bel Air, MD: Astrology Classics, 2005. First published 1822.

Reuchlin, Johann. *On the Art of the Kabbalah: De arte cabalistica*. Translated by Martin and Sarah Goodman. Lincoln: University of Nebraska Press, 1993. First published 1517.

Rochberg, Francesa. *Babylonian Horoscopes*. Philadelphia: American Philosophical Society, 1998.

Savedow, Steve, trans. *Sepher Rezial Hemelach: The Book of the Angel Rezial*. York Beach, ME: Weiser Books, 2000.

Shaw, Gregory. "Theurgy: Rituals of Unification in the Neoplatonism of Iamblichus." *Traditio: Studies in Ancient and Medieval History, Thought, and Religion* 41 (1985): 1–28.

Skinner, Stephen. *The Complete Magician's Tables*. Singapore: Golden Hoard Press, 2023.

Skinner, Stephen, and David Rankine, trans. and ed. *The Goetia of Dr Rudd*. Singapore: Golden Hoard Press, 2007.

Tester, Jim. *A History of Western Astrology*. Suffolk, UK: Boydell and Brewer, 1987.

Torijano, Pablo A. *Solomon, the Esoteric King: From King to Magus. Development of a Tradition*. Leiden, Netherlands: Brill, 2002.

Trachtenberg, Joshua. *Jewish Magic and Superstition: A Study in Folk Religion*. Philadelphia: University of Pennsylvania Press, 2004. First published 1939.

Index

About the Author

Jaime Paul Lamb is a consulting astrologer and occultist, practicing in the context of the Western esoteric traditions. He is a member of the American Federation of Astrologers (AFA), the International Society for Astrological Research (ISAR), and the National Council for Geocosmic Research (NCGR). He is certified in Hellenistic astrology through Chris Brennan's Hellenistic Astrology Course, has studied with renowned medieval-Renaissance astrologer Christopher Warnock, and is also the instructor of astrology at the Institute for Hermetic Studies, founded by Mark Stavish in 1998. Lamb is the author of *Myth, Magick & Masonry: Occult Perspectives in Freemasonry* (The Laudable Pursuit, 2018), *Approaching the Middle Chamber: The Seven Liberal Arts in Freemasonry and the Western Esoteric Tradition* (The Laudable Pursuit, 2020), and *The Archetypal Temple and Other Writings on Masonic Esotericism* (Tria Prima Press, 2021). Lamb resides in Phoenix, Arizona, with his wife and their many animals.

For more information, please visit his website at **jaimepaullamb.com**.